RIDEAU WATERWAY

Rideau Waterway

ROBERT LEGGET

Revised edition

University of Toronto Press

TORONTO AND BUFFALO

All photographs, with the exception of those noted,
were taken by the author

In tribute to the

Builders of the Rideau Canal

1826–1832

Workers, Contractors, Engineers

and, in particular,

the Superintending Engineer

Lieutenant Colonel John By

Royal Engineers

Acknowledgments

THE PLEASURE of bringing together the many strands of varied information which have been woven into this account of the Rideau Canal has been immeasurably increased by the personal associations which the search has given. In journeys up and down the Canal, in Kingston and Ottawa, in Smiths Falls, Perth, and the many smaller towns along the Rideau, and even in a few far distant places, I have found friendly people who share my interest in the Waterway. Without exception, they have willingly given of their time in telling me what they knew of the Canal and in suggesting further avenues to explore. Some have kindly loaned to me treasured old documents and books. To all these associates, some of whom I have come to know well, some of whom I do not even know by name, I am most grateful.

My interest in the Rideau Canal was first awakened when I was a resident of Kingston; my first studies for it were made in the library of Queen's University. Residence in Toronto allowed me to explore the libraries of the city and the University there. More recent years spent in Ottawa have given me some limited opportunity of dipping into the treasures of the Public Archives of Canada where are the invaluable "C" volumes in which so many of Colonel By's original letters are to be found, and of using the civic library. Visits to Montreal have provided opportunities to use again the library of McGill University and to study the Redpath papers in the McCord Museum. To those in charge of all the libraries mentioned, and to their most courteous and helpful staffs, I am greatly indebted.

Local newspapers have been found to contain a wealth of information upon even so restricted a subject as that of this book.

They have therefore been a fertile field for study but my use of them has been limited. The Women's Institutes of the Rideau district, through their Tweedsmuir books, have, as elsewhere in Canada, made a fine start at collecting and recording details of local history. Several of the Institutes made available to me extracts from their records and for this service I also extend my thanks. Their members would probably be the first to agree that there is still much to be done in this field of local and regional history. If this book should stimulate others to explore similar local aspects of Canadian history, it will serve a double purpose.

Although the book deals with a subject not unrelated to building research, it is the product of leisure time spent in a manner far removed from official duties of recent years. At the same time, friends and colleagues in the Division of Building Research of the National Research Council have been most kind, not only in their understanding interest (and patient acceptance of possibly too frequent references to the Canal in general talks) but also in such varied assistance as reading parts of the manuscript, stimulating discussions, and help with the final typing. It would be invidious to mention names other than that of T. N. Blackall, whose skilled assistance with the illustrative maps has added much to the appearance of this volume, but I wish N.R.C. colleagues in Washington and in London, England, to know that this personal acknowledgment extends also to them.

It was with the aid of the latter that a memorable visit was paid to Frant when Mr. W. S. Darlington, in the absence of the Rector whose warden he is, served as a welcome guide to his lovely church and village. A similar introduction to Mr. P. W. C. Stratton, Records Liaison Officer in the British War Office, led to a useful examination of old military records. A letter published in *The Times* resulted in singularly helpful correspondence with many interested in old military history, some of whom went to great trouble to furnish me with information, particularly about Colonel By. To all of these overseas friends of the Rideau, I am much indebted.

As this book approached completion, a number of friends were good enough to take the time to read one or more chapters; in many cases they gave me the benefit of their informed criticism. Among those who have so kindly assisted me in this way are: Colonel Wilfrid Bovey, Mr. L. W. Clarke, Dr. H. T. Douglas, Mr. D. Forgan, Colonel J. H. Jenkins, Mr. Eric A. Millar, Major

W. Lawson, Major General G. Turner, Mr. D. Watt, Major A. R. Whittier, and Dr. Esther C. Wright. Colonel C. P. Stacey, Director of the Historical Section, Canadian Army Headquarters, has been good enough to read the entire manuscript in its final form, after giving me helpful advice following his examination of early drafts. In a similar way, Dr. Charlotte Whitton, Mayor of Ottawa, has found time amid her many official duties to give me the benefit of her own wide knowledge of local history, following her reading of the manuscript. The final work has been improved greatly by all this most valued assistance for which I am indeed grateful. It gives very special meaning to the usual and proper disclaimer— that, despite all such help, the errors which remain are my own responsibility. Errors there must be despite the careful checking which has been done, if only because the records here dealt with are so widely scattered. Advice regarding errors and omissions which are noticed will be most welcome.

The finished appearance of the volume is testimony to the care which has been devoted to it by the staff of the University of Toronto Press, but it fails to indicate the personal attention which the project has received continually from the Director of the Press, Mr. M. Jeanneret, and his Assistant Director, Miss Eleanor Harman. Only they and I know how much the finished text owes to the skilled editorial assistance and very real interest of Miss Frances G. Halpenny, Associate Editor.

Finally, I am under a special debt to two ladies. Mrs. B. M. McCrohon of Montreal has typed most of the book in its various stages of development, always with a lively understanding. My wife has exercised a degree of forbearance far beyond that usually required of the wife of an engineer, in the course of journeys which are now known as "lock-hopping," and as the book itself has taken up an increasing number of leisure hours. Without her assistance, and continued encouragement, it could not have been completed.

R. L.

Ottawa
September 29, 1955

Note to the Revised Edition

ALTHOUGH the historical background of the Rideau Waterway does not change with the years, its surroundings do. Since this book was first published the St. Lawrence Seaway and the associated power development at Cornwall-Messina have been built; on the Ottawa River, the Carillon hydro-electric development has been completed; and new bridges and highways have been constructed in the vicinity of and across the Canal. In this Revised Edition the references to these contiguous works have been brought up to date. In addition the appendices have been fully revised to give the latest information and regulations relating to fishing, maps and charts, and the Waterway generally.

It is fortunate that the timing of this new edition has permitted appreciative reference to be made to the statue of Colonel By that is now to be found in Major's Hill Park in Ottawa. The Historical Society of Ottawa demonstrated in this very practical but delightful way their admiration of this great man, in tribute to whom this book was written. It has been a continuing pleasure to share with members of this Society and with other readers who have so kindly spoken with me, or written to me, the delights of this ancient but increasingly useful Waterway.

February 1972   R.L.

Contents

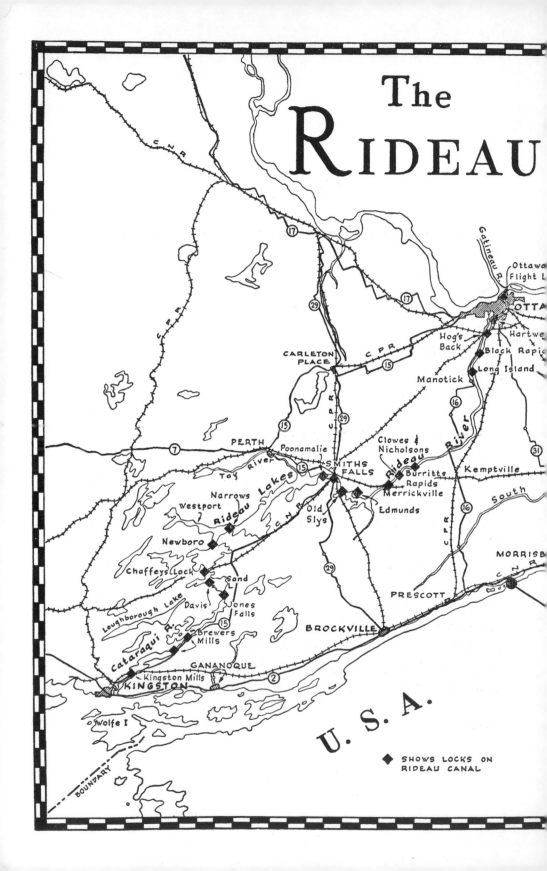

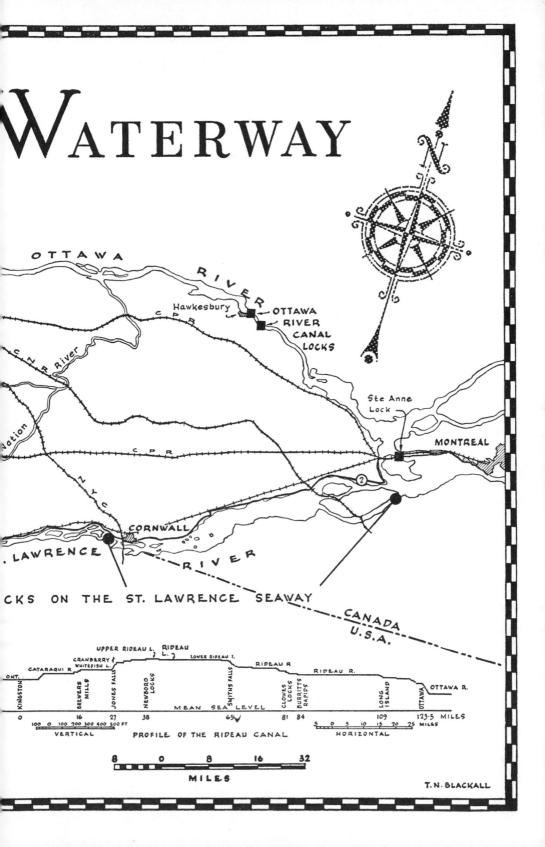

WATERWAY

OTTAWA RIVER

Hawkesbury

OTTAWA RIVER CANAL LOCKS

C P R

C N R River

Nation

Ste Anne Lock

MONTREAL

C P R

N Y C

②

CORNWALL

. LAWRENCE RIVER

CKS ON THE ST. LAWRENCE SEAWAY

CANADA U.S.A.

UPPER RIDEAU L. Rideau L.
CRANBERRY
WHITEFISH L.
Lower Rideau I.
CATARAQUI R.
RIDEAU R
Rideau R.
ONT.
BREWERS MILLS
JONES FALLS
NEWBORO LOCKS
SMYTHS FALLS
CLOWES LOCKS
BURRITTS RAPIDS
LONG ISLAND
OTTAWA
OTTAWA R.
KINGSTON
MEAN SEA LEVEL

| 0 | 16 | 27 | 38 | 65 | 81 | 84 | 109 | 123·5 MILES |

100 0 100 200 300 400 500 FT
VERTICAL
PROFILE OF THE RIDEAU CANAL
5 0 5 10 15 20 25 MILES
HORIZONTAL

8   0   8   16   32
MILES

T. N. BLACKALL

RIDEAU WATERWAY

Rideau Waterway

THERE IS a lovely waterway in Old Ontario. The Rideau Canal is
its official name but a greater contrast with the murky industrial
trafficway which the word "canal" immediately calls to mind, it
would be hard to imagine. Rather is this canal a silver chain of
rivers and lakes, linked by small locks and winding channels. Let
us call it the *Rideau Waterway*, a gracious name for one of the
most beautiful of all the inland water routes of North America.
A canal it is in part, of course, although for well over a hundred
miles of its total length it is but a well-marked channel—up the
Rideau River, through the headwater lakes, and then down the
Cataraqui River into Lake Ontario. Stretching from Canada's
capital city of Ottawa to the ancient city of Kingston at the foot
of Lake Ontario, it converts into an island a great triangle of land,
bounded also by the Ottawa River and the great St. Lawrence,
an island which forms the eastern tip of Ontario with the famed
district of Glengarry at its centre. The Waterway was built well
over one hundred years ago, long before thought had been given
to any sort of industry in this land of forests, lakes, and streams.
And it has retained much of its natural beauty. Even today it
passes through country which is still virtually untouched by
commerce.

The Waterway presents many paradoxes. It was built by the
Royal Engineers of Great Britain as a military work of great
urgency, to counter a real threat of attack from the United States
by providing an alternative route for the transport of military
stores and troops from Montreal to Kingston. In the late
eighteenth and early nineteenth centuries, Kingston was of great
strategic importance since it guarded the Great Lakes for the

British by means of its forts and naval dockyard. The coming of peace to this continent removed the need for such an alternative route and so the Canal was never extensively used for its original purpose. Today, its most enthusiastic users are guests of Canada from the United States, many of whom know it better than some of the Canadians who live on its banks.

The Canal was to connect Lake Ontario with the sea. Water travel up to Kingston had had to follow the St. Lawrence with its many portages and swift waters. Once the Rideau Canal was built, steamboats could navigate easily from Montreal to Kingston. For almost twenty years fleets of busy little steamers, plying the triangular route from Montreal to Kingston by way of Ottawa, made it truly the original St. Lawrence Seaway. Only when the first St. Lawrence Canal system was complete (in 1851) did it lose this unique position. Today, another St. Lawrence Seaway has been built, not only as an international venture but with its first locks on both sides of "the frontier," to assist in the defence of which the Rideau Canal was constructed.

Although the Canal was built to provide a water route to Kingston, few residents of that city and even fewer visitors ever give thought today to the nearby waterway, if, indeed, they know it is there. But at the other end of the Canal, at the remote spot on the banks of the Ottawa River where at first there was no settlement of any sort, has grown the modern city of Ottawa. Today, the Canal and its surrounding gardens are an enviable feature of the nation's capital, a pleasant attraction for residents and visitors alike.

During its early history, the Waterway carried much freight—timber from the forests around, until these were cut down, and then large quantities of coal to a town known for its link with the Canadian Pacific Railway. So close were early relations between waterways and railways that, on one famous occasion, the Rideau Canal carried a steam locomotive in order that a new railway line might be opened. The days of such happy co-operation between rival means of transportation have long since disappeared. The railways now carry their own coal, and all freight services on the Canal are a thing of the past.

The centenary of the Canal was celebrated not by tributes to its years of service but by a demand that it be closed down, its dams in some way demolished and its locks abandoned. This was in 1932, when economy was necessarily a national watchword.

Fortunately this impossible suggestion was not insisted upon. Today, the Canal is as busy in summer months as it has been for many a long year, and its traffic steadily increases. But the boats which now sail its waters are in search of pleasure, small craft of all types, of diverse sizes, and from destinations as far away as Florida and New Orleans. For, even though located in the heart of old Ontario, the Waterway is linked through other canals with most of the inland waterways of the eastern United States— paradox indeed when the military imperative of its construction as a defence against the Americans is remembered.

These are all material aspects of the Canal. Like many another work of engineers, it has its human side also and here, too, is paradox. Not only was it the last but it was certainly also the greatest work of British military engineers to be carried out in eastern North America. Despite this, it was completed—so it seems today—with no real authority from the British Parliament, the only authorization being for a preliminary expenditure of £5,000. In due course it was ceded by the Imperial government to the Province of Canada, ten years before Confederation, another of the gracious gifts from the Old Land to the New.

Many men worked on its construction. Many lives were lost, owing surprisingly, not to the rigours of the Canadian winter, but to fever in the hot and humid swamps of the Rideau Lakes. Some of the main contractors became leading figures in the life of the Canada of their day; their descendants carry names still well known in Montreal and eastern Canada. One of them built the mansion which is now the residence of Canada's Governor-General. Another built one of Canada's most famous churches while he was completing his work on the Canal. Many of the masons employed on the canal works continued their craft after their discharge and endowed this part of Canada with a legacy of some of the finest stone masonry houses to be found today anywhere in the Dominion.

But perhaps the greatest paradox is provided by the man who, above all others, was responsible for the building of the Canal. Lieutenant Colonel John By was sent from England to be the Superintending Engineer. In less than six years he had finished this work, gigantic in scope for its time, building it through virgin forests and along untamed rivers without the aid of any modern equipment and machinery, using mainly the materials he found in the area adjacent to the route of the Canal. Not only did he finish the project as planned, and almost as scheduled, but at a cost which today seems almost unbelievable, about £800,000 (or $2,500,000 in terms of the present day) for a waterway extending over one hundred and twenty miles, with forty-seven masonry locks and many dams, including masonry structures up to sixty feet in height. His achievement can well be regarded as one of the great engineering works of the last century. Colonel By arrived in Canada to start the canal in 1826. With his family and friends he sailed through the completed canal at the end of May 1832. Four days before this triumphant cruise started, an order was issued by the British government recalling him to England for questioning before a Parliamentary Committee, not in recognition of his meritorious achievement but because expenditures had exceeded those authorized. He was exonerated but the honours which should have been his never came his way and he died four years later, worn out by his zeal.

The following pages present the story of the Rideau Canal. Fully to appreciate its quiet beauty in high summer today, we need to know something of the way in which it was built, and to know this means knowing something of the strange story which led to its construction. We shall look first at the setting of the Canal and the country around it. (The reader is referred to the maps in the text and on pages xii–xiii for aid in visualizing the route of the Canal.) The next chapters trace briefly the reasons for building the Waterway and show how it was built, before recounting something of the man chiefly responsible for its successful completion. People are always more interesting than things or places but to see the men of the Rideau Canal at their full stature we must know too something of the work they did. With these men in mind, we then take an imaginary journey through the Canal finding ourselves tempted by such names as Indian Lake, Cranberry Lake, Chaffeys Lock and Brewers Mills, conscious as we pass through the locks of the smooth blocks of stone which were hewn in the bush more than a century ago to form this fine masonry, and noticing some of the tombstones in the quiet countryside which mark the graves of men who died in the building of these locks. It is hoped that this journey may add to the enjoyment of those who know the Canal already and possibly lead others to come to know its pleasant waters. So closely has the development of Canada's capital city been associated with the Canal that some account of Ottawa must, finally, be included. This is not intended to be even an abbreviated history of Ottawa but rather to show how the city owes its start and its initial planning to Colonel By and that what was once a rather nondescript little town has, because of the care with which the Canal within its limits has been developed, become a singularly lovely city.

The Setting

IN ORDER to visualize properly the setting in which the Canal was built, we have to look back well over a century. Fortunately it is not difficult to do this in the case of the Rideau Waterway. To-day one can paddle a canoe on any one of the Rideau Lakes past scenes which have not altered a great deal since they were first seen by the early explorers. The character of the trees has changed, since the noble white pine is no longer dominant, but the closely wooded shores, the rocky islands, and the quiet are as vivid and timeless today as they were two hundred years ago. Country typical of the Waterway can be surveyed to good advantage at Ottawa, meeting place of three rivers. Standing at the top of the Peace Tower of the Parliament Buildings, on a clear day one can trace the Ottawa River, through its broad expanse as Lac Deschenes, over the Chaudière Falls, and eastwards on its way to Montreal. Looking over to Quebec, one can pick out the course of the Gatineau River as it comes to join the Ottawa from the hills and forests to the north. And in the south, the thin line of the Rideau River can just be distinguished as it flows in a grand sweep from the fertile plains of Carleton County to join the Ottawa over its famous falls. Up in the valley of the Gatineau, one can stand and look upon miles of wooded shore line, re-splendent in its colours of the fall; early travellers would have passed in their canoes along rivers just such as this. Or one can stop at the lookout on the old Ottawa to Montreal highway, just to the east of Hawkesbury, and, forgetting the highway and automobile and several undistinguished bridges, enjoy the mag-nificent sweep of the Ottawa Valley with its rolling terrain, its cover of trees deceptively widespread when viewed from a distance, and imagine the great river plunging over the rapids which once were here, now submerged by the Carillon Dam.

In the days of its eminence, the Ottawa River was the direct water route from Montreal to lands of adventure to the west and to the north. There are many vantage points within the city limits of today (notably the Rockcliffe Lookout) where a still summer evening invites one to overlook the few modern buildings within sight and picture the great canoe flotillas of the past as they carried explorers on their way to the unknown, or brought back *coureurs de bois* with their loads of fur and tales of great achievement. Champlain saw the site of the capital in 1613, and many *voyageurs* were to follow him along the Ottawa. Etienne Brulé, Jean Nicolet, Radisson and Des Groseilliers, d'Iberville, Duluth, La Mothe Cadillac, La Vérendrye, Alexander Henry, Joseph and Thomas Frobisher, Peter Pond, Simon McTavish, Alexander Mackenzie, Lord Selkirk, and John Franklin—all have sailed these waters, all have portaged the Chaudière Falls, all have passed the mouth of the Gatineau and the lovely falls of the Rideau. Some of these early travellers may have heard that the Indians regularly used the Rideau River as a route to some of their hunting grounds and for their own tribal travelling. The Ottawa and the St. Lawrence, however, provided two such wonderful waterways, from their junction at Montreal, that they satisfied all the needs of the early white settlers for transportation routes into the west.

Montreal is indeed the real beginning of a description of the Waterway, and part of the reason for its construction. Throughout the days of water transportation in Canada, it was the focal point of all but local journeys. Even today, and despite the great changes in transportation facilities, it is still the hub of a network of communications that is unique in Canada and unequalled elsewhere in more than a very few locations. It was the necessity of portaging around the first rapids on the St. Lawrence which led to the founding of the city. Stopped on their sail up the great river from the sea by the rapids at what is now Lachine, the early explorers found a confusion of channels in the country around. These were soon made out to be the two rivers which form the great island of Montreal and the neighbouring Ile Jésus, flowing out of the Lake of Two Mountains, itself at the junction of two mighty streams. From the southwest came the St. Lawrence River, one of the most remarkable rivers of the world in the well-regulated flow of its water from the Great Lakes, and one of the largest in its length and drainage area. From the west, flowing directly into the Lake of Two Mountains, came the Ottawa River, here a tributary of the St. Lawrence but itself almost seven hundred miles long with a drainage basin equal in area to that of Nova Scotia and New Brunswick combined.

To the first white travellers in Canada, these were routes leading only to the unknown. The very name Lachine—*La Chine*—is a constant reminder of the hopes of early travellers that up these great rivers would be found the long-looked-for gateway to the Far East. This was not to be but they proved instead to be doorways to a new continent. Explorers continuing up the St. Lawrence discovered the Great Lakes and through them the Mississippi and the mid-west. Those who ventured up the Ottawa came also to the Great Lakes by the portage into Lake Nipissing but, of more importance to Canada, they were led by the river itself to the headwaters of streams which flowed into James Bay and Hudson Bay, and so to the North.

The St. Lawrence River forms such an obvious natural boundary that it was used as an international frontier almost from the time when the United States and Canada first came to define their limits. Most of the stretch of the great river from Lake St. Joseph to Lake Ontario has thus served as a part of one of the longest international boundaries since 1783. In time of war, it became a critical supply line, in constant danger of attack, but for well over a century now it has been developed with no thought of military need but only as one of the great commercial waterways of the world. The Seaway, jointly built by two good neighbours, increases still further its international service by making it possible for large ocean-going vessels from many lands to sail upon it. The Ottawa, on the other hand, is wholly a Canadian river. It, too, has seen fighting but only with the Indians: the tale of the stand of Dollard des Ormeaux and his sixteen French companions against the Iroquois at the Carillon Rapids of the Ottawa has become a Canadian epic. The Ottawa was the great canoe route to north and west and was so well used by travellers that, at the same time that the first St. Lawrence canals were being built (and also at the time of the building of the Rideau Canal), the first report was made on the possibility of developing a canal route using the Ottawa River and the portages from it over to Georgian Bay. For many years the Georgian Bay Ship

Canal as an alternative to the international St. Lawrence route was a live issue in Canada. A glance at a map of eastern Canada will show how natural a route it appears to be, on paper. Plans were drawn up, even test borings were made, but it was never built.

Today, the Ottawa River carries no through river traffic; the St. Lawrence has become an international enterprise, one which reaches its culmination in the great power dam and locks of the Seaway. But it is the two rivers which continue to give Montreal its eminence as the hub of a great transportation network. When the railways came, they followed the rivers from Montreal—the Grand Trunk (now Canadian National) along the St. Lawrence to Toronto, Chicago, and the mid-west, and the Canadian Pacific (now joined by the Canadian National) along the Ottawa to North Bay and the west of Canada. Main roads followed the same pattern when highway transportation came into its own. And today, the planes which take off from Montreal's great airport at Dorval, almost within sight of the Lachine Rapids, follow the same two rivers to the same familiar places.

This importance of the junction of the two rivers is in no way reflected by the actual meeting of the waters. They are so large and the land is so flat at their confluence, that there is no opportunity for drama. There are, it is true, the two mountains at Oka from which the Lake of Two Mountains takes its name but in general the entire area has few distinguishing features. The underlying limestone rock has been covered by deep deposits of soil, much of it laid down when this region was invaded by the sea some thousands of years ago. The five Monteregian Hills, one of which—Mount Royal—gives Montreal its name, are the remains of ancient volcanoes which broke through the crust of the local bedrock, but they stand out noticeably from the great St. Lawrence plain which forms a wide area around the meeting of the two rivers and along both their banks for some distance above. The plain between the rivers extends for well over one hundred miles to the west of Montreal and in this plain the northern part of the Rideau Canal has its course.

Above the Lachine Rapids, the St. Lawrence widens out into an open stretch of water which was early called Lake St. Louis. At its western end are the Ste Anne Rapids leading up to the Lake of Two Mountains and the Ottawa River and, on the south side of Ile Perrot, the main river flowing into the placid waters of the lake from a stretch of fast water which includes three rapids—Cascades, Cedars, and Coteau. On the north bank of the St Lawrence, these rapids were once circumvented by the Soulanges Canal and on the south side by the great canal feeding the Beauharnois Power development which has ingeniously become the new ship canal. At the head of the Coteau Rapids, the river again widens out, this time into Lake St. Francis which stretches for twenty miles to the foot of the relatively narrow international section of the river. For about sixty miles, the great river flows here between low-lying banks, still through the St. Lawrence plain, the north bank in Canada, the south in the United States. The water level of the river used to rise gradually as one went west, through a series of rapids, which included the Long Sault, all of them circumvented by a series of small Canadian canals built in the nineteenth century and large enough only for small ocean-going vessels and lower lake freight vessels. Large freighters used to trans-ship their cargoes of grain at Prescott into the grain elevator, the smaller vessels then taking it to Montreal. Now all the rapids and canals are drowned out by the great power dam at Cornwall-Mesina, navigation for the largest lake vessels and large ocean-going vessels being through the new Seaway locks.

Soon after Brockville there is a striking change in the scenery. Small islands increase to such numbers that this stretch of the river has been happily named the Thousand Islands section. The river breaks up into numerous channels, some of which flow between quite high cliffs. Advantage has been taken of this unusual terrain to build a series of bridges across the several channels; from the two high-placed suspension spans of the Ivy Lea international crossing the bolder character of the countryside can clearly be seen. Gradually the scenery reverts to its former flat pattern near Kingston, lying sheltered by the largest of the islands, Wolfe Island; the ship channel passes on the south side of this island and enters Lake Ontario almost immediately. The level of the lake is normally 245 feet above sea level, or about 225 feet above the water level at Montreal. Kingston, established early at a site known to the Indians as Cataraqui, was the guardian of the lakes for the British, in the warlike years of the late eighteenth and early nineteenth centuries, the site not only of an important fort but of the main naval dockyard. Travel to Kingston, however, was possible only along the route just briefly described—up the St. Lawrence with all its portages and swift waters. The Rideau Canal, built to provide an alternative route for military transport between Montreal and Kingston, joins the St. Lawrence here, through the estuary of the Cataraqui River which forms a part of the modern harbour of Kingston.

But let us return to Montreal in order to take a look at the Ottawa River before dealing further with the Canal. Above the Lake of Two Mountains the Ottawa flows, as does the St. Lawrence, between low-lying banks in the St. Lawrence plain. Rapids were encountered first at Carillon, twenty-seven miles from Ste Anne de Bellevue, and again at Grenville amout six miles further upstream. Three small military canals built in the 1830's by the Royal Staff Corps used to circumvent the rapids. Rapids and canals have now been drowned by the damming-up of the river by the great Carillon power dam of Hydro Quebec, completed in 1962. Beyond the Long Sault Rapids, however, the river was navigable for a further fifty-six miles all the way to the Chaudière Falls at what is now Ottawa. The Chaudière Falls, and the rapids immediately upstream of them, constituted the first real barrier on the Ottawa River, necessitating in earlier days a long portage even for canoes; it is here that the Gatineau River joins the Ottawa from the north and the Rideau River from the south. It is not surprising, therefore, that the first settlement of any kind in this region should have taken place near the foot of these falls: Hull was founded here by Philemon Wright in 1800.

The scenery along the Ottawa, upstream from Montreal, is not dissimilar to that along the St. Lawrence. To the south, the St. Lawrence plain stretches as far as the eye can see. The land on the north bank is similarly flat but a few miles west of the Lake of Two Mountains a range of hills appears to the north. This is actually the southern edge of what we now call generally the Precambrian Shield, the great exposure of the oldest rock types in the world which extends over almost one half the land area of Canada, from the Mackenzie River in the far west to Labrador in the east, and from the Ottawa area in the south to the Arctic wastes of the north. The Laurentian Mountains is the name often given to that part of the Shield north of the Ottawa River; they gradually approach the river but even at Ottawa they are still a few miles away. Some distance beyond the Chaudière Falls the Ottawa River actually crosses the southern border of the Shield. Then it changes its character. Rapids and swift water have abounded in this upper part of the Ottawa, but most of the fall is now tamed in a series of great water power stations.

The south bank remains flat all the way between the island of

Montreal and the site of Ottawa. The map shows how a gradual change in its course sends the river parallel to the St. Lawrence and at a distance of about fifty miles from it. Drainage from this level plain is limited and so there are only three tributaries to the Ottawa of any note from the south, the little Rigaud River, the South Nation River, and the Rideau. Most of this great triangular

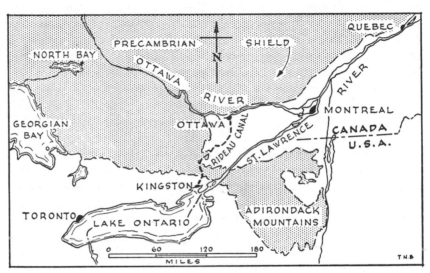

The Rideau Canal in relation to major cities and the Precambrian Shield

plain is drained by the South Nation, an unusual river since its headwaters are only three miles from the north bank of the St. Lawrence and but a few feet above. This oddity is explained, however, by the fact that the St. Lawrence is here 240 feet above sea level whereas the Ottawa, at its junction with the South Nation, is only 70 feet above sea level, so that there is enough drop for the South Nation River to flow in the way it does. We can begin to see also how it was possible to join the Ottawa with the St. Lawrence across this great plain.

Apart from the fact that it drops into the Ottawa River over a waterfall about thirty-five feet high, the Rideau is very similar to the South Nation for its first fifty miles. It flows peacefully through a flat plain and is joined, in turn, by a number of tributary streams. The Jock River is the largest of these, others being Kemptville Creek (or the South Rideau), Steven Creek, and Irish Creek. At Smiths Falls, the Rideau begins its flow out to the

Ottawa from the Rideau Lakes. A few of the many Rideau Lakes
are so located that they drain towards the St. Lawrence, their
outlet streams combining to form the small Cataraqui River and
the nearby Gananoque River. One of the early schemes for the
Rideau Canal involved using the Gananoque River, instead of
the Cataraqui, and joining it to the Irish Creek just mentioned as
a tributary of the Rideau, but the project was found to be impracticable.

At Smiths Falls a great change occurs in the nature of the
Rideau River and also in the scenery. The border of the Precambrian Shield has swung round: an outlier of this great rock
mass appears well below the normal line of its southern limit and
crosses the St. Lawrence River to form the Adirondack Mountains
of northern New York. All who are familiar with the beautiful
Adirondack region will recognize its similarity to the Laurentians
north of Montreal. Similar too is the Rideau Lakes area from
which the Rideau River emerges. The Kawartha Lakes, to the
northwest of the Rideau Lakes, have just the same rugged charm.
The Precambrian rocks dominating these various landscapes account also for the Thousand Islands: they are the tops of rocky
hills like those in the Adirondacks or the Laurentians which long
ago were almost concealed as the relative levels of land, sea, and
lakes slowly changed with the melting of the great ice masses
which once covered this area. This band of Precambrian rock is
of great significance to geologists: they know it as the Frontenac
Axis, so called because it is a prominent feature of Frontenac
County in which the city of Kingston is located. Kingston itself
is out of the Precambrian area; it is at the eastern extremity of a
low-lying plain very similar to the St. Lawrence plain, which is
composed of deep soil deposits resting upon just the same type
of underlying bedrock. There is no need for us to dip much
further into geological matters but the influence of this extension
of the Shield had so profound an effect on the Rideau River, and
thus on the route and construction of the Canal, that this explanation is a necessary preliminary to an account of the Waterway.

From this general background we may select certain aspects
which became of special importance when the Canal was projected. We have seen that the Ottawa River is joined, about one
hundred miles above its junction with the St. Lawrence, by the
Rideau River. This tributary, coming from the south, flows for its
lower fifty miles through flat and fertile agricultural land. It has

its source, however, in the Rideau Lakes which lie almost three
hundred feet above the level of the Ottawa River at the mouth
of the Rideau. The Lakes drain also to the south, into Lake
Ontario, one of the outlets being the small Cataraqui River which
enters the lake near the city of Kingston. Owing to the elevation
of Lake Ontario, there is a fall of only one hundred and sixty
feet in the Cataraqui River in its course from its headwaters in
the Rideau Lakes. The lakes are so interlaced that only small
portages are required to get from those which drain into the
Rideau River into those which drain to the south. When, therefore, an alternative water route was required between Montreal
and Kingston, there was a possibility of coming up the Ottawa
River, then up the Rideau into the Rideau Lakes, and then down
the Cataraqui to Lake Ontario.

But if this waterway was to carry anything more than canoes,
some means had to be found of surmounting the many rapids on
all three rivers. This could be accomplished by using the device
of locks, first invented (so it is said) by Leonardo da Vinci as one
of his many master designs. The operation of locks is extremely
simple in essentials, and will be familiar to all readers of this
book. It is necessary to have water at the foot of the lock deep
enough so that a boat may sail into the lock when the water in it
is lowered to the level of the river downstream and, correspondingly, to have the level of the water upstream of the lock so
controlled that, when the lock has been filled, the vessel being
"locked up" can sail out and on up its channel until the foot of the
next lock is reached. This controlling of water levels is achieved
by means of dams, built across rivers at points where there is a
steep enough fall to call for the use of a lock, or for groups of
locks, the dam "drowning out" the rapids or small falls which have
to be surmounted. Locks had been used in a small way on canals
built before the Rideau but Colonel By built locks and control
dams on a scale previously unheard of, even in early American
engineering circles. Not only did he build locks and dams on the
main rivers but also control dams on side streams in order to
provide the equally essential reservoirs from which would come
the necessary water to replenish that discharged downstream
every time a lock was used.

The Waterway which resulted is 123½ miles long, measured
from the beginning of the chain of locks at Ottawa to the bascule
bridge across Kingston Harbour which may be taken as the

junction of the Canal with Lake Ontario. About eighteen miles of this total length are really an artificial waterway, the remainder being the ordinary courses of the two rivers and the lakes which form a part of the route. There are a number of so-called branches, one up Kemptville Creek to the town of Kemptville and four on the Lakes to give access to small towns once served by the Canal, and there is one real branch, constructed just after the Canal proper had been completed. This leads from Big Rideau Lake to the town of Perth; it is almost seven miles long, and has two locks with a total lift of 26 feet.

On the main Canal, there are altogether forty-seven locks with a total lift, up and down, of 439 feet. Thirty-three of these locks are required for the ascent from Ottawa to the summit level of the Canal which is in Upper Rideau Lake, with a lift of 277 feet. For the descent from Upper Rideau Lake to Kingston, only fourteen locks are used, the drop being 162 feet. The difference in the number of locks for the two sections matches the more gradual rise from Ottawa to Upper Rideau Lake, the average lift in each lock on this section being only 8½ feet, and the steeper descent to Kingston, the average lift of these locks being 11½ feet. The locks all measure 134 feet long and are 33 feet wide, but the maximum size of vessel permitted through the Canal is 110 feet in length with a 30-foot beam. The official limiting draught is five feet but boats drawing up to five and a half feet may normally go through all parts of the Waterway. The main channel of the Canal has a minimum width of 60 feet at the bottom and 80 feet at the top, but the rounded bottom sections of some of the locks limit the size of barges which can be moved through the Canal to somewhat less than the minimum size for normally shaped boats. Bridges over the Canal limit the overhead clearance for masts, the critical section being at the Ottawa end where the limit is 22 feet.

At the Ottawa end the Canal starts with a flight of eight locks which have become a familiar sight through popular photographs showing them adjacent to the Parliament Buildings. This great water stairway, with a total lift of over eighty feet, is necessary in order to overcome the drop of the Rideau Falls into the Ottawa. The flight brings the Canal up to the level at which it is seen along Ottawa's Driveways and in Dows Lake. Still within the city limits of Ottawa are the next locks, a set of two at Hartwells, and another set of two at the Hog's Back Dam. Two more sets

of locks come within the next few miles, and there is also at
Long Island one of the notable arched masonry dams which are
so striking a feature of the engineering works of the Waterway.
Then follows a stretch of water over twenty miles long in which
the Canal is the river itself, as it flows gently through the level
fertile farms of this part of Carleton County. A succession of
locks in the next twenty miles leads to the two sets, one a flight
of three, at Smiths Falls. Here, too, is a fine arched dam near the
centre of the town, but the interested visitor must search for it.
The lock which follows those at Smiths Falls lifts the Canal to the
level of Big Rideau Lake, the first and largest of the Rideau
Lakes. It is from this lake that the Tay Branch to Perth takes
off, the Beveridge Lock being located at the mouth of the Tay
River. A lock at The Narrows connects Big Rideau and Upper
Rideau Lakes; the latter is the summit of the Canal and so the
link between the Rideau River system and the Cataraqui River.
What used to be a portage became a cutting through the height
of land into Newboro Lake, whence the Canal descends through
Opinicon, Sand, Whitefish, and Cranberry Lakes. A large bog
between the last two of these lakes was submerged when the
water level was raised by the building of a dam at Brewers Mills;
it was the site of some of the greatest difficulties in building the
Canal. Between Sand and Whitefish Lakes is the outstanding
piece of engineering of the entire system, the great arched dam
and flight of four locks at Jones Falls. Still but little known except
to fishermen and the occasional visitor, this giant curved stairway of locks, flanked by a dam which is a noble structure even
by modern standards, is perhaps the most striking testimony to
the skill of Colonel By and those associated with him in the
construction of this Waterway through the bush. Below Brewers
Mills, the Canal is formed by an artificial lake created by the
flooding of the old course of the Cataraqui River by the dam at
Kingston Mills, where there is another flight of three locks in a
beautiful narrow gorge. The last of these locks discharges into the
estuary of the Cataraqui at the level of Lake Ontario, and from
this point it is a sail of about six miles to the bridge over Kingston
Harbour which marks the official end of the canal route.

From what has been said, it will be clear that a good water
supply is necessary for Upper Rideau Lake, from which locks
descend at both ends to the two river systems. Fortunately, a
chain of lakes feeds into Upper Rideau Lake; known as the

Wolfe Lake system, it includes Clear, Wolfe, and Sand Lakes, the waters from all of which therefore drain both into the St. Lawrence and the Ottawa Rivers. These lakes enter Upper Rideau Lake at the town of Westport; they come in from the west but their headwaters are only a few miles from Kingston.

There are no less than fifty-three lakes in this one small area, varying from one to fifteen miles long. With some relatively unimportant exceptions, all the lakes lie to the west or northwest of the canal route so that the Waterway can be thought of as on the side of a gentle slope to the southwest, with most of the lakes draining into it and through it into the Rideau and Cataraqui Rivers; the few exceptions drain directly into the St. Lawrence. A look at this integrated pattern of lakes and interconnecting streams on a large map, or better still from the air, demonstrates the skill of the engineers in selecting for the Canal what is clearly the best route without benefit of any detailed maps, and with access to the entire area only by water.

It would add little to this account to detail all the tributary lake systems which feed into the Canal. Mention may, perhaps, be made of the Tay River system since it is one of the most important feeders. Bobbs Lake is one unit of this system which supplies water to the Ottawa eventually, and yet the lake is located not twenty-five miles from Kingston. The source of the Loughborough Lake system, which admittedly feeds eventually into the Cataraqui, is only seven miles from Kingston. A final note on this maze of natural waterways: allowance was even made for the possibility that the Rideau Waterway might be getting too much water for there is a small overflow or spillway dam at Morton, just below the great flight of locks at Jones Falls, which serves as a "safety valve" to the system; water which flows over it, should the lake level behind it get too high, moves down Morton Creek into Lower Beverley Lake and eventually into the St. Lawrence by way of the Gananoque River.

Some of the names which we have mentioned have included the word "Mills." It was only natural that with two rivers dropping rapidly in level, the power of the falling water not used for the locks should have been utilized. This was done in the early days by the erection of water-mills at most of the locks but almost all the old individual mills have now ceased to operate. There are, however, some small modern hydro-electric plants along the Canal, the most recent having been built just a few

years ago below the great dam at Jones Falls. Thus the early
military work brought in its train civilian conveniences for the
district through which it was built. Each of the locks became the
nucleus of a modest settlement since there had to be a staff for
lock operation. And the necessary maintenance of the Canal has
given work throughout the years to a small group of men, many
of whom have been skilled workers at their special trades.

The Rideau Canal completes, as will now be seen, the triangle
formed as the Ottawa and the St. Lawrence Rivers come together
to join above the island of Montreal. Starting at Montreal, or
rather Lachine, one can sail up Lake St. Louis to the locks at
Ste Anne de Bellevue, then up the Lake of Two Mountains, up
the Ottawa River using the little Carillon and Grenville Canals to
get around the rapids, right up to the entrance to the Rideau
Canal, beneath the shadow of the Parliament Buildings at Ottawa. By diverting up the Rideau Waterway, one can proceed to
Kingston on the St. Lawrence and then by a sail downstream,
using the Canadian St. Lawrence canals on the way, one eventually completes the triangular tour and gets back to Lake St. Louis
at Montreal.

Further choices are, however, available. Below Montreal, one
may turn up the Richelieu River at Sorel and from it reach Lake
Champlain, Lake George, and so the Hudson River, which in
turn leads to the great Inland Waterway serving the south of the
United States. If, alternatively, one turns upstream at Kingston,
there is the New York State Barge Canal which can be entered
at Oswego, leading again to the Hudson through the Mohawk
Valley. Course may also be set up Lake Ontario to the Welland
Canal for access to Lake Erie and the other Great Lakes, and so
also to the Chicago River with its link with the Mississippi and
all its tributaries. The Rideau Waterway, therefore, is much more
than a small canal running through lovely country between
Ottawa and Kingston. It is part of a great network of inland
waterways in Canada and the United States which permit safe
and pleasant journeys over half the continent.

Why the Canal was Built

THE STORY of the Rideau Waterway may really be said to start on that day in April 1760 when the last battle was fought at Quebec. At the signing of the Treaty of Paris, three years later, Canada became a colony limited to an area about two hundred miles wide stretching on either side of the St. Lawrence from Gaspé to near Cornwall, including the Ottawa River and just touching Lake Nipissing. Most of what lay beyond these strange boundaries was unknown. It may be disconcerting to some to think that even the site of Toronto was not included in the original land of Canada. Little more than ten years after the Treaty of Paris came the Quebec Act which extended the boundaries of the young colony southward to the Ohio and westward to the Mississippi. With the coming of peace after the Revolutionary War and the Treaty of Versailles, 1783, the shape and size of Canada were changed again. The fertile but unpeopled territory south of the Great Lakes was given to the United States but Britain's sovereignty north of the St. Lawrence and the Lakes was now unchallenged. These had been unsettled years for the colony and the problem of security had been ever present in the minds of the authorities.

An immediate result of the period of peace after the American Revolution was the start of the northward movement of the Loyalists into the Maritimes, Quebec, and what is now Ontario. Many began to settle along the Canadian shore of what had just become the international section of the St. Lawrence but the problem of finding other suitable locations, not only for the Loyalists but also for discharged soldiers, became a matter of great concern to the government. One result of this concern was

the first move in the long series of studies which eventually led
to the building of the Rideau Canal.

In 1783 the British government sent two military officers to
explore the country on either side of the Ottawa River. Lieutenant
Jones travelled along the north bank of the river as far as the
Chaudière Falls; he crossed these and returned to Montreal along
the south shore. Lieutenant French had a more interesting assignment. With two canoes for his party of seven soldiers, two Canadians, and an Indian as guide, he came up the Ottawa and
portaged the Rideau Falls on October 2. He followed the Rideau
River to its source in the Rideau Lakes, made the portage into
the "Gananoncoui" River, and sailed down it to the St. Lawrence
and then back to Montreal. Both officers found a large amount of
land suitable for settlement; their reports contain references to
the good quality of the soil along the Rideau River and to the
great variety of trees: maple, elm, butternut, ash, cedar, and pine.
No official action appears to have been taken on the basis of their
reports, settlement being generally confined to the St. Lawrence
Valley, but the journey of Lieutenant French had shown that a
through route did exist between the Ottawa and the St. Lawrence.
This was known previously only from the reports of Indians who
regularly followed it from Lake Simcoe on their way to the
Ottawa. It was not an obvious route for the journeyings of the
voyageurs, although the site of the beautiful Falls of the Rideau,
cascading into the Ottawa just before the Chaudière portage,
must often have attracted the attention of early travellers to the
west.

The Report of Lieutenant French is the first written record of
the Rideau Waterway. It might well have suggested to the more
penetrating military minds of the time that here was an alternative route between Montreal and the Great Lakes, and one of
significance in view of the increasing importance of the fortress
and dockyard at Kingston. There are some grounds for believing
that plans for a military canal route between Montreal and
Kingston, utilizing the Rideau River, were submitted to the British
government in 1790. European affairs, however, were keeping
that government fully occupied at the time. In Canada the Con-
stitutional Act of 1791 would tend also to divert attention from
such possibilities, in view of all the difficulties attendant on the
introduction of representative government and the splitting up
of the colony into Upper and Lower Canada.

The opening of the nineteenth century found the colony just emerging from all the uncertainties of its political development since the Treaty of Paris, and the first signs appearing of the basic changes in its simple economy which the century was to witness. Settlements were still small, Quebec City having even in 1825 a population of only 22,101, Montreal 22,357, Kingston 2,849 and York (as Toronto was to be known for some time yet) only 1,677. Settlement was, however, beginning to spread beyond the immediate valley of the St. Lawrence. In 1800, Philemon Wright founded the little village of Hull and began rafting big timber down the Ottawa River. Montreal was still the great fur-trading post but its eminence in this regard was being challenged by the steady upsurge of general trading. Travel was still entirely by water, with rough tracks around important portages. But the first simple canals had been constructed, a small one at Coteau-du-Lac just below Lake St. Francis having been completed about 1780, followed by a series of little "ditches" at Cedars and the Cascades. These could take only flat-bottomed *bateaux* but they were an important factor in the break-away from the universal use of the canoe. Indeed, even the *bateaux* were being superseded on the St. Lawrence by Durham boats, large flat-bottomed scows which could carry several times more freight. Timber rafts were now a familiar sight, the beginnings of the great days of the timber trade. And in 1809, the first steamboat on the St. Lawrence, the *Accommodation* of John Molson, made its way slowly from Montreal to Quebec. It was probably regarded as a freak but by 1813 the *Swiftsure* (also owned by the Molsons) began a regular service between the two leading Canadian settlements. Export trade had started and flour and wheat were being sent overseas in appreciable quantities.

This development, and all the promise it held for the colony, was rudely broken by war with the United States from 1812 to 1815. Fighting on land was accompanied by naval warfare on the Great Lakes, particularly on Lake Ontario, and this again directed attention to the vulnerable position of Kingston, the site of the British naval dockyard. It was naval superiority which enabled Brock to gain his victories in 1812 and the corresponding lack of naval strength in Lake Erie which led to the loss in 1813 of the western part of Upper Canada. As the war progressed, both sides entered into a phenomenal ship-building programme. It is surprising to learn that in 1814, Sir James Yeo, the British commodore, flew his pennant in a three-decker vessel more powerful than Nelson's flagship at Trafalgar. The Americans were said to be then building two ships which would have been the largest in the world. It is small wonder that communication between Montreal and Kingston became indeed a lifeline—and this was apparent not only to the British but finally also to the Americans. We now know that the latter had intended to cut the St. Lawrence had the war continued. This was told by an American general, Jacob Brown, to the commandant in Upper Canada, Major General Sir Frederick Robinson, and he reported the plan to the British government through Lord Bathurst, shortly after the end of the fighting.

This detail of military history is so specifically responsible for the construction of the Rideau Canal that it seems advisable to say just a little more about it. Colonel C. P. Stacey (Director of the Historical Section, Canadian Army Headquarters) who has made a special study of the matter, reports that Sir James Yeo, after the coming of peace, went so far as to say (in a letter to Viscount Melville) that victory was due not only to the mutual exertions of the British Army and Navy but also "if not more to the perverse stupidity of the Enemy." It seems almost incredible that the American strategists did not concentrate all their efforts on breaking the St. Lawrence line of communication, but they did not and the war ended with Kingston still intact and in full supply. But the Americans had not been entirely blind. Colonel Stacey discovered in the confidential Letter Book of James Monroe, appointed Secretary of War in September 1814, a complete plan dated February 1815, which, had it been used, would have changed the entire course of the war and so of much other history. The plan appears to have been drafted by Monroe after discussions with General Jacob Brown and was given to the General in the form of a long letter. The letter makes interesting reading today, especially when Monroe says that "there are two routes by which we may enter Canada, one by passing the St. Lawrence at some point between Kingston and Montreal, the other by Lake Champlain." Fortunately for Canada, this plan of campaign was thwarted by the coming of peace.

The British government took to heart its critical experience. Even before the end of the fighting, Sir George Prevost, then commander of British forces, had written to Lieutenant General Sir Gordon Drummond at Kingston, enclosing plans for a Rideau canal system and asking for comments upon these and for further information. General Drummond's reply gave reports from three local officers and the opinion that the difficulties in the way of building the canal would be immense and the expense "enormous." So also, however, was the cost of transporting freight up the St. Lawrence. This, from the head of the island of Montreal to Kingston, was in 1815 from £4 to £4-10-0 per ton (at least $20). The Durham boats, which carried about eight tons, were each manned by six men. The upstream journey took twelve days on the average but only four days were required for the return trip. Possibly reference to a single freight bill will show more clearly how costly was this transportation system. It is reported that it cost about one thousand dollars to trans-ship a 24-pounder cannon from Quebec to Kingston! The cost of shipping a frigate from England, complete with guns, cables, and ammunition, all in pieces, would be extremely high even by modern standards, but a small frigate was so shipped all the way across the Atlantic, and formed a part of the British naval squadron which once sailed the waters of Lake Ontario.

Following upon the report of Sir George Prevost, Lord Bathurst sent instructions on October 10, 1815, to Sir Gordon Drummond to get "estimates of expense of the Lachine Canal, and of the Ottawa and Rideau being made navigable, in order that His Majesty's Government may decide as to the propriety of undertaking these works, either separately or simultaneously." This original instruction shows clearly the intention to consider the entire question of navigation from Montreal to Kingston of which the Rideau Canal was to be only a part, although quite the most substantial part. Not only would the Lachine Canal be necessary, but locks at the Ste Anne Rapids at the head of the island of Montreal and small canals to circumvent the rapids on the Ottawa River between the Lake of Two Mountains and Hull. General Drummond passed on his instructions to Colonel Nicholls, then Commanding Officer of the Royal Engineers in Canada, directing him to send an officer to explore the route between Kingston and the Ottawa River and to report upon it generally. Lieutenant Joshua Jebb was selected for this unusual task. His instructions were "to follow up the course of the Cataroque from Kingston Mills, and, keeping a northerly direction, to penetrate into Rideau Lake, and descend the river which flows from it to its confluence with the Ottawa." He was further directed "to return up the river as far as the mouth of Irish Creek, and trace the waters of which it is the outlet to their source, and from thence to follow up the best communication he could find to Kingston Mills, or to Gannanoque, and suggest any temporary expedients for improving the navigation, so as to render it available for batteaux." He was also directed to "take note of the country, with a view to its being deemed eligible or otherwise for the establishment of military settlements." This was quite an assignment for one young officer to carry out but the task was completed as directed between April and June 1816.

The impatience of the times, and the urgency with which military communications were being viewed in official quarters, are shown by the fact that, after initiating this survey, Lord Bathurst wrote to the Lieutenant-Governor of Upper Canada early in 1816 saying that His Majesty's Government were "most desirous that preparatory measures should be taken for the performance of this important Work." He expressed his pleasure at the steps which were being taken to settle "industrious and useful" families in the Rideau region. He went on to order the local government to advertise for the construction of the canal by contract, presumably without plans of any sort. A notice regarding this strange request appears in the *Upper Canada Gazette* for February 27, 1817, but somewhat naturally, nothing resulted. Almost at the same time, James Monroe, now President of the United States, made a personal inspection of the northern frontier of his country, including the international section of the St. Lawrence, and a result was the construction of two military roads to this part of the St. Lawrence, one running westwards from Plattsburg, and the other to the east from Sackett's Harbor. These roads were quite clearly intended to provide for the movement of American troops to the Canadian border should hostilities recommence. Canadians must have known about them, yet, despite this, it was to be almost ten years before the start of construction of the Rideau Waterway, the only way of avoiding the dangers of attack and ambush across the international waters.

It was at this time of unrest that Lieutenant Jebb made his report. In it, he stated that both the routes he had examined were practicable but indicated his preference for the shorter (by way of Irish Creek); he gave general outlines of the works he considered necessary and a rough over-all estimate of cost. Curiously enough, he had been requested to survey the route for the passage of *bateaux* only, even though steamships were now in regular operation between Montreal and Quebec. By the year 1821, the St. Lawrence Steamboat Company ("The Molson Line") and another competing company had between them six steamboats on the run between the two cities. There were two large steamboats on Lake Ontario, and others were building. We may be puzzled as to why the idea of steamboat navigation should not have been immediately considered in relation to the design of the canals of those days, but the revolutionary character of steam motive power must be remembered. The slow acceptance of it will be again indicated when we come to consider the size of locks adopted for the original design of the Rideau Canal.

The Jebb report did not lead to immediate action with regard to the Canal, but in the next year or two the first military settlements in the "interior" of Upper Canada were laid out, at Perth, at Richmond, and at Pinheys Point in the Township of March. Lots were granted to officers and men of regiments discharged after service in the 1812 war: in Perth to men of the old 99th Regiment, in Richmond to those from the old 100th Regiment, and in March Township to men of the 97th Regiment. Perth was probably selected because it was the portaging point from the Tay River (a tributary of the Rideau) over to the Mississippi (the Canadian Mississippi, a tributary of the Ottawa); it is today a county town with much of its Old World style still remaining. Richmond was on the Jock River, another small tributary of the Rideau; it has not retained its former eminence but is now a small village on a secondary road. The March settlement included some retired naval officers. Although it had what now appears to have been almost the best of all the sites, a farmhouse, an old graveyard, and the ruins of a lovely little church are all that remain to mark the site of this pioneer community. These military settlements were established as a sort of "second line of defence" in support of the United Empire Loyalist settlements along the international section of the St. Lawrence.

The next move was made not by the British government but by the government of Upper Canada. Canal building was in the air and canals were thought of as the answer to all transportation problems. Contemporary reports suggest that Canada and the United States were entering upon something akin to the "railway mania" of two decades later in Great Britain. In July 1817, ground had been broken for the canal from Lake Erie to the Hudson

River, later to become the New York State Barge Canal. It was opened in the fall of 1825 when Governor De Witt Clinton splashed a barrel of Lake Erie water into the ocean. The Champlain Canal, finished in 1822, linked Lake Champlain with the Hudson River, the start of what is now the Richelieu-Hudson international canal route. And, nearer to the Ottawa, the Lachine Canal had been started by the government of Lower Canada when it was found that the Imperial government was not going to build it, and after the Lachine Canal Company had petitioned the government to take over the work of construction. Under John Richardson, an heroic figure of the time, the Canal Commission broke ground on July 17, 1821, at a ceremony at which the band of the 60th Regiment performed and beef and beer were distributed to the assembled guests. Even as the project was initiated, the threat of diversion of the traffic from the west by way of the Erie Canal was regarded as serious, but the Lachine proved to be the first link in the long chain of the St. Lawrence system of canals. Further to the west, William Hamilton Merritt's enthusiastic advocacy of the Welland Canal was at last bearing fruit. Shortly after this, the first joint report on the St. Lawrence route was made by a joint committee of the legislatures of Upper and Lower Canada. A St. Lawrence Association was formed to promote the navigation facilities on the great river, the threat of traffic diversion to the Erie Canal acting as the spur to this foreshadowing of the St. Lawrence Seaway of today.

It was at a time of such activity in canal building that the Legislature at York in 1821 passed an act "to make provision for the improvement of the internal navigation of the province" and appointed commissioners to determine the practicability and to report upon the estimated expense of such undertakings as they might propose. The Commission, headed by the Hon. John Macaulay of Kingston, worked for four years. Quite naturally, it concentrated its initial attention upon such major obstacles as Niagara Falls and the rapids of the St. Lawrence, but the Rideau route eventually came in for attention. Samuel Clowes, a civil engineer of some experience, was engaged to make surveys for the Commission and reported in considerable detail in April 1824. He decided to abandon the idea of the alternative route by way of Irish Creek on account of the scarcity of water supply, and the depth of the requisite summit cutting, and prepared estimates for canals with three different sizes of locks, all using the route followed by the canal of today.

The first estimate was for a canal 7 feet in depth, 40 feet in width at the bottom of channels and 61 feet at water level, the locks to be of stone masonry, 100 feet long and 22 feet wide; cost £230,785. The second was for a depth of 5 feet, widths of 28 and 48 feet respectively, and stone locks 80 feet long and 15 feet wide; cost £145,802. The third estimate was for a very modest canal indeed, 4 feet deep, 20 feet and 32 feet wide at bottom and surface of channels, with locks built only of timber, 75 feet long and 10 feet wide; cost £62,258. These figures will appear ridiculous, even for a century ago, as the cost of a canal system almost 130 miles long with 47 locks having a total lift of over 400 feet. The sums may be compared with the final cost of the work, with much larger locks, of about £800,000.

All the reports of the Commission were considered by a joint committee of the Legislative Assembly and the Legislative Council and they were published in April 1825. The final report naturally refers to the vital military aspects of the proposed Rideau Canal but has also this interesting comment:

In the event of war protracted as the last, the safety and the saving of transport conducted by such a channel would, it is believed, fully compensate to the nation the charge of the improvement, and it is most evident that to give full effect to the sound and liberal policy which has created the military settlements on the Rideau and introduced since the war a loyal population of more than ten thousand souls where there was before no inhabitant, and which is now surmounting, at a considerable expense, the interruptions of navigation, on the Ottawa, it is necessary to perfect the water communication removed from the enemy's frontier and leading in truth from the ocean to Kingston, which is the key to Lake Ontario and the principal military station in the province.

This reference to the local inhabitants is the first indication that consideration was being given to the canal proposal for any reasons other than those purely military. As events turned out, it was the local function which the Canal was called upon to fulfil rather than its military purpose, but the use of the word "enemy" in this official report shows that tempers were still hot, and the necessity for defence measures still keenly felt. Reports of the hardships of the early military settlements make one wonder why their needs were not more strongly urged. The bands of discharged soldiers who came from Quebec to establish them-

selves in Richmond and the Township of March had to come up
the Ottawa River from Montreal, with its several portages. They
disembarked at the Chaudière Falls and left their wives and
children there in camp, while they pressed on to clear the forest
on their lots and get simple shelters erected. Everything had to be
carried, apart only from timber which was in plentiful supply.
Mills had been established at Burritts Rapids in 1793 and at
Merricks Rapids just before the settlement of Richmond was
started but all the lumber obtained from them had to be floated
down the Rideau River and then up the Jock River, this being
then the only means of communication. It was at Burritts Rapids
that the first bridge across the Rideau was erected, in 1824 just
after Samuel Clowes had completed his surveys, the cost being
defrayed "by subscription" with some assistance from the court
at Perth which had quickly become well established. There were
trails through the forest from Brockville to Perth, and from
Prescott through Merricks Mills to Richmond and so on to the
banks of the Ottawa, where there was as yet only the small settlement at Hull. Although these routes are marked on old maps,
such as that reproduced in this book, written accounts of the life
of the early settlers leave no doubt that they were little more than
walking trails and, even at that, impassable at certain seasons of
the year. Travellers had often to sleep out in the open and one
reads of women sleeping in the trees in order to be safe from
bears.

Some idea of the state of the country at the time can be gained
from an account of an unusual incident (related in Gourlay's
book on the Ottawa Valley) which has decided relevance to the
planning of the Rideau Canal. The Duke of Richmond, then
Governor-in-Chief of Canada, on a visit to this region "determined to travel on foot over the route advised by the Duke of
Wellington as the location of the Rideau Canal. Two attendants
accompanied him, carrying his camp bed with the et ceteras. He
reached Perth and rested there on the night of August 17, 1819.
Next morning he started for Richmond as an exercise, a walk of
thirty miles on a road only blazed and cleared of brush; one may
consider he had an interest in the place and the people to undertake the like. He reached Sergeant Vaughan's tavern at dark and
put up there whilst his two men plunged through the swale
and struck Richmond at midnight." This remarkable journey had
a tragic ending for two days later the Duke died, as a result of

hydrophobia, contracted from a bite in his heel from a pet fox; he was buried in the Anglican Cathedral at Quebec. The Duke had much to do with the start of work on the Canal, in keeping with his concern for defence measures generally. He was probably responsible for the active interest which the Duke of Wellington took in the Rideau project.

The interest of the Iron Duke in the Canal may seem to be surprising but he was now Master General of the Ordnance and so was bringing to bear his military genius on all the far-flung operations of the British Army. As early as 1819 he had addressed a very strong memorandum to Lord Bathurst urging the importance of the Ottawa-Rideau project. It is almost certain, therefore, that the Duke knew of the studies being made for the government of Upper Canada.

The Macaulay Commission's report was submitted to London through the Governor-General during the summer of 1825. The British government offered a loan of £70,000 (at 5 or 6 per cent interest, it was said) to assist with the construction of the Rideau Canal but this the Legislature refused, preferring that the St. Lawrence route should be developed first. Since the Rideau Canal was still being considered primarily as a necessary military work, it was to be expected that the Imperial government should wish to keep control of it in their own hands. After apparent failure to come to agreement with the government of Upper Canada, the British authorities therefore directed a special military Commission which had been sent out to Canada to report on the defence of the country, to bring home with it an estimate of cost for the Rideau Canal, with locks the same size as those for the Lachine Canal which had just been completed.

This Commission, headed by Major General Sir James Carmichael Smyth, had as its other members Lieutenant Colonel Sir G. Hoste and Major Harris of the Royal Engineers. They accepted the line of Samuel Clowes and used his levels and details but amended his estimate by the addition of £20,000 to allow for the increased size of locks (108 feet long by 20 feet wide with a depth of 5 feet). Towpaths were also to be included in the design since the use of steamboats was still not contemplated. The Commission traversed the entire route of the proposed canal and finally recommended that it should be built by the British government itself. The officers attempted to work out some co-operative arrangement with the government of Upper Canada, in

view of the strong recommendation which had been made in
the report of the Joint Legislative Committee that the canal
should be built. But they had to make a negative report on this
aspect to the Duke of Wellington:

In compliance with Your Grace's command, we have endeavoured to ascertain what assistance, if any, could be procured from the Provincial Government towards carrying out this important work. . . . We regret, however,
to say that there does not appear to be the slightest chance of any pecuniary
aid from the Province of Upper Canada. The settlers are very poor and the
Province is still in its infancy. Excepting it is undertaken by His Majesty's
Government we are afraid it will never be executed. Companies are forming
and cheap and temporary expedients are likely to be resorted to for improving navigation of the St. Lawrence in order to enable the produce
from Lake Ontario to be forwarded to Montreal and Quebec, with less
trouble and risk than at present. The important advantages of such a communication in the rear of the frontier are not likely to be appreciated by the
bulk of the inhabitants of the Province; nor is it probable that for the
attainment of a remote good they will agree to any tax or immediate
pecuniary loss.

Though the advantages of the St. Lawrence route were making
themselves felt, the fear of military attack was still so strong that
immediately upon receipt of this report, the British government
authorized the military authorities to undertake the construction
of the waterway. The report of the military Commission followed
by only a few months the submission of the Upper Canada official
report, and authority for construction of the Rideau Canal was
almost immediately granted. This speedy action after the pre-
ceding delays seems to indicate the firm hand of the Iron Duke
who was now a commanding figure in the British scene. He was
soon to be Prime Minister; it was under his short-lived government (1828 to 1830) that much of the important construction
work on the Canal was carried out.

Another reason for immediate action, once the Upper Canada
report had been received, was that the British government had
already taken steps regarding other links in the route which had
to be made navigable in order to provide this alternative passage
between Montreal and Kingston. The Lachine Rapids on the
St. Lawrence, above Montreal, were already circumvented by the
Lachine Canal project of Lower Canada. At the head of the
Island of Montreal are the rapids around Ile Perrot, to avoid
which the St. Andrews Steam Forwarding Company had built a
small private canal with one timber lock at Vaudreuil, on the

south side of the island, giving a depth of water of five feet. This lock was to serve until the first Ste Anne Canal was built by the Board of Works of Upper and Lower Canada from 1840 to 1843, with a depth of six feet. From this point, through the Lake of Two Mountains and up the Ottawa River, there is navigable water for twenty-seven miles. Then come the Carillon Rapids and within the next few miles, the Long Sault Rapids. Once past these stretches of swift water, the river is again navigable all the way to Ottawa. Work on the Grenville Canal, which bypassed the Long Sault Rapids, was started as early as 1819 when, by authority of the Duke of Richmond, ground was broken by the Royal Staff Corps. This canal was to be six miles long with seven locks originally giving a total lift of 43 feet. In 1829, the short Carillon Canal was similarly started by the Royal Staff Corps; it was to be over two miles long, with three locks giving a lift of 14 feet. Then, there was another short canal at Chute à Blondeau with one lock, but it was abandoned when the main Carillon Dam was built about 1880 to give a depth of nine feet in the Carillon Canal. With the authorization of the Rideau Canal, therefore, a complete navigation route from Montreal to Kingston, with a depth of five feet, was in definite prospect.

The man who supervised the building of the Rideau Canal was to face one of the most challenging tasks ever given to an engineer —the construction through virgin forest, along untouched rivers and lakes, far removed from any of the amenities even of the new colony, of a waterway almost one hundred and thirty miles long, with speedy construction imperative. The man selected by the British government for the task was Lieutenant Colonel John By of the Royal Engineers: in the following chapters is recorded the way in which he met this challenge.

Building the Canal

COLONEL BY landed at Quebec from England on May 30, 1826. His instructions were to complete a water communication having a uniform depth of five feet, from the Ottawa River to Kingston, along the route suggested by Samuel Clowes, that is to say not using the shorter of the two main routes, by way of Irish Creek, but the route which the Canal follows today. The locks were to be the same size as those on the Lachine Canal and on the Ottawa River canals which were already under construction by the Royal Staff Corps when By arrived. He was warned not to bring the Canal down to the St. Lawrence by way of Cornwall, as he would be pressed to do by merchants and others interested in the commercial development of the St. Lawrence route. The work was to be constructed to Kingston, which was a well-fortified stronghold, located on Lake Ontario and not just on the St. Lawrence. It is clear that the threat of war with the Americans was still strong, clear also that even in such uncertain days "pressure groups" had already made themselves evident. The British War Office wrote to the Colonial Department about By's departure. The Secretary of State for the Colonies (under whom Canada was then administered) also wrote to the Lieutenant-Governor of Upper Canada asking him to afford every assistance in the carrying out of the project. The local government rendered very real assistance when once the work was under way.

Quebec was the headquarters of the Royal Engineers in Canada, and By first reported to Colonel Durnford, his commandant. Then he lost no time in moving up river to be closer to the scene of his work. He reached Montreal in August 1826 and apparently opened a temporary office there, for it is on record that he soon commenced discussions with prospective contractors for the canal works. Shortly after his arrival he wrote to his superiors in London to say that he was quite sure that the Canal could not possibly be built for the estimate then standing, £164,000, and suggested that it would cost more like £400,000. This was his conclusion without even having visited the site of the work. But he was soon on his way up the Ottawa River, in order to see for himself something of the area in which he was to reside and labour for the next six years. He landed at the little settlement of Hull on September 21, 1826.

Hull had been founded in 1800 by Philemon Wright, a New Englander from Concord, Mass., who came into Canada in the closing years of the previous century, it is said with thirty thousand dollars, and explored much country before deciding on his future home. He cleared more than a thousand acres and worked hard to improve the breed of his cattle. Widely known, he kept an extensive store and soon had a saw mill and a grist mill working. He was a favourite of the Governor and the colonel of his own company of militia. This fine figure of a man, about six feet tall, described as having a "wonderfully strange, quick, reflective and wild eye," was about seventy years old when Colonel By arrived at Hull. Since it is said that he was the first to have suggested the possibility of building the Rideau Canal, he must have been pleased to welcome the man who was charged with its construction.

Not only did Wright have a substantial home by the year 1826, but the settlement itself had become well known. Its streets were lively with the activity of a frontier community. A fine hotel, the Columbian, had been built, with livery stables attached. A steamboat service had been started on the river. There was an armoury, "richly filled with cannons, muskets, and swords." Three churches and minor chapels had been built, as well as schools. But, standing on the wharf and looking across the river, Colonel By would have seen that along the rocky south bank stretched the solid front of the forest, reaching in places to the water's edge, at others to the rim of the precipitous cliffs.

The Governor-in-Chief of British North America, His Excellency the Earl of Dalhousie, had also travelled up to Hull in order to select the canal entrance with By. The fact that the Governor made this journey, repeating it about a year later in order to see the progress of the work, is clear indication of the importance with which the work was viewed officially. The location of the entrance was selected by the two men, actually on the ground, and was confirmed in a letter from Lord Dalhousie which is still in the records, dated September 26, 1826. This day may well be regarded as that on which the city of Ottawa was founded.

So thick was the bush on what is now the Ottawa side of the river, only one or two small clearings having then been made apart from that at Richmond Landing, that it is unlikely Colonel By had any opportunity to see much of the area in which he was to work, except the portion which now forms the centre of the city of Ottawa. He would, however, have been able to get first-hand descriptions of the country between Hull and Kingston, along the route of the Canal. Fortunately we have available today such accounts of what the country was like before construction began. One of these was written by John MacTaggart who had been sent out from England to be the Clerk of Works on the canal project; he was instructed by Colonel By, during this visit to Hull, to survey the alternative routes for the start of the Canal and later to go through the whole route and report upon it. More will be said later about this remarkable man; suffice it to say now that he stayed in Canada for three years but had then to return to England after removal from the works by Colonel By; he also had fever. He wrote a book upon his experiences (*Three Years in Canada*) in which he included, whether with permission or not is not clear, copies of his reports to Colonel By.

His description of the route of the Canal, in his report of August 3, 1827, is too long to be quoted in full. So also is another account written by one of Colonel By's young engineer-officer assistants. By condensing their descriptions, however, it is possible to give a picture of the country which had to be penetrated by the Waterway. From the Falls into the Ottawa River, as far as the Hog's Back rapids, a stretch of river now wholly within the city of Ottawa, the Rideau River was almost completely impassable. Details will later be given, in MacTaggart's own words, which will show how thick and impenetrable was the bush along the banks of the river in this section. So troublesome was travel through this bush that MacTaggart had to postpone his survey of it until the ground was frozen. It then took him five days to get from the banks of the Ottawa to Dows Great Swamp, where he and his companions spent Christmas Day of 1826 camping out in the cold.

Rapids continued from Hog's Back intermittently to Black Rapids which were important enough to have been named even though the forest came to the water's edge and there was yet no settlement there. Above Black Rapids, lay the Long Island still-water where the uninhabited banks of the river were high and woody. Long Island had rapids along its full length of about four miles, with a fall of about twenty-four feet. A "paltry" saw mill, the property of a Mr. Hurlburt, existed near the Island but the country generally was still untouched forest. A twenty-mile stretch of still-water was met above Long Island and then came three small settlements at Burritts Rapids, Nicholsons Rapids, and Merricks Mills. A limestone quarry had been opened up at the latter point by James Clowes, whose name is today perpetuated in one of the locks. At Merricks Falls, the first connection with any other settlement was reached, a rough trail from Prescott here crossing the Rideau River on a simple bridge, close to a low mill dam which had been erected by Mr. Merrick. Small settlements followed along the river, in view of the road connections, at Maitlands Rapids, Edmunds, and Slys. Most of these so-called settlements were little more than the house of the settler whose name has now been adopted for the locality. One or two of the settlers operated ferries for itinerant travellers through the bush. Along the eight miles between Merricks Falls and Maitlands there were no clearings and the banks of the river were low and swampy. At Maitlands (as may be seen from the sketch map) an extension of the road from Brockville crossed the river by means of a ford. Beyond Old Sly's house, the river descended about thirty-five feet in a few hundred yards, in a rocky channel little more than fifty feet wide. A settler had established here a small saw mill and a mill dam but no other development was then to be seen at this striking point in the river, now the busy town of Smiths Falls.

Three miles of almost continuous rapids followed, extending to the First Rapids on the Rideau, two miles below its exit from Rideau Lake. Two narrows were passed in the twenty-three miles of the lake, at Olivers Ferry (now Rideau Ferry) and at the Upper Narrows. The trail from Brockville to Perth, then well established as a small military settlement, crossed the lake at

SKETCH

showing the COMMUNICATION between the

RIVER OTTAWA and LAKE ONTARIO

as it existed prior to the Construction of the

RIDEAU CANAL.

The dotted line shews the present Steam Boat
route between Montreal and Kingston.

GATINEAU RIVER

CHAUDIERE FALLS

CHAUDIERE LAKE

RIDEAU FALLS

MOSS BACK

BLACK RAPIDS

LONG ISLAND

GOOD WOOD R.

RICHMOND

RIDEAU R.

SOUTH NATION RIVER

SOUTH BRANCH

BURRITTS RAPIDS

NICHOLSONS

CLOWES QUARRY

MERRICKE MILLS

MAITLANDS

BARBER'S CREEK

PRESCOTT

OGDENSBURGH

ST. LAWRENCE RIVER

S T A T E   O F   N E W   Y O R K

LONG SAULT

FIRST RAPIDS

COCKBURN CREEK

OWL STREAM

SMITHS FALLS

SLYS

OLD SLUYS RAPIDS

EDMUNDS RAPIDS

OLIVERS FERRY

IRISH LAKE BRIDGE

PLUM HOLLOW

BROCKVILLE

PERTH

RIDEAU LAKE

UPPER NARROWS

WEST LAKE

ISTHMUS

MUD LAKE

CLEAR LAKE

ISTHMUS

INDIAN LAKE

CHAFFEY'S MILLS

SAND LAKE

JONES' FALLS

WHITE FISH LAKE

BREWERS UPPER MILLS

BREWERS

LOWER MILLS

ROUND TAIL

RELIGES

RIFTS

BLACK RIFTS

KINGSTON MILLS

CATARAQUI RIVER

MUSQUITO LAKE

DAVIES MILLS

CRANBERRY LAKE

GANANOQUI RIVER

GANANOQUI

FT. HENRY

KINGSTON

WOLFS ISLAND

Olivers Ferry. To get across the Isthmus, canoes had to be portaged about a mile and a half into Mud Lake and so across the height of land. This led into Clear Lake and then, by another small portage, to Indian Lake. A winding creek led from Indian Lake past Chaffeys Mills, where a dam had been built to secure the necessary head of water for a saw mill and a distillery. Apparently such a pioneer installation was necessary to supply the few scattered settlements in this region! Mosquito or Opinicon Lake came below Chaffeys and then another small fall, a dam, and a saw mill operated by a settler named Davis. A narrow rocky channel, in which the stream fell over sixty feet in less than a mile, led into Cranberry Lake.

MacTaggart called this Cranberry Marsh rather than Cranberry Lake and refers to it as "this infernal place." It was to cause more real trouble in the building of the Canal than almost any other location. About eighteen miles long and up to two miles broad, it was almost completely covered by extensive flats of cranberry bushes, with long tangled roots, so buried in the bed of the swamp that the bushes themselves floated on the surface. Small canoe channels existed through the marsh, leading to one outlet at White Fish Falls and another at Round Tail Falls. The first of these outgoing streams became the Gananoque River, and the second the Cataraqui, both of which flowed down to the St. Lawrence. Just below a small dam at Round Tail were two important mills owned by a Mr. Brewer, two miles apart. Thence to Kingston Mills the stream was generally sluggish, with only two shallow rapids (or riffles); it wound between low-lying clay banks, and occasionally passed through large swamps in which were standing dead trees killed by the flooding of the land by the dam at Kingston Mills. This dam had been erected by the government in order to provide power for a saw mill which was installed to supply lumber for the dockyard and other operations at Kingston. A fall of twenty-six feet from the mill-pond brought the stream to the level of Cataraqui Bay, a channel leading across the Bay to Kingston.

Such was the country through which the Rideau Canal was to be constructed. Settlement was meagre; access to the area was by a few rough forest trails or a difficult water route. Rapids and waterfalls had to be dammed and controlled, and locks had to be built. Channels had to be excavated along extensive stretches of the watercourses and through the portages, and swamps, dangerous to health, had to be penetrated. It was a task to shake the confidence of any ordinary man; to Colonel By it appears only to have constituted a challenge.

Before returning to Montreal from his visit to Hull in the fall of 1826, By arranged for an obvious piece of preliminary work, a bridge across the Ottawa River at the Chaudière Falls which would provide access to the site of the canal works from Hull. Design and supervision of this bridge was MacTaggart's first actual assignment on the canal works and he was very proud of his part in this successful enterprise. He called it the Union Bridge, since it was the one bridge uniting Upper and Lower Canada, by linking together the rocky islands which then made, and still make, the Chaudière Falls so picturesque. The bridge consisted of eight spans, five of sixty feet and two of seventy feet, with a major span over the gap then called the Big Kettle; this gap measured 200 feet across—soundings to a depth of 300 feet failed to reveal its bottom. Colonel By had solved the initial problem of crossing the Big Kettle by shooting over it a missile with a cord attached to it, which was then used to pull over progressively larger ropes and cables. Thomas McKay was the contractor for the masonry of the first two spans built as stone arches; he had already made his reputation at such work on the Lachine Canal.

By the middle of October 1826, one of the arches was completed but the coming of winter forced a slower pace. Masonry work continued, however, since the arches were built as dry-stone structures. Snow had to be swept from the masons' platforms each morning and special guard kept against the dangers of floating ice. On two days no outside work could be done at all. MacTaggart says that his hands were frost bitten while he was shaving in a room with no fire and that, on this same day, mercury froze in many thermometers. Only one man, however, was frost bitten on the job. A safeguard was the serving of grog to the men, once, and sometimes twice a day—a practice perhaps fortunately without a modern counterpart.

The entire bridge was finished by March 1828. Ice, however, damaged the scow which was supporting the centre of the big wooden span over the Kettle, and it collapsed. By the end of the year it had been replaced. The bold design provided a roadway thirty feet wide, and despite signs of weakness the bridge served throughout the period of the canal building and until 1835. It then finally collapsed, and was eventually replaced by the famous suspension bridge designed by Samuel Keefer.

During his initial visit to Hull, Colonel By also laid out the first parts of his headquarters. Under MacTaggart's energetic direction, land was cleared on either side of the valley in which the entrance locks now lie. The first buildings were erected and two wharves were built at the foot of the valley, on the Ottawa River shore, for the landing of government supplies coming to the Canal. Colonel By had selected the location of his own house, near the site of the Château Laurier of today, and had suggested that a fort or battery should be built on the opposite hill. An area had been set aside for a workyard, and the first workshop buildings were started. Land adjacent to this working area had been subdivided into lots. Two small villages were laid out, the start of Upper Town and Lower Town, and before the winter was far advanced, all lots had been taken up.

MacTaggart joined his chief in Montreal in March 1827 and doubtless took part in the final planning of construction. This concerned chiefly the necessary contract arrangements. A statement was published in the local newspapers explaining the system to be used with the suggestion that "it is best to allow no contractor to have anything to do with them [the works], be his cash or consequence what they may, unless he is well known as a practical artist, competent for what he professes." It also included this concise summary of the work to be done: "The works of the Rideau Canal seem to divide themselves into the following great branches; building and finishing locks of heavy masonry, excavating earth and clay, excavating rock and gravel, constructing heavy dams across the Rideau of rough rubble masonry, framing aqueducts and bridges of wood, etc." It was explained that a subaltern's command of sixty soldiers would always be stationed near each contract work, that surgeons would be engaged and furnished with all necessary medicines, and that plenty of spirits and provisions of all kinds with camp equipment would be supplied by the government.

The arrangements outlined in this document are surprisingly similar to those adopted in modern days for unusual and isolated contract works. The actual contract agreements, of which one at least still exists, are not very different from those of today. They stipulated that the agreement was between the Commissary General to His Majesty's Forces (in Canada) for and on behalf of the King, and the named contractor who guaranteed to carry out the work stipulated for the unit sums noted in the document. The agreement which is in the Public Archives at Ottawa is that made with William Hartwell and covers the clearing and excavation of the necessary channels between Rideau Lake and Mud Lake and between Indian and Clear Lakes. The "unit prices" are £20 per acre for chopping down trees, clearing and grubbing the ground, £4 for chopping alone, 4s. per cubic yard for rock excavation and 1s. per cubic yard for earth excavation. These were the prices to be paid to the contractor for each of the units noted, the total amount of his work having to be measured, by the engineers, when it was complete, and the quantities multiplied by the unit prices to give the total amount due to him. The excavation prices, though they were for hand labour, are not very different from today's unit prices for the largest contracts. Modern earth-moving equipment has only succeeded in keeping unit (or total) costs approximately steady, since labour costs have mounted higher and higher in the years between.

If the requirements in the newspaper notice about the contract system had been strictly followed, and if the administration of the contracts had remained with Colonel By, the works might well have been completed even more expeditiously than they were, and certainly with less difficulty for By himself. But the contracts, as in the example cited above, were between the contractor and the King as represented by the Commissary General, and it was the Commissary General who handled all contracts from his offices in Montreal and Quebec. It is almost certain that Colonel By had a good deal to say about the main contracts, especially for the masonry, but as the work went on, and after Charles Forbes was replaced by C. J. Routh as Commissary General, it is easy to see from the records that many administrative difficulties developed.

It was not hard to get experienced men for the masonry contracts since experience was so obviously necessary in this kind of work that only an expert contractor would think of applying. For the excavation, however, all too many men with no real experience at all applied and some were awarded contracts which resulted in nothing but trouble. Several of the contracts awarded had to be changed during the course of the work, with consequent legal tangles. It was not the first time in the history of engineering, and by no means the last, that the apparent simplicity of excavation work attracted the unwary with disastrous results. All but four of the original contractors eventually went bankrupt or had to have their contracts terminated.

Before Colonel By left Montreal in the spring of 1827 to take up his permanent residence on the banks of the Ottawa River, all the main contracts had been arranged and by the middle of the summer all the work was "under contract." It was essential, of course, for Colonel By to have the necessary legal power to use the land required for the canal construction. Although the work was for the Imperial government, the government of Upper Canada co-operated to the extent of passing a special Act of its Legislature, on February 17, 1827, giving Colonel By as a representative of the King, all the powers which the Upper Canadian government would have had, had it undertaken the work. He was given specific permission to purchase land immediately, when it could be acquired reasonably under the terms of the Act, in a letter from the Military Secretary to the Governor, dated December 19, 1829. Despite the comprehensive nature of the Act, and the scrupulous care with which Colonel By used his powers under it, many legal battles were to follow by reason of the efforts of some landowners to profit unduly. By says in one of his letters that after long negotiations "the various Proprietors appeared to have altered their opinions, and generally speaking are now willing to take the real value of their property instead of asking ten times its value." This, too, has been a not unusual feature of construction work through the years, but one would not have imagined that members of the legal profession in the river towns of Brockville, Prescott, and Cornwall would have been party to some of the obviously obstructionist tactics which the records clearly reveal. Colonel By was vilified unmercifully, and even assailed in court, the most remarkable legal ingenuity being displayed in attempting to show that he had taken actions which were not specifically authorized under the Act.

With By in residence on the Canal, and the start of actual work in the summer of 1827, real efforts were made to obtain an accurate idea of the extent and probable cost of the entire project. Colonel By himself went through the whole route of the Canal for the first time in the month of May. MacTaggart completed his initial survey of the route, with rough levels and quantities, in June and July; "after labouring hard in the wilderness," as he says, "he got back to the Ottawa alive," and sub-

mitted a report to his chief dated August 3, 1827. His estimate
of the total cost of the work was £486,000. Since a more accurate
picture was required for the satisfaction of the Board of Ordnance
in London, one of the young Royal Engineer officers, Lieutenant
Pooley, was sent through the route of the Canal in July and
August of the same year, with a survey party, with instructions
to prepare accurate general plans and estimates. A revised estimate of £474,000 was arrived at. It may assist our appreciation
of what was then involved in such work to note that the list of
food given out to Lieutenant Pooley's R.E. survey party included
only flour, biscuits and bread, fresh beef, salt pork, pease, indian
corn, salt, and rum. This contrasts strangely with the standard
food supplies for a survey party of today. Simple as the list was,
Lieutenant Pooley had a lot of explaining to do to the Commissary
authorities as to why he had used such large quantities. He at-
tributed it to the appetites of his Canadian *voyageurs.*

Pooley must have been a most trusted assistant to his commanding officer since he was sent over to London, later that year,
in order to present in person the revised estimate of cost, and
Colonel By's report, to the Board of Ordnance. With the estimate
went a strong recommendation from Colonel By that the size
of the locks should be increased above the original authorization
of 100 feet by 22 feet wide with a depth of five feet over the
lock-sills. He urged that the locks be built of such a size that
they would take naval steamboats and also the wooden spars
which were still required for the British Navy from the forests
of Canada. His request was finally granted after a study of the
problem on the site.

In the meantime the organization of construction continued.
Two companies of the Royal Sappers and Miners had been raised
in England especially to work on the Canal, each of which consisted of 81 men. The 15th Company arrived at the site on June 1,
1827, the 7th Company on September 17. They camped under
canvas on Nepean Point until the barracks being erected for them
on Barracks Hill (now Parliament Hill) were ready. The 7th
Company was moved to Newboro in 1829 but the 15th remained
at Bytown (as it had then become) throughout the entire work.
Commanding officers were Captains Victor and Savage and they
were assisted by Lieutenants Denison, Briscoe, Frome, Benjamin,
and Simon, with two regimental officers attached, Captains Cole

and Gale of the Royal Engineers. These soldiers were called upon to undertake many and varied tasks, including guard duty at the various works, and even construction operations when special work had to be carried out, as in the rebuilding of the Hog's Back Dam.

In many of his letters, Colonel By refers appreciatively to these officers and their men. As early as August 1828, and in keeping with his solicitude for those working under him, he recommended to the Master General of the Ordnance that ". . . all who wish it [of the Royal Sappers and Miners] should receive their discharge [after the work was completed] and one hundred acres of land; this I am humbly of opinion would have a good effect in checking desertion and secure their services as loyal subjects to His Majesty for life." The recommendation was based on previous experience of desertions among men working near the American border. It was adopted, and no desertions took place after the ruling went into effect. Even before this concession was made, only 16 out of the total of 162 men had deserted, a truly remarkable record if all the circumstances be considered. The members of the two companies received their discharges on June 30, 1831, when the canal works were almost complete. Many of them settled along the route; they and their descendants provided a thin chain of British settlers through the still untouched bush between Bytown and Kingston. An examination of the full influence of this unusual settlement would provide a singularly interesting social study.

Contractors were, in this summer of 1827, getting their work organized and started. During the winter of 1826, which Colonel By spent in Montreal, he had had many discussions with contractors and he then took the point of view that they could not lose on the work since he would see that they were removed from their contracts if they could not properly carry on. By also arranged, at that time, that every workman on excavation contracts would be expected to provide his own shovel or wheelbarrow in order to avoid the excessive loss which might be experienced if the government provided such tools. Construction generally began at the two extremities of the Canal; a later start was made at works in the centre, from Newboro which is just at the summit level and to which access could be gained by the bush roads up from the St. Lawrence. Contracts were given for

masonry work separately from excavation. It is almost correct to
say that Colonel By had no trouble with any one of the major
masonry contractors but nothing except trouble with most of
the excavation contractors. When the work commenced, it was
only a matter of weeks before some of the contractors found that
they were losing money. The prices submitted by the excavation
contractors were often too low but with the blind optimism of
the ignorant they usually continued long after they should really
have ceased work, or been stopped if their financial situation had
been known. The provisions in the contract documents clearly
spelled out the responsibility of the contractors but despite this
Colonel By was almost continually besieged by contractors who
had failed, or their creditors. The contract signed by the contractor guaranteed the completion of the work, described in the
respective document, by the contractor at the prices he stated;
and the contractor certified that he knew the character of the
work upon which he was tendering. If he made any error in
estimating his costs in advance of construction, that was clearly
his own responsibility and this he guaranteed by the signing of
his contract. All this, however, was conveniently forgotten by
those who made claims upon Colonel By when, as was so frequently the case, he had to remove them from the project they had
started because of unsatisfactory progress.

The nature of the work is easy to appreciate even for those
unfamiliar with engineering construction. Excavation of soil was
by hand with picks and shovels; wheelbarrows transported the
earth to suitable dumping areas. The only haulage available was
that provided by oxen at a few locations. There is no mention,
in any of the records of the work, of even so primitive an aid to
manpower as a horse-drawn scraper. Rock which had to be removed from cuttings, or as it was required for the stone masonry,
was excavated by drilling holes which were then filled with gunpowder and blasted. No cacophonous air compressors or powerful
rock drills were available, or even thought of, when the Rideau
Canal was built. All the holes required were drilled laboriously
by hand; each hole was drilled separately, with a sharp-pointed
rock chisel and a heavy sledge hammer, the chisel being steadily
turned during the driving. Three men usually made up a drill
team. The speed of drilling, as recorded at the time, varied from
12 feet in a day for three men at work on a 1¾ inch diameter hole
to as little as 4 feet in a day for a 3-inch hole. Holes thus made

were filled with powder and tamped (or packed down), and the charges were then set off with slow-burning fuses. Simple gunpowder (or "Merchants' blasting powder") was the only explosive then known; it consisted of a mixture of three parts of "nitre" to one part of a mixture of sulphur and charcoal. The old device of the "plug and feather," by which the swelling of wooden plugs when wetted was made to split rock, was probably used, but the holes would still have had to be laboriously drilled by hand. There is no reference in any of the old records to the use of the expansive power of ice for splitting but in view of the ingenuity displayed in so many other directions on the canal works, it is almost certain that the Canadian winter climate was employed to good effect in this way.

The excavated rock had then to be broken up into small enough pieces for removal by wheelbarrows unless the location was such that simple hand hoists could be used for lifting the heavier pieces of stone. As anyone visiting the Canal today can see, the stones used for lock construction were quite large, too large to be handled by hand; they were set in place by means of simple hand cranes. This part of the rock work is not too different from practice today, nor was the actual finishing of the stones to proper dimensions, since masons still use hand tools for much stone work, just as they did in the eighteen-twenties.

The other major part of the work was the fabrication of the necessary lock gates and sluices with their essential iron fittings. Flat iron was obtained from England and worked in the usual way by blacksmiths. Iron castings, however, were obtained from foundries in Lower Canada. Timber was available on every hand, and its working was the one thing in which many Canadians were well skilled. Most of the gates were built by small teams of carpenters on a contract basis, the usual price for a pair of lock gates, complete (the government providing the iron and timber), being £100; this sum included also the hanging of the gates in place. Such a price seems ridiculous, even allowing for a change in the value of money, until it is realized that wages for skilled workmen varied up to a maximum of only 7s. per day for the very best stone masons. Labourers received 2s. 6d. a day; carpenters 5s. a day; blacksmiths up to 6s. a day.

With such a vast amount of hand work necessary for even the simplest construction operations, contractors for the canal work naturally needed a large labour force. There was no local population upon which to draw. Canadians using the Ottawa River were experienced river men or skilled in woodcraft; they were therefore generally employed at work in which these skills could properly be used. Some Canadians were engaged on masonry work but these were brought up from Montreal and Quebec. To supply the great bulk of the manpower, large numbers of Irish immigrants were employed. One writer mentions a total working force of six thousand men but another estimate of two thousand men is more probably correct. Peter Robinson, founder of Peterborough, brought out two shiploads of Irish immigrants, all of whom settled along the banks of the Rideau.

The hazards under which these inexperienced men carried out their work in an unfamiliar setting are vividly described by MacTaggart.

Even in their spade and pickaxe business, the [men] receive dreadful accidents; as excavating in a *wilderness* is quite a different thing from doing that kind of labour in a cleared country. Thus they have to *pool in*, as the tactics of the art go—that is, dig beneath the roots of trees, which not infrequently fall down and smother them. . . . Some of them . . . would take jobs of quarrying from contractors, because they thought there were *good wages* for this work, never thinking that they did not understand the business. Of course, many of them were blasted to pieces by their own *shots*, others killed by stones falling on them. I have seen heads, arms, and legs, blown in all directions; and it is vain for overseers to warn them of their danger, for they will pay no attention. I once saw a poor man blow a red stick, and hold it deliberately to the *priming* of a large shot he had just charged. I cried out, but it was of no use. He seemed to turn round his face, as if to avoid the smoke; off went the blast . . . he was killed in a moment.

MacTaggart also describes efforts which had to be made to prevent such fatal occurrences. "At length we got the matter so systematized, that a number of shots were always prepared to be *fired* at once; a person stood at a distance and kept blowing a horn, so that all quarriers got out of the quarry to a respectable distance before the mine was sprung." Respect for human life might not have been quite the same a century ago as it is today, especially on construction, but the elements of safety engineering were given some attention in the building of the Rideau Waterway.

The entrance locks to the Canal from the Ottawa were naturally the focal point of early construction. They were built in succession, to provide a total lift from the level of the Ottawa River of eighty-one feet. All were of solid masonry upon inverted stone arches, the stone being quarried from the limestone cliffs on either side of the line of the locks. Excavation for the flight was done by a contractor named Pennyfather of whom little is known, but the masonry work was carried out by Thomas McKay, as one part of his major contribution to the project. The excavation work was in stiff clay in which boulders and sand seams were encountered. The flow of underground water through these seams, in the form of springs, caused considerable trouble but this, too, was overcome. The locks themselves were constructed, at first, with the limestone blocks just laid on one another with no bond between them. Water, however, forced itself through the walls and in some instances moved the stones. They were therefore secured with iron wedge bolts and straps. Then the walls were "grouted" using a quite modern method, that is forcing a liquid grout by means of long "tin tubes" into all the joints; this proved very successful and the system was then used for most of the masonry throughout the Canal. Of unusual interest is the fact that the cement used for this purpose was obtained from a quarry "on the opposite side of the Ottawa, which, being burnt and ground very fine, proved a better water-cement than some obtained from the States, and far superior to the Harwich cement, which was nearly spoiled before it reached the canal." The great modern cement works of the Canada Cement Company at Wrightville uses today the same quarry but the Company seems to have neglected in its publicity this very early tribute by one of the officers of the Royal Engineers to the quality of its product.

With the locks in such a commanding position on the Ottawa River, it was natural that they should attract the attention of visitors and travellers up the great water route to the west. Probably the most interesting was Captain (later Sir) John Franklin. Returning to England from his expedition to the Mackenzie River, in August 1827, he naturally stopped to see the new works and it was arranged for him to lay the first stone. This he did on August 16, 1827, the stone being in the invert of the third lock up from the river. Exactly one year after the day on which the site for the entrance had been decided, the Earl of Dalhousie, then approaching the end of his term as Governor-in-Chief, returned, accompanied by the Countess, to see the progress of the work. They landed at Hull on the anniversary of September 26, 1826, and spent some time examining the new works. On the 29th day of the month, at three o'clock in the afternoon, the

Earl of Dalhousie laid the corner-stone, a block weighing nearly two tons, several feet under the level of the river, on the east side of the Canal. The ceremony was performed inside a coffer-dam, a temporary wooden dam which kept the river water out of the work. The event was duly celebrated by the workmen and a small gathering of local residents.

Interest was, of course, not confined to the first locks but continued as the Canal gradually took shape. Colonel By's senior officers in Canada gave him the encouragement of personal visits, all of which appear to have resulted in cordial expressions of appreciation for the work he was doing. Colonel Durnford, commanding the Royal Engineers in Canada, made a regular inspection trip through the Canal at least once each year. This was no pleasure cruise, especially in summer months, owing to the fetid swamps which had to be negotiated and the flies for which there were then no convenient repellants. His Excellency Sir James Kempt (who was soon to become Administrator of the government of Canada) went through the Canal in the early summer of 1828 as one member of an official commission of inquiry. Sir John Colborne (then Lieutenant-Governor of Upper Canada) paid a similar visit one year later. Two of the contractors for the Welland Canal, then being started, came to see if they could use the system of construction developed by Colonel By for the reconstruction of the dam at Hog's Back. They told him that they declined to consider it after seeing the Hog's Back job, as they would be afraid to try it! Naturally the Royal Navy gave attention to the work, so specifically designed for the conveyance of naval vessels; Admiral Sir Charles Ogle went over the works in 1829 while on a tour of Upper Canada from his flag station in Halifax. When it is remembered that all such visits necessitated the long journey up from Montreal to either Kingston or Hull, by canoe, it is clear that the fame of the works, and the Superintending Engineer, must have been well established in the country.

The building went steadily forward, up the Rideau River from Bytown, and up the Cataraqui from Kingston Mills, as the lower works were brought well along to completion. The young officers under Colonel By were stationed at the more important of the scattered works, Lieutenant Pooley, for example, being in charge of the fine arched dam and other works at Smiths Falls. Lieutenant Colonel Boteler had been sent out from England as the chief assistant to the Superintendent; he was placed in charge of

the works at the Kingston end and his services were greatly
appreciated by his chief. The main office of the works remained
at Bytown throughout the entire period of construction, but
Colonel By himself was often away, travelling up and down the
entire route of the Canal several times a year. He had other visits
to make also, occasionally to Montreal and one, at least, to York
by steamboat from Kingston. Quite possibly this was his first
venture by a regular steamship service, even though the citizens
of Kingston had started a steamboat service between their city
and Prescott some years before the building of the Canal was
started.

Colonel By regularly sent progress letters to the Governor at
Quebec, usually addressing them to the Military Secretary, Lieutenant Colonel George Couper, who became his close personal
friend. More formal reports went to General Mann, the Master
General of the Ordnance, in London. In September 1828, for
example, he reported for the information of Sir James Kempt that
"the fever on the line of the Canal is subsiding and the men are
returning to work; I therefore hope by the 15th of next month to
have the Bridge across the Great Kettle of the Chaudière Falls
completed; and I trust that I shall have also three locks at the
entrance to the canal, on the approved scale in a very forward
state by that time; the mound at Dow's Great Swamp is proceeding gradually . . . the lock at Black Rapids will likewise be in a
forward state, and I should feel highly flattered if your Excellency
would honour the Works at this end of the Canal by inspecting
them this Autumn."

The reference to the fever is a recurrent note in almost all of
the reports. It is variously described, but usually as the "swamp
fever," and this term will be used when it calls for mention. It
appears to have been a very severe type of malaria, doubtless
caused by the humid conditions of work in high summer in the
swampy areas of the Canal, coupled with poor sanitary conditions.
Colonel By was himself attacked by it. Many died from it, how
many will never be known. It was not peculiar to the canal works,
even though very prevalent in their locality; Kingston, York, and
other towns and villages were also visited by the scourge.
Throughout the summer of 1828, the fever was especially bad
everywhere in Upper Canada, and particularly so along the Canal,
almost all the work being completely shut down for weeks, at
certain places even for months. John MacTaggart had so serious

an attack in 1828 that it was one reason for his return to England from his important post on the canal staff. In his book MacTaggart gives a graphic account of the symptoms, with special reference to its occurrence amongst almost all the workers in the Cranberry Lake area. "Sulphate of Quinine, a preparation from bark, is what the doctors administer for the cure of this wearisome distemper; it seems to be a very potent medicine, but being very dear, poor people are at a loss to procure it. The Indians are never troubled with anything of the sort." The foul conditions at Cranberry Lake must certainly have been a great cause of worry to those in command. Small dams at the two outlets had raised the water level in the swamp about eight feet, thus giving it some claim to the name of "lake." In the summer, a blue mist was seen to lie over the surface, which vanished only in the midday sunshine. The smell always given off was "very nauseous, like that of a cadaverous animal in the last stages of decomposition." On one occasion, Colonel By was passing through the swamp and his canoe became grounded. His *voyageurs* jumped over the side to release it and sank up to their waists in the blue slime, which exuded an almost unbearable odour. All but two died from the fever shortly afterwards, and Colonel By was struck down by one of the worst attacks he ever had; indeed his life was actually despaired of for a time. Cranberry Lake was not the only noisome place, however. One of the very worst spots on the whole canal was that known as the Isthmus, the portage between Mud Lake and Rideau Lake. In 1830, Colonel By ordered a wide strip of forest to be cut down in order to generate a current of air between the two lakes so as to provide a condition in which his men could work. This led to one of his many troubles with irate landowners but he states quite clearly that he regarded this step as absolutely essential for the good progress of the work.

The two doctors attached to the Canal must have had a busy time, especially in the summer months. One of them, Dr. Robinson, the assistant surgeon who was stationed at the Isthmus, wrote to Colonel By on July 18, 1830, asking if he could have an extra supply of forage for his horse since he was having to ride through the bush frequently in order to visit a man at Long Falls who was seriously ill. Colonel By had to send this request on to his commandant, Colonel Durnford, at Quebec City since he was not permitted to authorize such an item from the Commissary General's department. Then the application had to be approved by

Dr. Joseph Hill, the Inspector of Hospitals. And in the same letter it is related that there are fifty-five men ill with the fever at Kingston Mills, and that it has now spread to Jones Falls!

Such an absurd example of "red tape" was trivial compared with other administrative requirements imposed upon Colonel By, in almost all cases by the office of the Commissary General. This gentleman, C. J. Routh, appears from the records almost to have had as a major objective in his life that of rendering difficult every aspect of the provision of supplies for Colonel By. Those who become restive about having to fill out modern business forms in triplicate may take courage when they read that Colonel By had to submit all his requisitions, even for minor items of stationery, with two or three copies—all written by hand—to his headquarters in Quebec. They had then to be approved by the Military Secretary, the Commanding Officer of the Royal Engineers in Canada, and three other officers of the Commissary General's department, before issue could be made. In the Public Archives at Ottawa, there is such an order, dated 30th October 1830, for some quills, wafers, letter books, and Imperial drawing paper, with the six signatures upon it . . . and the final date of 24th December 1830, two months later! The wonder is that the Canal ever did get finished.

But it was over money matters that the "system," and the Commissary General, really showed what could be done in the way of making life difficult. Contractors, for example, were to be paid in dollars at Montreal, the money in general circulation at that time being chiefly dollar bills (provincial bank-notes) and American half-dollars, large silver coins. Early in 1829, Colonel By wrote to his commanding officer to say that the contractors on the upper part of the works complained of the risks that they had to run in conveying money (by canoe) from Bytown up through the line of the Canal. They had therefore advanced the eminently reasonable suggestion, which he endorsed, that they might be paid by cheque at Kingston. This request had of course to be referred to the Commissary General, who replied that it could not be granted since "it would embarrass the system of accounts" (a phrase that has a strangely familiar ring to it). It was explained that the only possible way would be to issue cheques payable in British silver money, and that this would give the contractors an advantage of 8 to 9 per cent, which was unthinkable.

Page after page of the old letter books contain similar frustrating records. Colonel By must frequently have been driven to distraction by such pettifoggery when, daily, he was facing major problems in the conduct of the work. But never once does he betray any impatience in his letters, always being "the most obedient servant" of those to whom he wrote. One more of his administrative problems may be mentioned, for it casts a revealing light on the difficulties of the contractors on the more isolated parts of the work. A. C. Stevens and Company had probably the most isolated location of all. In January 1829 they wrote to Colonel By asking if they might have the customs duty remitted on supplies they might bring in from the United States. Wheat had been very scarce so they had been forced to use a lot of corn. They therefore wished to bring in 350 to 400 barrels of flour and from 1,000 to 1,200 bushels of coarse grain across the St. Lawrence at Prescott and then by the winter trail through the forest to their camp. Ever dutiful, Colonel By sent on the request to Quebec City for official consideration, and that seems to have been the last that was heard of it.

Despite all such problems, the work went on. Colonel Durnford paid one of his obviously welcome visits in May 1828 and wrote to Lieutenant Colonel Couper from Bytown reporting generally satisfactory progress even though no dams were yet quite complete. He suggests that they should set up a committee to deal with land claims and so save Colonel By the vexation of the repeated prosecutions which were now being aimed at him personally. The Superintending Engineer's own report to General Mann at the end of the same year suggests that the whole job is now three-fifths complete and ventures the date of August 1831 as that by which navigation would be possible (a very close estimate it proved to be). The swamp fever has been very bad, Colonel By says, so that contractors were rushing their works to get them completed as fast as possible; he would therefore need a good supply of cash in 1830. He has reconstructed the dam at Hog's Back and has been twice through the Canal despite two very severe illnesses.

Six months later, in his next report to General Mann, Colonel By is able to state that he hopes to have the first fifty miles from Ottawa open for navigation by September of that year, and the through route completed by June of 1831. It is reported that a steamer did reach Kemptville late in the year 1830. Certainly by 1831, parts of the Canal were in regular operation. So sure was

Colonel By of the official opening being in 1831 that he had four silver cups made in London engraved with the date 1831, and sent out for presentation to the four principal contractors! Unfortunately, Mr. Merrick, proprietor of Merricks Mills, interfered with these carefully laid plans and chose the fall of 1831 to dam the Rideau River in order to effect some repairs to his mills. This so lowered the water level farther down the river that navigation was impossible, and the long-anticipated opening had to be postponed until the spring of 1832. There was still a lot of minor work to be done on the Canal, however, even in the summer of 1832, so possibly Mr. Merrick should not be blamed too severely for the delay in the opening.

The military character of the Waterway was never lost sight of during the years of building. Not only were small contingents of soldiers stationed at all critical points throughout the period of construction but blockhouses were erected at strategic locations along the Canal as a defence measure. As early as 1829, Colonel By had written to Quebec to say that in connection with the town planning at Hog's Back, he had managed to secure the land "necessary for a Fort for the protection of the Locks and Dam." One of By's difficulties with regard to land was that the Act of the Upper Canada Legislature gave him power to expropriate land for the project of building the Canal but not for purposes of defence. Despite this, in his usual cautious manner, he managed to procure most of the land which he deemed necessary for this purpose. In many of his letters to Quebec, he urged the necessity for continuing attention to the defence of the Canal. About a year after the letter just quoted, for example, he wrote again to Colonel Durnford that "it appears to be absolutely necessary that Block Houses or some works of defence should be erected wherever there are embankments or otherwise they could readily be destroyed by an enemy." Though Colonel By must have been well aware of the possibilities which the Canal presented for peace-time traffic, this emphasis on necessary defence is but another example of his close attention to his official duty as he saw it.

The blockhouses at Merrickville and Kingston Mills are now the most vivid reminders of the military character of the Waterway but there were originally many other military buildings along the Canal, such as the splendid log blockhouse at Jones Falls which was still standing within the memory of many local residents. Some of these were built to the orders of Sir John Colborne during the disturbed period following the rebellion of 1837, as an anti-sabotage measure. That this concern for defence against possible attack was still widespread, even beyond 1830, is indicated by construction at Kingston, to which fortress the Canal was to give alternative access from Montreal. Fort Henry, now happily restored to its former grandeur, was erected in 1836 to replace a smaller establishment. The famous Martello towers were not built until as late as 1846, more than thirty years after the cessation of hostilities with the United States: they constitute monuments to the Oregon Boundary Dispute. The Rideau Waterway was not, therefore, alone in its military significance.

Final touches were made to the canal works during the winter of 1831–32, all hopes being then centred on an official opening in the early spring of 1832. One would have expected that the completion of such an important work in the young colony would have attracted wide public attention but the newspapers of the time gave very little space to reports of the event. The reason for this neglect was a tragic one; public attention was then being diverted to the cholera which, starting at Quebec, was sweeping its way into Upper Canada. Fortunately, however, none of the principal actors in the drama of the Rideau Canal were touched by the plague and so preparations were finally made for the first unbroken voyage from one end of the Canal to the other. Many recent references to the Rideau Waterway state that this first journey was from Bytown to Kingston; actually the triumphal passage was in the reverse direction.

When spring came to Canada in 1832 Colonel By took his family and some of his fellow officers down the Waterway to Kingston so that all might share the final joy of participating in the opening. Robert Drummond had his vessel the *Pumper* all ready for the occasion, and indeed even changed its name temporarily to the *Rideau*, thus providing another cause for confusion in later years. At about noon on May 24, the great journey commenced, the *Rideau* having a forward escort in the naval dockyard cutter *Snake*, and herself creating a rear escort by hauling two barges. The barges and the cutter went only as far as Jones Falls. The excitement of the occasion must have been translated into speedy action on the part of all those involved, both on the vessel and at the locks, since the *Rideau* arrived at Smiths Falls at six o'clock on the morning of the 25th. Many of the small group

of settlers then resident at the Falls had waited up all night to see
the arrival. One member of the equally small military garrison
had arranged to fire a welcoming shot from a cannon but this was
so well loaded that, when fired at the climactic moment, it burst
into fragments. Extra passengers were taken on at Smiths Falls.
The rate of progress now slowed up considerably for ahead were
the new little towns of the Rideau settlements to be visited.
Merrickville was an important stop and here more entertaining
took place. Eventually, on May 29, 1832, the little vessel sailed
triumphantly to the wharf at the head of the flight locks at Bytown. The Rideau Waterway was complete; the Ottawa had been
linked with Lake Ontario. When the Ottawa River Canals were
ready, as they were to be in 1834, steamboats would be able to
sail up from the sea to Montreal, on to the Ottawa River, through
the Rideau Canal and so into the Great Lakes. The first St.
Lawrence Seaway would then be a reality.

Financial Worries

THERE IS only one blemish on the long record of the Rideau Canal over the years of its construction, maintenance, and use. This was in connection with its cost, and with the necessary allocation of funds for its building from the British Treasury in London. When estimates of cost for modern engineering works in Canada are under discussion, it is not uncommon to read some pointed comment to the effect that original estimates have always been very much less than the actual cost of engineering works "ever since the time of the Rideau Canal," with the implication that poor engineering judgment was responsible for financial difficulties on the Rideau works. The long neglect of Colonel John By, despite his great achievement in completing the Canal, is without doubt attributable in some degree to the fact that he was recalled to face a Parliamentary Committee of Inquiry. Something very much more than a trifling financial irregularity must have been involved. All too frequently, however, references to what happened are partial and incorrect. It seems advisable, therefore, to review here briefly the chain of circumstances which finally led to the misfortune of the implied censure of Colonel By.

This part of the story must start with the three rough and very preliminary estimates of cost made by Samuel Clowes for the Macaulay Commission of Upper Canada, on the basis of his reconnaissance survey in 1824 of the possible routes for the Canal. These estimates were for canals with smaller dimensions than that actually built, and the Carmichael Smyth Commission had increased the size, and their estimate. But although even Clowes' maximum sum of £230,785 was a preliminary estimate and was undoubtedly far too low, his figures were apparently used as the

basis of the original discussions about the construction of the
Canal by the Imperial government, and must be held responsible
for much of the misunderstanding which developed subsequently.

In anticipation of a decision to build the Canal, the Ordnance
Department had had inserted in the estimates presented to the
British Parliament in the year 1825 (the year before Colonel By
was sent to Canada), the sum of £5,000 for preliminary work on
the Rideau River. This item was passed by the House of Commons. Since it was such a small sum, it is perhaps natural that it
was passed without any special attention being given to it. The
best method of carrying out the construction of the Canal was
considered very carefully by the Ordnance Department; they
instructed By to undertake it by contract. It has since been
pointed out that this really should have meant asking Parliament
for the entire sum required for the project since contractors could
not be expected to wait for their payments until an annual amount
was authorized each year by Parliament. The Ordnance Department, however, apparently assumed that since the sum of £5,000
had been approved, the entire canal project had been approved,
and that it would not therefore be necessary to wait each year
for the annual building grant to be submitted to and approved
by Parliament. In these days of strict Treasury control of all
public funds, such an assumption is astonishing but the available
documents seem to leave no doubt that it was made. When, however, this original sum was granted, no estimate of the total cost
had been presented to the British House of Commons and the
House did not have the opportunity until it was too late of considering whether or not such a costly work as the Canal was to
prove to be should be carried out with funds from the British
Treasury. What probably started out as a simple assumption in
the interests of getting ahead with an urgently required military
work, far removed from the legislative halls of Westminster, was
to lead to repeated troubles about unauthorized expenditure and,
finally, to the reprimanding of Colonel By, the one man who most
certainly was not responsible for the original action.

Fortunately, we have a record of Colonel By's own understanding of his position from one of the aides-de-camp to the Earl of
Dalhousie, Major Elliot. He wrote on June 16, 1826, to his friend
Captain George Burke who had settled at Richmond, and included in his letter this statement: "I saw Colonel By on his way
through this place [Quebec City] and gave him all the informa-

tion in my power and with it my printed copy of the Clowes survey. Colonel By told me that he was not at all limited as to the sum to be expended, and that he hoped the work would be finished in five years." Despite this understanding, Colonel By was meticulous with regard to all his expenditures, and in his own letters he frequently refers to the measures he is taking in order to ensure the strictest control of the public funds for which he was responsible.

From the start of the work, he submitted the most detailed estimates to his superior officers. He did this by means of complete statements of cost, written out in beautiful copper-plate writing, in Indian ink, on large sheets of Imperial drawing paper. Several of the "progress estimates" (as they would be called on construction work today) still exist in the official records at Ottawa. They show, in the clearest manner possible, how carefully the Superintending Engineer was watching every item of cost, and how meticulously he reported every aspect of the financial part of his work to official quarters. The statements have significance in another direction. They are all made out in a standard form, a number of columns being ruled on the paper, the lines across the table presenting the figures for each lock and major structure on the Canal. The tables show the original estimate of cost, the amount spent to date, the estimated cost of completing the work, the estimated total cost, and then the difference between the original estimate and the anticipated new total, with explanatory notes following. The statements thus provided a control and record of the way in which the cost of the work was developing. This is the standard way in which construction progress estimates are made out today and are described in modern text-books on cost accounting. Such texts often suggest that the method is an innovation of the twentieth century, but it was in faithful use throughout the building of the Rideau Canal over one hundred and twenty years ago.

The actual expenditure of money on the job took several forms. There were the obvious costs of the necessary supplies and the salaries and wages of the military and allied civilian staffs engaged on the work. All these payments were subject to direct control by the Commissary General and his staff and so could not be questioned. Colonel By was responsible for authorizing the payments to be made to the contractors on the work, and also for the purchase of the land needed for the construction of the Canal.

That the project would eventually exceed the figures mentioned in preliminary discussions was clear to Colonel By from a very early date. Just after his arrival in Canada, as we have learned already, he sent a warning to London that the Canal was likely to cost in the neighbourhood of £400,000. As soon as the work was under way in 1827 he made efforts to get more reliable estimates. The first, prepared by John MacTaggart, was £486,000. Colonel By decided to have this checked independently by sending Lieutenant Pooley over the entire course of the Waterway. The revised estimate so obtained amounted to £474,000 but it is to be remembered that this was for a canal with locks measuring only 100 by 22 feet and not the larger size now recommended strongly by Colonel By. To report this figure and explain how it was obtained, Lieutenant Pooley was sent by his chief to London, and he took with him in the late summer of 1827 the first complete report of the Superintending Engineer on the estimated cost of the entire project.

This report, with its greatly increased estimate of cost, caused consternation in the Ordnance Department in London, despite the advance warning which Colonel By had previously submitted. It was intimated in these high official quarters that the original estimate of Samuel Clowes had been "made out from the reprehensible motive of endeavouring to benefit the Colony by embarking His Majesty's Government in this undertaking upon the faith of an estimate which the author of it, himself, admits he considered to be fallacious and inadequate." Similar doubt was cast upon Colonel By's position and work but a special committee of engineers (in London, of course) to whom the whole matter was quickly referred, reported that Colonel By had not deviated from his instructions and that they could find nothing in his plans or estimates to criticize in any way. The Committee were obviously impressed by the daring of By's plans, especially the way in which he was going to flood out some of the rapids and falls with singularly high dams. They pointed out that, although this system had previously been used, the Americans having a dam 28 feet high for this purpose, the Rideau works were going to include dams 45 and 48 feet high respectively at Hog's Back and Jones Falls. Acknowledging this bold advance in engineering design, they commended the work and its superintendent.

The British government, however, were still concerned about the whole project and were not satisfied with this report. They therefore appointed a special commission of military engineers under the chairmanship of Lieutenant General Sir James Kempt, then Lieutenant-Governor of Nova Scotia, with Colonels Fanshawe and Lewis of the Royal Engineers as members, to examine the details of the Rideau Canal on the spot and decide upon the recommended changes. They were instructed to stop the work unless they were sure that the project was practicable and that it had been designed and was being conducted economically. They were also authorized to approve the larger size of locks which Colonel By had recommended if they agreed with him on this point after a full study of the whole project. The Commission made the complete journey along the canal route and submitted their report, which was signed in Kingston in the month of June 1828.

While these studies were being carried out, another winter went by, giving Colonel By more opportunity for the development of his plans and the carrying out of more accurate surveys. As a result of this further work, he was able to submit a revised estimate of cost of £576,757 to the Commission. They reduced the figure to £558,000 but recommended that this be accepted as a reasonable estimate and stated that "they have every reason to believe [that it] will be found ample to meet any probable contingency which may occur." Of special interest today is the reference in their report to Colonel By himself: "Economy had not been lost sight of by Colonel By, and he has, in accordance with what he believed to be the spirit of his instructions, pushed forward the work and excited a degree of exertion throughout the whole Department which few individuals could have accomplished." They therefore ordered him to proceed with the work, as he had planned it, and authorized building of the locks to the new size, 134 feet long by 33 feet wide (with the same depth of five feet); any parts of the smaller locks already started were to be taken down and rebuilt, and the contractors were to be repaid for the work they had done. This report cleared the way for construction to proceed without further interruption.

Colonel By had still to worry about difficult landowners and their fantastic claims which got more unrealistic as work progressed. He even had trouble on this account with the Royal Navy; in November 1830, he had to send to Colonel Durnford a copy of a letter which he had received from Commodore Barrie, at Kingston, saying that "the Naval Department will look to the

Ordnance Department for the payment of all damages done to the said property [at Kingston Mills] by the Ordnance Department." Nevertheless, no more commissions or committees were sent out from England. A Select Committee of the British House of Commons was appointed in 1831 to review the accounts and papers of the Rideau Canal; it heard witnesses who knew the canal works, several of whom spoke highly of Colonel By. The resulting report, however, mainly concerns the way in which the project had been handled by the London authorities and contains no criticism whatever of the Superintending Engineer.

At the end of 1831, By submitted to London his final estimate, based on the very careful and accurate estimates which he had regularly presented. Apparently it was lost in the mails for he submitted a duplicate copy in February 1832. The total was £715,408, this being £22,700 more than had been voted by the British Parliament. In addition, he calculated that it would require £60,615 to complete the entire project, with all its ancillary defences. His total estimate for the work (£776,023) thus exceeded by £216,023 the estimate of £558,000 accepted and approved by the Commission of which Sir James Kempt was chairman in 1828, but the cost of extras which had been found to be necessary as construction progressed, such as the adoption of waste weirs, and the enlargement of dams and embankments following the unfortunate failure of the first dam at Hog's Back, accounted for all this increase in cost apart from about £30,000.

When it is considered that the whole Waterway project was carried out without benefit of any detailed preliminary surveys, that construction was subject to all the hazards of the Canadian climate in summer and winter, and that the scourge of sickness had seriously impeded the work for months at a time, the closeness of the final cost to the estimate approved by the Commission is indeed quite remarkable. The Lords of His Majesty's Treasury in London, however, did not take this view. The Secretary to the Board of Ordnance forwarded Colonel By's final estimate and accompanying papers to the Treasury on May 19, 1832. Six days later, a Treasury Minute was issued which said, in part:

My Lords have under their serious consideration the Letter from the Secretary of the Ordnance. . . . My Lords will take into their future consideration these voluminous Accounts and Papers; but they can not delay expressing their opinion to the Master General and Board of Ordnance on the conduct of Colonel By in carrying on this Work. . . . In order, therefore, to complete the Work, Colonel By has, upon his own responsibility, thought proper to expend no less than £ 82,576. . . . It is impossible for My Lords to permit such conduct to be pursued by any public functionary. If My Lords were to allow any person whatever to expend with impunity . . . a larger amount than that sanctioned by Parliament and by this Board, there would be an end to all control and My Lords would feel themselves deeply responsible to Parliament. They desire, therefore, that the Master General and Board will take immediate steps for removing Colonel By from any superintendence over any part of the Works for making Canal Communication in Canada, and for placing some competent person in charge of those works, upon whose knowledge and discretion due reliance can be placed. . . . My Lords further desire that Colonel By may be forthwith ordered to return to this country, that he may be called upon to afford such explanation as My Lords may consider necessary upon this important subject. Let copies of these Papers, and of this Minute be forthwith prepared, with a view to their being laid before the House of Commons.

These were the comments upon pioneer work in the Canadian bush, controlled with a diligence and rectitude which is fully revealed in a careful reading of original letters. The Lords of the Treasury did not wait to examine with any thoroughness all the papers submitted to them before making their Minute; six days only elapsed from the date of the Ordnance letter to that of the Minute. No opportunity for explanation was given to anyone, and this damning indictment was submitted officially to the House of Commons. Colonel By was recalled; the House of Commons appointed another committee; it heard evidence, including that of Colonel By. He was exonerated and the faults in Ordnance accounting procedure became evident; but the damage was done. The honours which should have come to the builder of the Rideau Canal were never bestowed upon him. He retired from the Army and his name was soon forgotten, amid all the excitement of the reform of the British Parliament. And there is a further tragic footnote to this story. Some of those who were being brought over from Canada to testify before the Parliamentary Committee, and whose evidence might have done something to ameliorate the treatment accorded to Colonel By, were drowned when the vessel bringing them from Canada, the *President*, was lost with all hands.

Colonel By's own letters show clearly, as we have said, the unusually rigid views which he held, and upon which he acted, with regard to the expenditure of public funds on the works under his direction. It was his misfortune to be responsible for very large expenditures of public funds at a time when the British Parliament was being reformed not only in its constitution but in the attention which it gave to such procedural matters as financial control. Making every allowance, however, for all these special circumstances, it is still difficult to understand how he could have been involved in such an unhappy end to a great undertaking. The explanation which has been usually given is that By was made a political scapegoat, especially by the Board of Ordnance in London, the members of which were certainly less than frank in their submissions to the British House of Commons with regard to expenditures on the Rideau Canal. Government officials, however, must have been particularly conscious of the keen criticism in the British press generally of the Rideau Canal as a flagrant waste of money in a distant and unimportant colony. One of the typically vituperative pamphlets of the time contrasts the money spent on the Rideau Waterway with that which had been requested (but not granted) for certain improvements to navigation in Ireland.

Despite official uneasiness, however, some of the invective about the project, it would seem now, can be traced back to a more personal effort against Colonel By. We have seen that Colonel By had to submit to London a duplicate set of his final statements for the year 1831, and this appears to have been the only occasion, throughout the history of the works, when such a loss of official papers occurred. Of itself, the incident might not be significant. But there were, apparently, other losses of papers of which Colonel By appears to have had no knowledge. One of the rarest of the relatively few publications dealing with the Canal and its builder suggests these further losses. This is a small pamphlet published and printed at the office of the *Patriot,* in Kingston, Upper Canada, in January 1832, the title of which is worth quoting in full: "The Following Notices of *The Rideau Canal* in which is made clear, the exalted worth of the Superintendent of that stupendous work, *Colonel By,* of the Royal Engineers; Who for its grandeur of design—its indefatigable prosecution—and rapid, and successful completion amid, not only, artificial obstructions, caused by intrigues of envious men, has merited, and enjoys, the gratitude of the present and secured for himself a Renown, imperishable in future Ages. And respectfully dedicated to the public, by its obedient humble servant, *The Author*." This magnificent title, the punctuation of which must make Fowler turn in his grave, heads an anonymous production which is subscribed "A Friend to Justice and to Merit." The author appears to have written at white heat over the vilification of Colonel By which was taking place in certain Canadian newspapers; his invective is a joy to read for all who feel keenly about the injustice to which John By was so obviously subjected. Towards the end of the pamphlet, it is related that attacks on Colonel By in October 1831 were directly attributable to a young man called Burgess who had gone to London with the stated intention of impeaching him. Burgess's journey is referred to in extracts from the *Montreal Gazette* and the *Liverpool Chronicle*. From these it seems clear that the young man had been connected with the Rideau works, since it is stated that he had taken with him to London from the canal office copies of many vouchers which he had presumably stolen.

More information about Mr. Burgess has been found in the Public Archives at Ottawa. In July 1831, Colonel Couper, the Military Secretary to the Governor at Quebec, sent to Colonel By a printed pamphlet which had been mailed to him from Montreal, asking for an explanation. The leaflet is quite beautifully printed, on thin India paper, and is a copy of a letter signed by Colonel By, dated November 29, 1829, at the Royal Engineers' Office, Rideau Canal. It is addressed to a Colonel Howard and starts thus: "Sir, Mr. H. Howard Burgess, a young man recommended to me by the Lord Bishop of Quebec in August 1826, and who has continued with me from that date to the present moment, having mentioned to me that it would afford him great satisfaction if I would give him a certificate of his good conduct, during the time he has been employed in my Office, I have the honour of assuring you that no young man could have conducted himself more to my entire satisfaction. . . ." A warm commendation follows.

Colonel By's letter of explanation to Colonel Couper, in his own handwriting, is so important that it must be quoted in full:

My dear Couper,

In answer to your enquiry relative to the enclosed printed letter, I can only say that it appears to be a copy or something like one, of a letter I wrote in favour of Mr. H. H. Burgess when he [Mr. Burgess] was 1st clerk in the Ryl. Engrs. Office at By-town, to Col. Howard his godfather. I gave the letter unsealed to Mr. Burgess to forward to Colonel Howard; but since my writing the letter attended to, the young man has been out of his senses, and has entirely given himself up to drinking; so much so that I have been obliged to suspend him from his situation and it appears he has left this place much in debt. I can only attribute his publishing my letter to a wish to impose on the Bishop of Quebec, who took great interest in his welfare; for not wishing to injure the young man I have taken no further notice of his ill-conduct than suspending him, which I did early this spring as also his Brother Mr. P. Burgess for neglect of duty.

Believe me, My dear Couper,

Yours faithfully,

JOHN BY.

Against the background presented by these letters, we may now look again at the record of the visit of Mr. Burgess to London. An English newspaper of the time published a statement about this young man and his connection with the Rideau Canal, which contained these words: "These [flagrant abuses on the Canal] have reached such a height that the Chief Clerk of Works, Mr. H. H. Burgess, who was appointed to that situation by the Hon. Board of Ordnance in London, determined to be no longer a party to such shameful, and fraudulent proceedings, &c. has come to this country for the express purpose of apprising Government of the impositions, which have been practiced upon them." Mr. Burgess was certainly not the Chief Clerk of Works; he was, however, in possession of a considerable quantity of vouchers which he had removed from the office at Bytown in which he had worked, and he was discharged from that office for drunkenness. The contrast between the newspaper description and what we know to be the true state of the conduct of the Rideau works indicates Mr. Burgess's capacity for mischief. He may well have had a good deal to do with the strange proceedings in London.

We should allow Colonel By himself to close this part of the Rideau story. In the records at Ottawa is a letter which he addressed to his great friend and fellow officer of the Royal Engineers, Colonel Durnford, after he had retired to Frant. He has this to say of the final inquiry: "The present Government throw blame on me for not waiting for the Parliamentary Grants, forgetting that it was ordered by his Grace, the Master General, and Board that I was not to wait for Parliamentary Grants, but to proceed with all dispatch consistent with economy, accordingly, the contracts were formed by the Commissary-General at Montreal; by which the Engineering Department was bound to pay for the works as they proceeded, which precluded the possibility of stopping the works, and thus laying the Government open for heavy damages. I was never ordered to stop the works until I was so unjustly recalled; when, thank God, they were all finished, and the Canal had been open to the Public for some months, or I should have been robbed of the honour of building the magnificent erection."

John By

IN THE HEART of the county of Sussex, England, near Tunbridge Wells, is the village of Frant. It is typical of all that one imagines an English village to be, with a village green dominated by an old parish church. A lych-gate lets the visitor into the churchyard, a pleasant garden dominated by old yew trees and favoured by a wonderful view over its low stone wall. Here is English countryside at its best, rolling land with neat hedgerows and villages nestling among the trees of the valleys. The atmosphere calls to mind at once Gray's *Elegy in a Country Churchyard*—it would be hard to imagine a scene more in contrast to the Rideau country.

A low porch in the church leads to a bright and dignified nave with a finely proportioned chancel and choir, all most obviously old but well kept indeed. A beautifully carved cover to the font is the work of two local ladies. Among the many tablets and memorials is a large white alabaster plaque, immediately to the right of the porch door, the inscription on which links this bit of rural England with Canada:

Sacred to the memory of
Lieutenant Colonel John By, Royal Engineers,
of Shernfold Park in this parish.

Zealous and distinguished in his profession,
tender and affectionate as a husband and a father,
and lamented by the poor, he resigned his soul to his Maker,
in a full reliance on the merits of his blessed Redeemer,
on the 1st February 1836, aged 53 years,
after a long and painful illness,
brought on by his indefatigable zeal and devotion in the service
of his King and Country, in Upper Canada.

This stone is erected by his afflicted widow, in remembrance of every virtue that could endear a husband, a father, and a friend.

In the churchyard, beneath a large granite tombstone, the builder of the Rideau Canal lies buried.

Shernfold Park is the "manor house" of Frant. To it Colonel By retired with his wife and family, following the completion of the inquiry in London; he had been placed on the unemployed list because of his failing health. The house is a dignified English country mansion, its high ceilings and beautiful proportions giving it an air of spaciousness which belies its relatively small size. The rooms all look out on to pleasant gardens. Amid these peaceful surroundings John By spent his last few years. No doubt his exposure to fevers, rough living conditions, and the rigours of six Canadian winters were the cause of his last long illness, but disappointment must also have broken his spirit. He was a modest man, as his letters show, but he would have been other than human had he not looked for some recognition of all that he did in the building of the Canal. Surely a knighthood was to be expected for him and promotion in the Army. No such honours were to be his.

Colonel By came from a family long connected with the public service, in the British Customs. His grandfather, John By, resided in Archbishop's Walk in the parish of St. Mary Lambeth in London, held the post of Chief Searcher in the London Customs House, and had four sons (John, George, Charles, and William) all of whom lived in Archbishop's Walk. All are buried in the churchyard of St. Mary Lambeth. His second son, George, married a Miss Mary Brian. They had three sons and several daughters, John being the second of their sons. He was born on August 10, 1779, and was baptized in the church to which his family had for so long been attached, St. Mary Lambeth. When he entered the Royal Military Academy at Woolwich, he broke away from the family tradition of Customs service. There he obtained his commission at the early age of twenty (on August 1, 1799), as a Second Lieutenant in the Royal Artillery. In December of the same year, he transferred to the Royal Engineers.

By's progress in the British Army was steady but not spectacular. He became a First Lieutenant on April 18, 1801, and a Second Captain on March 2, 1805. During the early part of this period, he served at Woolwich and at Plymouth and in August 1802 he was ordered to Canada. He was in Canada until 1811 when he was recalled for service in the Peninsular War in Spain and Portugal. While in Canada he secured also his next promotion, to First Captain, on June 24, 1809. For this first stay of nine years in Canada, he was attached to the Royal Engineers' establishment at Quebec City and had much to do with the building and extension of the fortifications at Quebec and with the reconstruction of the first small canal at the Cedars, on the St. Lawrence. How much he travelled in Canada at this time we do not know but, if his future activity is any guide, it is almost certain that he made it his business to examine as much as he could of the new land which he was helping to become settled.

He served with distinction in the Peninsular War, taking part in the great sieges of Badajos soon after his arrival at the battle front, in May and June of 1811. He was later recalled to England and placed in charge of the works at the Royal Gunpowder Mills at Faversham, Purfleet, and Waltham Abbey, positions he is said to have occupied with great credit from January 1812 until August 1821. During this period, he was promoted to be a Brevet Major (on June 23, 1814). He supervised the building of the new Army small arms factory at Enfield Lock in 1814, while in command at Waltham Abbey. In the same year, the Peace of Paris was celebrated in London by a great fireworks display in St. James's Park for which the Royal Laboratory, under the Board of Ordnance, was responsible and it is on record that Major By was asked to lend assistance with the necessary arrangements. It is a pleasure to know that he had a hand in at least one such celebration. His inventive turn of mind is well shown by the fact that, during this time, he designed a truss bridge with a span of 1,000 feet and even constructed a model of it which used to be in the possession of the Royal Engineers at Chatham, England. In 1821, owing to reductions in the strength of the British Army as a part of national economy measures, he was placed on the unemployed list. Depite this, he won his promotion to Lieutenant Colonel on December 2, 1824.

Is it stretching imagination too far to conjecture that the selection of him as the man to build the Rideau Canal was made by the great Duke of Wellington himself? His service in the Peninsular War would probably have brought him to the attention of the Duke. He could not have done what he did on the Rideau without having displayed similar ability at earlier tasks. The combination of any such demonstrated ability and his nine years of engineering experience in Canada would have made him an ideal candidate.

Colonel By was accompanied to Canada by his wife and two young daughters. His first wife, Elizabeth Baines, had died shortly after her relatively early marriage, leaving no children, and By had subsequently married Esther March, a daughter of John March of Harley Street, London, on March 14, 1818, while stationed at Waltham Abbey. The older daughter, Esther, must have been born within a year or two since she married the Hon. Percy Ashburnham, second son of the third Earl of Ashburnham, in 1838. Mrs. By and the little girls stayed with Colonel By throughout the duration of the construction work. Tiny tots when they arrived and not yet in their teens when they returned to England, the daughters must have had an exciting childhood in Upper Canada. Their education was probably, almost certainly, the reason why Colonel By, among his multitudinous duties, arranged for the start of a small school at Bytown. However, although the environment would have been novel, it could not have been healthy. The youngest daughter, Harriet Martha, was to die at 21, on October 2, 1842, six years after her father. She and her mother, who had died four years earlier (February 18, 1838), are both buried at Frant. Esther was not to survive her sister for long, and as both her children died in infancy, there are no direct descendants of the founder of Bytown.

But we must turn back to Colonel By, in all the vitality of his busy life on the Rideau works. As is so often the case with professional men, Colonel By left little behind him which tells us much about himself. We know that he was about five feet ten inches tall, stoutly built almost to the extent of being corpulent but with a decidedly military bearing. Mounted on a famous black charger, he was a familiar and generally respected sight around the little settlement of Bytown. His hair was dark, his complexion rather florid and he was jovial in appearance and good natured in character. No doubt his very definite sense of humour came often to his aid as it has done for many other men with such unusual burdens.

In keeping with his military and professional traditions, his official letters were strictly impersonal. In only one of the many which the writer has examined does he even mention Mrs. By, and the reference could hardly be more formal. It comes at the end of a letter of a rather more personal character than usual, since it was written directly to Sir James Kempt on July 23, 1829, clearly in reply to an inquiry by the Governor as to his health.

He says that Mrs. By joins him in sending regards, before subscribing himself, as usual, His Excellency's most obedient servant.

There are a few scattered references in the records to visitors to the site of the works, at the time of building, but one could wish that there had been more opportunities for description of life in this busy but remote community. Captain Alexander of the 42nd Highland Regiment was one such visitor and in his account of his visit he pays tribute to the welcome extended to him by Colonel By. He described his house as a "cottage ornée, tastefully decorated, with rustic verandahs and trellis work, situated on a high bank overlooking the Ottawa and opposite a lofty promontory on which stood the barracks." This confirms the location of this justly famous residence as having been in what is now Major's Hill Park. It was built of small boulders and moss, plastered with clay; the walls, of great thickness, were plastered with lime on the inside, giving a residence which was said to be comfortable at all seasons of the year. A similar but smaller house was built nearby for the use of Lieutenant Pooley, Colonel By's first assistant on the works. It is in keeping with the character of the man, and with his devotion to economy on all parts of the works under his direction, that a relatively cheap method of construction was used for his own residence but cut stone masonry for the official workshops and other buildings on the other side of the Canal. Most unfortunately, both of these historic homes were burned, Colonel By's in 1849 and Lieutenant Pooley's in 1869.

An even more intimate sketch of the By household is to be found in another rare record from the past which brings in to this tale the name of one of the greatest figures in Canada's commercial history of this period, Sir George Simpson of the Hudson's Bay Company. He was a relatively young man at the time the Canal was built, and on February 24, 1830, in London, England, he married his cousin, Frances Ramsay Simpson, a young lady well known in fashionable society. The young couple must have had a very short honeymoon in England for they crossed the Atlantic by sailing ship to New York, travelled overland to Montreal, and were at Lachine by the beginning of May. There they joined a party which had been assembled in the service of the Honourable Company and almost immediately set off on one of the great canoe journeys for which George Simpson came to be famous. They travelled from sunrise to sunset, covering almost incredible distances in single days of canoeing. Not only this, but the young bride, recently a darling of London drawing rooms, faithfully kept a diary of her journey. This still exists and delightful extracts from it have recently been published in a most appropriate medium, *The Beaver*, house organ of the Hudson's Bay Company. Under the date of May 4, 1830, we read an account of what she saw at Bytown, after sleeping on the banks of the Ottawa River at the mouth of the Lièvre River (in the open bush, of course), rising at sunrise, and being paddled sixteen miles by strong-armed *voyageurs* even before breakfast.

. . . Near this is situated the village of "Bytown" deriving its name from Colonel By of the Engineers with whom Mr. Simpson is well acquainted. He laid the first stone here, and is the principal superintendent of the great Rideau Canal, which connects the St. Lawrence and the Uttowas Rivers; also the upper and lower provinces of Canada. He was from home when we arrived, but we were very kindly received by Mrs. By (a very agreeable and accomplished young woman) who insisted upon our stopping to breakfast with her.

The house which stands in a good garden, overlooks one of the most beautiful spots I have seen in the Country; it commands an extensive view of the river, on the opposite side of which is the little village of Hull. The spires of the three Churches are visible through the trees, several bridges (one of which is very handsome) are thrown over the different channels of the River, formed by the islands and projecting banks of the Falls; from the upper storey are to be seen the fine and romantic Kettle [Chaudière] Falls and beneath runs the Rideau Canal. Mrs. By has resided here 4 years, and is to remain 2 more, until the works which are under the superintendence of the Colonel be completed; at the expiration of which time they return to England. After taking leave of our kind hostess we rode 9 miles in carts (not of the most elegant nor easy construction) with Buffalo Skins thrown over the backs and seats which we could readily have dispensed with, as the day was intolerably warm, without the addition of Furs. The road was so rough that it required some exertion to keep our seats, as the carts were without springs, indeed on rattling over a 'Stripe of Corduroy' here, we narrowly escaped cutting a Somerset over the horse's head, into a deep slough through which we plunged. Travelled till 8 p.m. and encamped at the Company's Establishment of the 'Chats' occupied by Mr. Thomas the Clerk in charge.

In this gracious tribute to Mrs. By and her home from a shrewd observer, we are reassured that the Bys were able to live in comparative comfort; the reference to the garden will interest those who know the floral splendours of Ottawa: the current horticultural interest of the city's residents is in a long tradition.

It is almost certain that Colonel By was absent on one of his inspection tours of the Canal when the Simpsons called at his home for he had made such a trip in May of each of the previous years. On these journeys, Captain Alexander tells us, Colonel By was conveyed by a picked team of Canadian *voyageurs* who were able to paddle as much as one hundred miles a day "on pork and pea-soup." The reference is in the spirit of what is known of the travelling habits of the Colonel. MacTaggart tells us that he was often accompanied on his trips by Colonel By, "a gentleman I shall ever esteem and value. He encountered all privations with wonderful patience and good-humour; was even too daring in some instances; would run rapids that his Indians trembled to look at; and cross wide lakes with the canoe when the Canadians were gaping with fear at the waves that were rolling around them. He could sleep soundly anywhere, and eat anything, even to raw pork."

Quite clearly, Colonel By was a man of iron constitution. But this was almost a necessity for the life he led, which exposed him also to several attacks of the dreaded swamp fever. In April 1829 he became ill after the disastrous failure of the first dam at Hog's Back. As will be seen later, Colonel By felt this failure very keenly, so that his sickness may have been the result of his excessive worry. He pays tribute to the skill of Dr. Tuthill, the senior doctor on the works, for he was idle for a few days only and went through the whole route of the Canal with his commandant, Colonel Durnford, two weeks after his attack. He was equally anxious to get about following the bad attack of fever which he caught "up the line" in September, and by which his life was seriously endangered. He was up again by the end of October, and was so far recovered as to be able to start up the Canal on November 9. A trip in an open canoe at this time of year is not an enviable task even for one in the best of health and with adequate modern equipment. By and his *voyageurs* got as far as Mud Lake; here they camped on an uninhabited island, on a night so cold that the water of the lake froze before morning. They had no shelter and little fuel but they had to remain for some time awaiting a change in the weather before they could get out.

Travellers in Upper Canada had, of course, to expect the unusual. Colonel By was once lost in Cranberry Marsh, before the works had developed to the point that a regular route was marked out, and was forced to spend several days in the bush. On another occasion, while travelling with John MacTaggart and some others in December 1827, he came to the large house of an American settler in the woods. They found the house so crowded with American and Irish immigrants that there was nowhere on the ground floor for them to rest. Colonel By and his party were so fatigued that, even though they disliked the atmosphere of the house, they sought out the landlord and asked if they could find a place to rest upstairs. Up a narrow, frail and dirty staircase they found a dirty attic which was kept cold by its broken windows. Looking around they saw a number of men asleep on the floor and a table with something upon it covered by a sheet. They lifted this to see what was underneath, and found the dead body of a young lad of about fifteen, terribly mutilated. Downstairs again, they could get no satisfactory explanation of the presence of the body. After spending a fitful night on the ground floor they departed the next morning, unable to do anything to assist the parents of the lad. He had been killed by a careless shot from a gun and the criminal laws of Upper Canada were such that they could not interfere in such a case.

One would have imagined that Colonel By's responsibilities on the Canal would have occupied all his time, but he managed also to discharge the duties of first magistrate with municipal powers for the new community of Bytown, until such time as regular appointments were made. The Earl of Dalhousie had directed him to survey the land around the start of the canal works, to rent lots to settlers, to open streets, and to adopt regulations for the building of houses. He had been advised orally by His Lordship to spend the money received from rents for the improvement of the town. It is reported that in 1831, permission was sought for the spending of £114 for constructing drains, building a new bridge, and starting a public wharf.

Application was made to the Governor in May 1827 for the appointment of regular magistrates and in due course Colonel By was succeeded by Captain Andrew Wilson, with others added to the bench soon afterwards. It was not long before unruly scenes began which were to dominate the local municipal picture for some years after the canal works were finished. This was probably inevitable, since the settlement was so closely associated with this major construction work and yet quite outside the control of the Superintending Engineer. All men who were discharged from the works, for example, would gravitate to the hostelries of the

little town and in view of the way in which men had to be recruited for the work it was not surprising to find evidence of some
resentment against Colonel By towards the end of his stay.

One incident is particularly revealing. In April 1831, Colonel
By found it necessary to remove in a summary fashion from a
government building which he had loaned for use as a bakery, a
man called Hill who was found to be selling spirituous liquors to
the men on the works. Hill was given twenty-four hours in which
to get out of the building. When he had not moved in forty-eight
hours, Captain Victor was ordered by his commanding officer to
remove the offending goods. The door had to be forced open and
this was observed by one of the local magistrates, though he did
not interfere. The sergeant and corporal in command of the party
which carried out this job were then arrested. It is said that the
next day Colonel By was himself arrested by the Deputy Sheriff
as being the instigator of a riot, £500 being asked for as bail
until the next assizes. Unfortunately, there the record stops!

Drunkenness was but one more of the problems with which By
had to deal in superintending his vast undertaking. There are
several references to excessive drinking in official letters but
one has to search into somewhat unofficial records to find what
it was that these hardy pioneers did drink. A distillery was regarded as an indispensable part of a new community, so that raw
grain whisky could be produced, at a cost of two shillings a
gallon, it is reliably reported, the flavour being improved by
frosty potatoes and yellow pumpkins. MacTaggart assures us that
this drink was extremely delicious but he has other language in
which to describe the more common liquor, also called whisky,
made from frosty potatoes, hemlock, pumpkins, and black mouldy
rye. "No hell broth that the witches concocted of yore can equal
it . . . this absolute poison of Upper Canada, the laudanum that
sends thousands of settlers to their eternal rest every season." He
blames the name "whisky," which has a peculiar charm for Irishmen and Scotsmen, for the prevalent use of this obnoxious potion,
the manufacture of which was soon to be prohibited. One of the
men who had to be discharged for repeated drunkenness was a
Sergeant Adamson. Such was the courtesy of the age that, in the
letter about his discharge, the Barracks Master Sergeant still
signs himself as the "most obedient servant" of the man he was
dismissing.

Expressions such as these may have been superficial but they give a particular tone to all the correspondence about the Canal, still happily in the records. A surprising aspect is the legibility, and indeed beauty, of practically all the Rideau Canal letters—in sharp contrast, it may be noted, to the letters written at the same time about the building of the Grenville Canal, down the Ottawa River, by the Royal Staff Corps. Colonel By's own letters, and there are many still preserved, are written in a fine clear hand, sure indication of his strong character even to the amateur student of calligraphy. Stenographers in their thousands are a very recent addition to the Ottawa scene; Colonel By wrote almost all his letters himself. The requisitions for stationery and office supplies remind one that the letters were all composed with quill pens, frequently by the light of candles or oil lamps, and were sealed with wafers. All copies of letters had to be laboriously written out individually by hand.

Despite the excessive formality of the official correspondence, and the necessity of following strict channels of communication (there is one record of a severe reprimand to By for writing directly to the Governor, whom he knew well, instead of to the Military Secretary!), the kindly character and warm disposition of Colonel By are evident behind the subject-matter of many of the letters. In January 1829, for example, he writes to his commandant, Colonel Durnford, asking if he may be permitted to sell supplies from the army stores to settlers in Bytown since there are so few there who are not employed in the public service and in view of the difficulty and cost of getting supplies in small quantities. As might be expected, the Commissary General refused to consider such a thing. A similar fate met another suggestion of Colonel By on behalf of his men, that labourers might be permitted to bank their savings in the Military Chest at Bytown. This idea was even endorsed by His Excellency Sir John Colborne who was visiting the work at that time. The "system" however, would not permit it and so the men had to go on keeping their savings in any safe place which they could find in their own quarters.

In addition to all that he was doing on the Rideau works, the Superintending Engineer was asked to undertake various other technical tasks. Reference has already been made to the visit to Colonel By of the two contractors from the Welland Canal. He was also consulted about the building of the Grenville Canal. This small work had been started by the Royal Staff Corps in

1819 and was far from finished when the Rideau works were started. Early in the summer of 1829, Colonel By took time off from his duties at Bytown to go down the Ottawa River to inspect the Grenville works, and the relevant papers, with Lieutenant Colonel Du Vernet of the Staff Corps. He reported to Colonel Durnford on June 30, in a singularly helpful letter, with very friendly references to his brother officer. It appears that at about this time the authorities were considering giving over the Grenville works to the Ordnance Department. Over a year later, By was again consulted and signed a joint report with the two officers just mentioned and some others. He was also consulted by a Mr. Shirreff who lived at Fitzroy Harbour, upstream from the Chaudière Falls on the Ottawa River, about the latter's proposal for a canal up the Ottawa to Lake Huron by way of Lake Nipissing; so began the long history of the projected Georgian Bay Ship Canal. Colonel By submitted a report from Mr. Shirreff to Colonel Durnford on this ambitious project early in 1829. In June 1830 he was approached by a contractor, Thomas Phillips, with an offer to build locks on the Back River, Montreal, for one shilling and a penny per cubic foot if free stone and sand were supplied to him. This offer he sent on to Sir John Kempt with his commendation, writing just half an hour before he left for a trip up the Canal with the Commissary General.

That Colonel By found opportunity for such sympathetic appraisements seems more noteworthy when we remember the barrage of claims from incompetent contractors, referred to earlier, which made such demands upon his time and patience. He dealt with all such "claims" in strict accordance with the contract agreements but this left many of the contractors unsatisfied and a steady stream of petitions to the Governor-in-Chief started on its way to Quebec. The petitions were duly sent back to Colonel By for his opinion. Some of them were many pages long; he had to go through them all and make detailed comments. In every case that the writer has seen, his comments are fair and reasonable, completely justifying the stand he had taken. The wording of some of the petitions has really to be seen to be believed, especially one series coming from Glengarry, since abuse of Colonel By seems to have been an accepted starting point. On one occasion only does By appear to have lost patience with this sort of thing; he comments on January 1829 in a letter to the Military Secretary, which deals with an eighteen-page

than he performs." He ad
simply flooded with false (

The final incident to be :
claim by the gentlemen fr
McMartin, is noted again
By had to write to the
about these two men, con
tion. By is led to express
should think it necessary
orders given during his vi
summer 'that all *just* clair
Governor's complaint, it
had been too lenient but
goes on to say that he co
resist unjust claims with
ments that may be mad
that no such unjust cla
Department "even shou
Government prove a 'cu

Despite the distractio
of close attention to da
in mind the role of th
quently considered way
its use. Even before he
bilities were evident to
British territory not or
the means of attacking
mistress of the trade
the Great Lakes which
manufactured goods."
its end, his hopes for
estimates of the traffic
her 1830, we find hi
about the appointmer
for the men who had
proceeds to suggest
quired each spring ar
He goes on to outline
through trip from K
shillings per hundred
possible freight and

closely written reply to his observations from the gentlemen in Glengarry, that he "regrets extremely that my duty should expose me to such unmitigated and uncalled for abuse."

The involved nature of some of this sordid business is shown by an exchange of many letters regarding the difficulties of one of the small firms of excavation contractors, obviously formed just for the Rideau work by a partnership between James Mc-Dermott and a Mr. Lynch who was a storekeeper in Kingston. Lynch seems to have provided the money but McDermott was in charge of the excavating. He was directed to cease work, on cancellation of the contract, in a letter from John MacTaggart dated September 23, 1827. Then the trouble began. The partners broke with one another and by December McDermott was lodged in the Kingston jail, on the suit of Lynch, presumably for breach of their agreement. But the creditors of the two partners were still unpaid. One of them was Thomas Dalton, of the Kingston Brewery, and he wrote directly to Colonel By on December 12, 1827, enclosing an authorized account for the work which had been done by McDermott on the Canal (signed, incidentally, by Arthur McLean, architect, of Brockville—reference to this profession is unusual at this early date). Dalton asked if payment could be made, since he himself had not received one shilling for the beer he supplied to the workmen on the contract, and even offered to go bail for McDermott, if this would assist in settling the matter. In Dalton's letter occurs a tribute to Colonel By which, even if it must be somewhat discounted since Dalton was a suppliant, is still of significance. Dalton refers to ". . . the resolution I understood you have formed and generally promulgated to pay no Contractor until you are assured that the workmen are paid or otherwise satisfied; a resolution worthy of the high character you have acquired, and of the confidential situation you fill, and which must unquestionably insure you the blessings of thousands." In February, Dalton has to write again to tell Colonel By that every action taken in trying to clear up the account seems to increase the hatred between Lynch and McDermott, with the result that the creditors have had to appoint three arbitrators, having bonded the two partners to the extent of £1,000. Mac-Taggart apparently got himself involved in this complex case in an unfortunate way since Captain Bolton had to write on March 18 to Dalton, trying very diplomatically to smooth over ruffled feelings which had developed from a scene in the officers' mess

at Kingston earli
MacTaggart. The
since Dalton had
plaining about a
In this same lette
in Kingston, had
effect that Colo
Kingston and ha
some funds. Da
pernicious tend
McDermott, m
submitting a pe
document bein
sent to By for
the company o
at Kingston in
he had to ad
from Kingston
anywhere wit
using Mr. Dru
as an interme
would ever ha

This incide
the sort of thi
By. Many sim
will be noted
ment is the
trouble and
with the cor
which to civ
more rock t
had expecte
higher wate
started the
sent back t
been over-l
Clerk of W
actually do
ment so th
petition; "
have no r

look forward to 2,000 passengers, 2,000 horned cattle and horses, 1,000 sheep and pigs, and quantities of dry goods, wines and spirits, liquors, grain, potash, softwood, and stone. He estimates an annual income of £41,762-10-0 and notes that this should be considered together with the intended military advantages of the Canal. And, to make use of the Canal to the fullest, he suggests that boats must be encouraged to go through it in order to use up the water which would be available for the supply of the Canal from the headworks. Against this watchfulness, his recall to England is a tragic incongruity.

Despite the increasing difficulties that Colonel By had to face as his great work approached completion, there were many who had begun to appreciate the significance of the Canal to the area which it penetrated. Notable among them were some of the citizens of Kingston who decided to honour Colonel By while he was still with them. They organized a public dinner which was held on Tuesday, March 13, 1832, in Carmino's Hotel at Kingston. Seventy diners enjoyed what was said to have been one of the finest meals that Mr. Carmino had ever prepared, and also the playing of the Band of the 66th Regiment which was in attendance throughout the evening. The Editor of the *Kingston Chronicle* described it as "the happiest, most convivial and harmonious assemblage that has ever been remembered of the inhabitants of Kingston. . . . The occasion, combined with the stimulating influence of copious Champaigne libations, rendered many a tongue loquacious. . . . 'For those who never spoke before, now spoke ten times more!'" Unfortunately no record of the speech of John By remains nor, indeed, is there a record of any of the innumerable speeches that were then declaimed since all that the diligent editor was able to procure for insertion in his paper was the text of one speech which its writer (a military man) "had intended to deliver." The Honourable John Kinley was in the Chair. The success of his direction of this function is indicated by another contemporary tribute which said that the dinner would "be remembered as long as the waters of Ontario and the Rideau are united and will form an era in the hospitable history of Kingston which never yet was backward in appreciating merit and rewarding the exertions of those who contribute to the success and prosperity of her enviable position."

Colonel By returned to Bytown a day or two after the dinner in order to carry on with the preparations for the official opening

Down the Years

"PASSED down ten Indian canoes." So reads the daily journal for Nicholsons Locks under date of Friday, June 15, 1838. Similar entries appear on many pages of this old leather-bound volume. The recent records for the same lock contain other repetitive entries regarding the passage of the M.V. *Radel II*, the experimental radar research vessel of the National Research Council, on its way to and from Lake Ontario for its secret experimental work. It would be difficult to imagine a more revealing contrast between the early traffic on the Canal and that which it now carries or a more vivid reminder of the changes which have come to the country served by the Rideau Waterway in the century since it was first put into use.

One could not wish for a more telling example of the truth of Kipling's succinct suggestion that "Transport is Civilization" than the Rideau Waterway. Built through virgin forests and at first completely out of touch even with the primitive pioneer civilization of the young colony of Canada in the eighteen-twenties, the Canal witnessed and was to some extent responsible for the founding and steady development of numerous little towns along its shores. The forest was cut back from its banks; farms were established, served initially by the Canal as a commercial waterway. The railways came; the Canal even assisted with the building of one line and with the servicing with coal of the great junction of Smiths Falls for many years. Then came the highway as the rival of the railways; the Canal helped again with the building of roads, though they were eventually to rob it of its last remaining chance to serve as a freight carrier. Its traffic waxed and waned, some new use always seeming to turn up as

of the Canal, and for his own long anticipated departure f
England. The unpleasantness of the public inquiry was w
ahead of him, and before that experience he was to enjoy anoth
happy celebration when he sailed with his family and some of 1
many friends from one end of the Canal to the other. We c
well imagine that some of those who dined with him at Carmir
Hotel were among his well-wishers as the *Pumper* pulled av
from the wharf at Kingston Mills little more than two mor
after this convivial dinner party.

Since no formal commendation followed Colonel By's exon
tion by the parliamentary committee, as would have been fit
the Rideau Canal itself must remain as the enduring monur
to his greatness as an administrator and as an engineer. Rec
such as have been quoted testify to his upright character
show that he was indeed a Christian gentleman. The st
perseverance with which he replied to his responsibilities
appreciated by a fellow military engineer, Sir Richard B
castle, who served in Canada during the rebellion of 183
wrote much about the colony's prospects. In his book *The Ca*
(1842) he well realized the magnitude of Colonel By's ta
ever man deserved to be immortalized in this utilitarian
was Lieutenant Colonel By. In an unexplored part of the c
where the only mode of progress was the frail Indian cano
a department to be organized, workmen to be instruct
many difficulties to be overcome, he constructed a truly 1
able work."

another declined. And in recent years, when other inland waterways have ceased to find any traffic at all, the Rideau carries its greatest number of vessels, which move up and down in search of the recreation it offers in absorbing plenty.

The passage of Indian war canoes through locks may seem incongruous but this new aid to navigation was frequently used by Indian travellers for at least the first decade of the Canal's service. There are records, too, of the assistance given by Indians during the course of construction. We know that they were then regularly using the Rideau River and Lakes as a waterway for their hunting expeditions and that appreciable quantities of furs, including even otter, were still being obtained in the Rideau country when the Canal was opened. An old man, who has spent most of his working life in the service of the Canal, has told me that he heard from his grandmother of an incident which took place when she was living, as a little girl, in the old stone house still in use on the east bank of the Rideau River near Clowes Lock. An elderly Indian, alone in his canoe, came paddling up to her home one summer evening soon after the Canal was opened. He asked her father for permission to berth his canoe at the piling ground, a common stopping point for Indians who wished to spend the night en route to their hunting grounds. He drew up his canoe as usual, turned it over, and proceeded to make his bed on the earth beneath it. In the morning, those in the house were surprised to see the canoe still in place when they came out, for the Indians were usually early risers. When no signs of movement were seen, her father went to investigate and found that the old Indian had passed to his final hunting ground in his sleep. He was buried in McGuigan's Cemetery nearby, a graveyard not now used but still to be seen beyond an adjacent orchard.

It is often said that the Rideau Canal was never used for its intended purpose of conveying troops and military supplies from Montreal to Kingston. This popular impression recently gained renewed publicity when, in the summer of 1951, three training vessels of the Royal Canadian Navy passed through the Canal from Kingston to Ottawa and were said to be the first naval vessels ever to use the Waterway. From the account which has been quoted of the initial voyage of 1832, we have seen that a naval cutter took part in that famous venture. Two gunboats are reported to have passed through the Canal in July 1838. And search through the old journals which still survive shows similar naval occasions in these early years.

The old records, maintained carefully at all the locks, some of which are fortunately still available for study, show clearly that the British Army also used the Canal in its early years. On Sunday, May 3, 1840, to give a specific example, the steamer *Bytown* passed down through the Merrickville stretch of the Canal with one barge in tow, on board which were the men of the 65th Regiment. Similar references are to be found to passage through the Canal of the men of the 1st Royal Regiment, the Royal Sappers and Miners, and of the 32nd, 34th, 73rd and 85th Regiments. The troops were sometimes conveyed in barges, sometimes in Durham boats. Among the journal entries (all in copperplate script), some make mention of ammunition as well as troops. It is, therefore, quite certain that the Canal did in a sense fulfil its intended function for almost two decades after the initial voyage of the *Pumper*, though never under the stress of war.

This military traffic on the Canal was not heavy, of course, and as the years went by it gradually became insignificant as compared with the commercial traffic. In the first few years after the Waterway was opened, up to about 1840, much of the freight was conveyed on barges, pulled by the new paddle steamers which were just beginning to revolutionize water transportation. Some of the strings of barges must have been impressive sights. There is on record one voyage of the steamer *Hunter* pulling no less than twenty-four. This must have been exceptional; there would rarely be more than ten barges behind any of the regular steam tugs. The barges had to be locked through in pairs so that, though there were relatively few steamers, the lockmasters and their men were on duty for twenty-four hours a day, even in these initial years. In 1840 appear the first references in the lock journals to "propelling barges," the first vessels to be driven by means of propellers instead of side paddle wheels. This advance in motive power came just when commercial traffic was beginning to increase. Within the space of two years, for example, a normal day's traffic had changed from a maximum of three steamers to a total of seven or eight. It was about 1840 that the business of the shipping companies which were associated for so many years with the Rideau Canal really commenced. (One of the many links between the Canal and Montreal is provided by the directorship which John Molson held in the first of the Rideau forwarding companies.)

These developments in freighting on the Canal reflected commercial activity elsewhere on a far larger scale. Traffic on the Waterway was, in fact, a good indicator of a great change in the economic life of Canada during the first quarter of the nineteenth century. In 1821 the Hudson's Bay Company had finally absorbed the Northwest Company, an event which marked the beginning of the end of the fur trade as the major economic activity of Canada. The first exports of grain had taken place two decades before this. As trade in commodities much more bulky than furs steadily developed, water transport had perforce to change. The coming of the steamship made this possible and, at the same time, directed public attention to the vital necessity for improving inland waterways. Rapids which could be safely navigated by canoes with their precious bales of furs could not be used by larger vessels with bulky cargoes. Canals, therefore, were in public demand wherever transport to the sea was impeded by restricted waterways and this led to the canal "fever" which has been referred to in an earlier chapter. On the New York State Barge Canal, the first of the great North American canals to come into use, over one million dollars in tolls were paid by vessels by 1830. We have already seen that the first Lachine Canal was opened for use in 1825 but further development of the St. Lawrence route was to be plagued by many delays, some of which were related to the choice of the main ocean port on the river. In 1824, for example, 613 vessels sailed up as far as Quebec but only 55 of these went on to Montreal, and these were all small boats. Agitation from the merchants of Montreal finally resulted in the formation of the first Montreal Harbour Commission in 1830; the available depth in the channel up to Montreal was then only nine feet. As the channel was improved the ocean traffic to Montreal increased, and this development in turn had its effect on the inland waterway traffic down from Upper Canada.

Agitation also for improvement of the insignificant little canals on the St. Lawrence between Montreal and Lake Ontario continued to mount. Vessels coming down from Lake Ontario could navigate with safety most of the rapids on the St. Lawrence but could not manage to sail up these stretches of swift water. Accordingly, before the St. Lawrence system was completed, vessels from Upper Canada journeyed to Montreal down the St. Lawrence, using the lower canals as they gradually came into use, and then returned to Lake Ontario by sailing up the Ottawa River to Bytown and through the Rideau Canal to Kingston. The serious depression of 1836–37 exercised a considerable influence upon the early development of commercial traffic on the Rideau Canal but by 1840, the effects of this economic set-back were disappearing and, as we have just seen, commercial traffic really began to increase. At the same time this early "Triangular Route" became the subject of much public controversy. For example, the freight rate in 1841 from Montreal to Kingston was from $13 to $15 per ton. Merchants were not slow to point out that this was exactly the same amount as was charged between Buffalo and New York for transport over almost twice the distance! The controversy sounds very similar to some of the arguments of today about adjustments of rates for bulk transport before the Board of Transport Commissioners.

In the year 1845 a fleet of no less than thirty small steamboats was regularly employed on the Kingston-Montreal-Ottawa-Kingston round trip. One company alone had a fleet of thirteen "puffers," as the early non-condensing steamboats were affectionately called. Another depression in 1847–50 slowed up this steady progress but with the turn into the second half of the century, traffic continued to increase, its peak being reached about 1860. This is the more remarkable in that the St. Lawrence canal system was completed in 1851, when the opening of the Junction Canal between Cardinal and Iroquois finally made it unnecessary for vessels to use the Ottawa and Rideau route in returning upstream from Montreal. In its issue of May 27, 1834, the *Patriot* (of Toronto) had had this to say: "The Rideau Canal has at length asserted its pre-eminence over the St. Lawrence rapids and seems destined for some years to be the chosen route from Montreal to the Western Regions." But despite such high hopes, the fate of the Rideau Canal as the St. Lawrence seaway had been forecast on a day in 1842 when *The Highlander* sailed into Kingston Harbour, having come up the St. Lawrence under its own steam through the rapids which still remained. This was almost a freak voyage but in 1851 navigation up the St. Lawrence from Montreal really became a commercial proposition. For the first few decades of its existence, however, the Rideau Canal had been a vital part of the St. Lawrence seaway, precursor of the route developed by the end of the century by means of the fourteen-foot canals of the St. Lawrence, and forerunner of the great international Seaway project of today.

Another development in the story of transportation was in the end of far more significance to the Rideau Canal than the opening of a rival water route: the steady progress of the railway as an efficient freight carrier, one which had the unrivalled advantage in Canada of being available for use throughout twelve months of every year. The combination of railways and the new water route at first gradually decreased the volume of traffic carried by the Rideau Waterway until about 1875. There were still busy little steamers passing up and down the Canal but the volume of freight which they carried not only did not increase, as on other water routes, but even diminished. This disappointment to those responsible for the operation of the Canal was temporarily reversed in the last quarter of the century, however, when the little settlement of Smiths Falls was selected by the newly formed Canadian Pacific Railway as its main junction in eastern Ontario. As a divisional point and junction, Smiths Falls quickly became an important railway centre, and thus used considerable quantities of coal. The Canal provided the community with a most convenient means of cheap transport for its bulk shipments of coal. Brought across Lake Ontario from American shipping points, the coal was trans-shipped at Kingston into barges suited to the locks of the Rideau Canal and these were then towed by sturdy steam tugs up the Waterway to Smiths Falls. Many thousands of tons were thus transported every year until well into the twentieth century. One of the men who spent all of his active life in sailing the waters of the Rideau has said that for over twenty-five years he brought more than four thousand tons of bulk coal into Smiths Falls every shipping season. The grimy barges regularly passed along the quiet woodland waters of the Rideau Waterway, through the locks and across the tranquil lakes, on their way to service the town built around this rival mode of transportation. The day came, however, when, with a changing pattern of labour and transportation costs, the coal traffic on the Canal began to decline. As labour charges mounted steadily, it became more economical to leave the coal in the cars in which it was originally shipped from the American mines and to bring it to Smiths Falls by means of one of the train ferries across the St. Lawrence. The last barge-load of coal left Kingston in 1920.

Water transportation has always provided the greatest service to commerce and industry in the movement of large bulk cargoes. The movement of coal on the Rideau Canal is but one example of this specially favourable aspect of freighting on inland waterways. Throughout the entire history of the Canal, its cargoes have reflected this feature. One commodity, for instance, which was a recurring item on the annual lists of freight handled was lumber, in its simplest form as trimmed logs, floated down from the shoreline nearest to the point in the forest at which it was cut to be processed in saw mills along the Canal, or more probably at Kingston or Ottawa. When the lumber trade was at its height, squared timbers were regularly brought down the Canal on the start of journeys to points as far distant as the British Isles. The old journals show that as early as 1840 the Canal was in regular use for the passage of rafts of logs; this traffic continued well into the twentieth century. Small movements of wood over the Waterway may still be seen today but the last major shipment was in 1933 when Wendell Brown, of Portland-on-the-Rideau, brought a raft of logs up from Morton, below Jones Falls, into Big Rideau Lake where they were converted into sawn lumber. A saw mill still operates on the shore of the lake at Portland but today it obtains most of its wood supply by means of trucks. Other waterways continue to provide an economical method of moving logs since their procurement and handling necessitates much hand labour for which no real substitutes can be found. If the forests around the shores of the Rideau Lakes are eventually rehabilitated, as they should be, we may yet see the Waterway again used for conveying logs down to the main rivers.

Other types of freight carried by the Canal have varied greatly, in kind and in time, as the years have brought changes to the countryside it serves. Products of some of the mines on its shores, now abandoned, have been moved out by barge. Near Ottawa, large quantities of sand for building purposes, and especially for road use, were regularly transported by barge down to the city until road transport by truck proved to be more convenient. One after another of these specialized cargoes have had their day in the history of the Canal, only to disappear as the years went by. A contemporary record comes from one of the Tweedsmuir Books faithfully maintained by the Women's Institutes of Canada. The Institute of Newboro reports:

The writer has seen [the Canal] crowded with boats carrying the produce of the country and bringing in such goods as were needed and the growing prosperity of the country could afford. *City of Ottawa* . . . *Rideau King* and *Rideau Queen* were some of the boats that carried passengers and freight and looked to one in their day like monsters of marine architecture. . . . Tugs were . . . *Swan, Elswood, Eleanor, Maggie May, Hirma Easton, Peerless* and many others towing 2, 3, and 4 barges; about 40 sailing scows carried out wood, lumber, pressed hay, grain, horses, cheese, whatever the country had to sell and brought in goods the merchants sold, the implements that were needed, the foodstuffs not grown in this climate and furnished employment to hundreds of men. Rafts of squared timber and of rough logs running up to hundreds of lock bands, built up with cook and bunk houses, stables for horses gouged by 20 or 30 men made their slow way to mills and market every year and left behind a fire menace. I have seen the men at Jones Falls at work without a break for over sixty hours. They slept on the grass while the locks were filling and ate their meals that had been brought to them sitting on a swing bar. They worked 24 hours a day [and] slept when they could. At first the lock men were paid 60c. a day for 7½ months each year. Later their pay was raised to $1.00 a day and there never was a time when there was any trouble in getting men to work on the lock. And now it is done. Not a passenger boat, not a tug or a barge or scow or raft plies the Rideau. In place of the musical steam whistle that could be heard for miles, we have the motor boat's raucous horn. The rhythmic puffing of the steam engine is replaced by the ill-mannered stuttering of the gas engine. Instead of never-ending industry furnishing a topic of conversation, you hear nothing but bait, bass and beer.

This typical memory of the past, possibly slightly distorted by the lure of alliteration's artful aid in the suggestion about the present-day limits of conversation, conveys something of the bustle of activity all along the Waterway during the summer months in years long past, and this impression is reinforced by other early records. The transport of farm products was a particularly important part of the normal traffic, and no product was more famous than the cheese of the Rideau area. By processing it into cheese, the severe limitations on early transport of milk were successfully overcome and many little cheese factories were to be found throughout Carleton and Leeds counties, even in the early years of the century. Cheese is still made, on a greatly reduced scale, but much of what is prepared now is processed in large plants and transported by road and rail. The advance in road transport has at once removed much of the necessity for making cheese, and made more economical the movement of the cheese that is still manufactured. The last of the "cheese boats," as they were called, sailed in 1930, so recent have been some of the technological changes which have transformed the nature of the Rideau Waterway.

The latter half of the last century was, then, the great period of Rideau Canal traffic. Many names have come down to us of men who made their fortunes and their reputations in freighting on the Rideau. One of these prominent figures earned for himself the undisputed title of "King of the Rideau." Moses Kent Dickinson was a native of New York, a grandson of the man after whom Dickinsons Landing on the St. Lawrence was named. He settled in Bytown near the middle of the last century and quickly established himself as a forwarder of freight on the Rideau Canal. At the height of his activity, he owned and operated a fleet of sixteen steamers and eighty-four barges but soon after 1860, possibly because he foresaw the change in canal traffic which was coming, he sold his entire freighting interests to Montreal and Chicago financiers. A leading citizen, he was Mayor of Ottawa from 1864 to 1866 and served later as a Member of Parliament for Russell County. His business acumen is indicated by the fact that he was the founder of the little town of Manotick, obtaining the rights to the use of the water of the Rideau River which flowed over the control dam at that point. He established his first mill there in 1859 and the little settlement quickly grew until it had a saw mill, a grist mill, and a flour mill which may still be seen today. The town itself is changing into an important "dormitory" for many workers in Ottawa who live in Manotick and drive to and from their work over the sixteen miles of highway between— another sign of the changing times which have affected traffic on the Canal.

Naturally, it is the passenger traffic on the Canal which really touches responsive chords in the minds of all those who knew the Canal in its hey-day. Although never a source of much revenue, the conveyance of passengers was an important function of the Waterway for almost exactly a century after the start of its operation. Most of the little steamers had some form of accommodation for passengers; even though this was rather primitive, it was widely used. We have to remember that for some decades after the Canal was opened, the Waterway provided the only satisfactory means of travel along the route which it followed. In the latter half of the last century, railways began their rival service to the travelling public of eastern Ontario but it was not until well into the present century that road traffic eliminated all possibility of any long continuation of passenger traffic on the Waterway. On November 2, 1935, the last passenger steamer, the *Ottawan*, pulled away from its wharf at Ottawa, on its way to close yet another chapter in the history of the Rideau Waterway when it reached Smiths Falls. This decline is a familiar pattern on almost all the inland waterways of North America, the lure of fast travel by automobile along the great network of highways which now covers the continent having drawn away the last remaining possibility of continuing passenger services by water. There are still a few queer folk (and I am one) who, when time permits, prefer the comfort and relaxation of travel by water to all the claimed advantages of automobile transport but we are in such a small minority that we cannot hope that our old-fashioned ideas will defeat the imperative of economic necessity. A few steamship services on inland waterways still remain fortunately, but not on the Rideau Waterway, even though one would imagine that the beauty of the countryside might draw enough patronage for at least one vessel plying between Ottawa and Kingston. Since that fall day of 1935, only those who have the privilege of owning their own vessels have made the passage of the Canal, except for those who use official vessels.

The standards of accommodation for passengers improved over the years from the crude bunks of the early steamers to fully equipped staterooms; rates increased astronomically, from the four shillings which purchased a single fare from Ottawa to Kingston when the Canal was opened in 1832. Passengers have included men and women from all walks of life, country folk on their way to and from their homes, commercial travellers about their business at the little towns along the Waterway, travellers from far countries seeing in this way something of the beauty of the Canadian countryside, and those in authority upon their lawful occasions. An early visitor was Sir George Arthur, the Lieutenant-Governor of Upper Canada, who is recorded in the old lock journals as having passed Burritts Rapids on the Bytown steamer on Thursday, August 16, 1838, on his way down the Canal. Governors-General of Canada have been regular passengers on the Waterway, the first being Lord Sydenham. One of his early visits was in 1843 when the selection of a capital city for the united Canadas was first under active discussion. The

Governor-General then paid a short visit to Bytown from Kingston, coming as usual by way of the Canal. Extensive decorations were put up in his honour on Barracks Hill, over Rideau Street, and above the Sappers Bridge. It is recorded that a few minutes before eleven o'clock the courier who had been stationed at the lookout at Hog's Back arrived at Sappers Bridge to announce the impending arrival of the Governor. Final preparations were hurriedly finished off and by the time the steamer reached the wharf near the bridge, the welcoming party was ready to greet His Excellency. It was headed by the Hon. Thomas McKay, one of the leading masonry contractors on the Canal, who then lived at Bytown.

Down through the years the same scene was repeated to some degree on innumerable occasions, for visitors of all estates. Official uses of the Canal gradually disappeared, however, and it became more of a local travel-way. In the early days of Ottawa, for example, the Canal provided a convenient local ferry service. When the Great Dominion Exhibition was opened in Lansdowne Park in 1879, many of the patrons travelled to the Park from the city on ferry boats on the Canal. The vessels which provided its regular longer services, to Smiths Falls, to Westport and Portland, as well as those between the terminal ports, were well known to all residents of the Rideau country. Those who grew up on Rideau shores will remember the unusual sound of the whistle of the old *Ottawan*. Above all will they remember the *Rideau Queen* and the *Rideau King* with their graceful lines and crowded happy decks. The names *Loretta* and *Agnes P.* were for long borne by steamers which were well used in the service of the Department of Transport in its work of maintaining the Canal. Their plaintive whistles were the only sounds which disturbed many of the more remote parts of the Waterway, and their high stacks were familiar sights all the way from Ottawa to Kingston Mills.

The vital task of maintaining the locks, dams, and channels of the Canal has been performed from 1832 to the present day by a variety of agencies as the responsibility for the Waterway has changed. It is the Canal Services branch of the Department of Transport which today carries the responsibility, and the Superintending Engineer of the Rideau Canal is a senior officer in that branch. Prior to 1935, the name of this department was Railways and Canals; the department itself had been formed by a subdivision of the federal Department of Public Works in 1879. The

Public Works Department is the oldest of all federal agencies, having assumed the functions of the Commissioners of Public Works of Upper and Lower Canada (including the supervision of the Rideau Canal). The Canal was built, as we have seen, by the Imperial government, at its own expense, in view of the military significance of the project, and it was at first maintained by that government. As the military importance of the Waterway gradually diminished, with the prospects of war with the American states gradually becoming more and more remote, the British government wished to pass over the responsibility for the Canal to the local government, especially in view of the steadily mounting commercial use being made of it. Though tolls were charged for all vessels using the Waterway, the amount so collected never equalled the amount which had to be spent on maintenance, so that the Canal was always a financial liability though an engineering work of steadily increasing local importance. Accordingly, the first approach to the provincial government of Upper Canada was made by the British government as early as 1848. After careful study by a board of engineers, the provincial government declined to accept the offer then made. A new approach was made in 1853 and was accepted, but only after a great deal of argument, and on the basis of the Canal being an outright gift. The Order-in-Council authorizing this transfer is dated October 1, 1853, but the actual legal transfer was not completed until some time later.

For thirty years, therefore, the Rideau Waterway was operated and maintained as a military enterprise by the British Army. The superintendence of the Canal, and the supervision of work required for maintenance, were carried out by regular troops from their barracks in Bytown. The men engaged originally on the Canal operation were old soldiers. For a number of these years lockmasters wore their Army uniforms even though they had officially retired from service, and thus added their own colour to the scene. Many of the members of the Royal Sappers and Miners who worked on the construction of the Canal took their discharge in Canada and accepted permanent positions on the Canal staff. The lockmaster at Nicholsons Locks, for example, Thomas Jenkins, had been the regimental tailor at Bytown during the period of construction. He probably arranged to secure Patrick Rails as his permanent lockman for Rails had been one of the tailors who had worked under him. Similar appointments were made at all the locks, not always with entirely satisfactory results. The lockmaster at Black Rapids, for instance, and I do not think that his name need be recorded, "having been reported for being repeatedly in a state of partial intoxication is suspended from his position"—on August 28, 1840. The remarkable thirst of the pioneer settlers appears again behind an order issued a year later, on July 3, 1841, which forbade the "locklaborers to sell beer." Any found so doing were promised an immediate discharge by John Burrows, then serving as Clerk of Works. These and similar orders can be seen in any of the old lock journals, for the method followed in communicating with the staff along the Canal was to issue a letter at Bytown to the lockmaster at the flight locks who copied it into his journal, initialled it, and then passed it on to the man at the next lock. So a letter travelled all the way to Kingston Mills.

This may seem to have been a very slow system—until the truly primitive state of the country in these early years on the Canal is remembered. We are reminded of this again by the records of some of the maintenance work which was carried out. The lockmasters made their own nails, for instance. Here is another typical entry: "Laborers at the Woods for a Seder log for making shingles to repair the roofs of the Government store." Naturally they cut their own wood, selecting suitable trees from the forests around, hauling them with oxen to the locks and there sawing them by hand into the sizes needed for the Canal lock gates and buildings. In those early days, it was possible for the men at the locks to find in the woods not only straight timber but also "knees," the smoothly shaped stumps of trees which could be split into three or four segments to be used as natural "knee-braces" for strength in building. Today in the old buildings along the Canal, and in old houses throughout the province of Quebec, this interesting structural use of a natural form is still to be seen, but such aids to building can now only be obtained in remote parts of the country.

Wood from the forests around, iron sent from the Bytown stores, and stone cut from the nearby quarries—these were the materials with which the small crews of men at the locks along the Waterway maintained the works in good condition. They were encouraged by regular visits from the Superintending Engineer and his assistants. The assistant engineers and paymasters always examined the journals and account books kept at the locks and signed them on each visit. These visits were not all made during pleasant summer weather when the Canal itself could be used as the channel of communication. At least one official trip was made to the chain of locks every winter, and this meant hard travelling under winter conditions, much of it on foot with the aid of snow-shoes. The contrast with modern practice on the Canal is, perhaps, nowhere more marked than in connection with these winter inspection journeys for today it is possible for the Superintending Engineer to travel the full length of the Canal from his office in Ottawa in a few hours, on a good highway kept cleared of snow for most of the winter. But though travelling time may have changed over the century the unusual care and attention given to proper maintenance by the Superintending Engineers and their staffs have not changed through the years.

As a result of this sound policy of continued maintenance, heavy expenditures on the Canal have not been necessary for many years. For some time the annual cost of maintenance has been somewhat less than half a million dollars a year. This sum of money, and a permanent staff numbering no more than 120, serve to keep in good repair and to operate throughout about six months of every year a waterway over one hundred and twenty miles along with all its associated locks and dams. It can readily be seen that public money is not being wasted. There are those, however, who have complained about the expenditure of even this sum on a route which carries no freight. Indeed, in the year 1932, exactly one hundred years (almost to the day) after the Canal was first opened for traffic by the initial voyage of Colonel By and his party in the *Pumper*, the proposal was seriously advanced in the Parliament of Canada that the Rideau Canal should be closed down as one of the economy measures which, of necessity, had to be considered in those hard days. It required little study, however, to show that, once built, a canal cannot easily be abandoned with safety, or indeed with economy, in view of possible damages which may result as dams and lock gates fall into disrepair, and land which has been flooded for a century is suddenly exposed to view with all the hazards to public health which would follow.

Fortunately, no such alarming forebodings were actually needed to win respite for the Canal but they should be mentioned since requests are still addressed periodically to the Government of Canada for the saving of the money spent on the Rideau

Canal. In the years since 1932, the true answer to such queries has been gradually strengthened in a most gratifying way, for traffic has been returning to the Canal. It is not traffic which would yield much revenue in the form of direct payment of tolls, were tolls still imposed, but it is traffic which brings indirect revenue to Canada which is now estimated to exceed by a comfortable margin all that is expended in keeping the Rideau Waterway in good repair and open for use from May to November of each year. The traffic is, as all readers of this book will now know, that of pleasure boats: the small craft of summer residents around the shores of the Rideau Lakes, larger vessels belonging to Canadians at Ottawa, Smiths Falls, and other larger centres, and, more particularly, those of American visitors who come now as most welcome guests of their neighbour to the north. Mention of the amount of money they spend when on this side of the international border may seem crude but it is made to show how well expenditures on the Rideau Canal can be defended as sound public investment. Sailing on the waters of the Rideau system any summer are to be seen not only trim craft from neighbouring points in New York State, which have just had to cross the St. Lawrence in order to enter the Canal at Kingston, but vessels from ports of registry all over the eastern half of the United States, and even from as far afield as Cuba and the Pacific Coast.

Many Canadians who do not appreciate the various inter-connections of the Rideau Waterway with other North American inland waterways, would be amazed to see a visiting American launch gliding along the Rideau Waterway with New Orleans, or possibly Tampa, Florida, emblazoned on its stern. Let them remind themselves that the Waterway leads not only to the St. Lawrence. From that river a boat can travel to the Hudson River and New York, either along the Richelieu and through Lake Champlain and Lake George or by the New York State Barge Canal from Oswego on Lake Ontario. At New York it has access to the Inland Waterway which then provides a safe route down the American coast all the way to Florida. Up Lake Ontario, through the Welland Ship Canal and so to Lake Erie, Lake Huron, Lake Superior, and Lake Michigan, a boat can sail to Chicago and there enter the strange but vital waterway which leads to the headwaters of the Mississippi. Once on that great river system, the way is clear down to New Orleans and the Gulf of Mexico, or out west to the upper navigable reaches of the

Missouri River. Small wonder, then, that vessels are to be seen each summer in the Rideau Lakes bearing names of cities from all over the North American continent. Indeed, ships have been passed through the locks from as far away as Bermuda and the Canal Zone. A large ocean-going cruiser registered in Seattle, Washington, once came round through the Panama Canal and then all the way up through the United States to this old military waterway. The largest pleasure vessel to be passed through the Canal in recent years has been the *Sea Wolf* of Cleveland which carried a crew of twenty-two men. So many have become accustomed to the idea of the Rideau Waterway as a pleasant sailing ground for small craft that mention of such large vessels may come as a surprise. It must be remembered, however, that the locks on the Canal are capable of taking vessels up to 110 feet long with a beam of 30 feet, dimensions somewhat larger than those of the boats of which most of us think when we consider boating as a recreation.

It is no exaggeration, therefore, to say that the Rideau Canal is still a seaway. Many of the larger pleasure vessels which have passed through it have spent some time at sea. There was no difficulty in passing the Fairmile training vessels of the Royal Canadian Navy through the Canal on their cruise of 1951. Another converted Fairmile, and a regular patron of the Canal, the *Radel II* of the National Research Council, was mentioned at the beginning of this chapter. Operated by the Division of Radio and Electrical Engineering of the Council, this vessel carries experimental radar and equipment under study for its use as an aid to navigation. It usually spends the winter at Ottawa; for open sea work, it sails down the Gulf of St. Lawrence and so is one of the few vessels regularly to use the Ottawa River canals; for freshwater work, Lake Ontario is the usual testing ground and the *Radel II* proceeds there through the Rideau Canal. The note of contrast with which this chapter started is reinforced as one thinks of this sleek white vessel with its special aerials and obvious research equipment in one of the locks in the heart of the Rideau country, Chaffeys or Poonamalie, for example. The sight of this most modern of experimental craft makes one wish that Colonel By and some of his young assistants could see the Waterway of today.

The Rideau Canal thus continues during the summer months of each year its silent service to eastern Ontario, providing quiet waters for the relaxation of a steadily increasing number of those who enjoy the outdoors and find a real attraction in the lakes and woods of the Shield country. In many respects, the Rideau Lake country seems like one of the national or provincial parks of Canada, and the operation of the Canal itself, now that its commercial function is so negligible, the equivalent of a park service. The Waterway is certainly a national asset of unusual value not only because of its historical significance, being a true "national historic monument" even though spread over 120 miles, but also because of the singular beauty of its course and of the convenient access it gives to many inviting lakes and much pleasant countryside. So well has it been maintained down through the years that its future service fortunately appears to be unlimited.

Cruising the Canal

KINGSTON TO CHAFFEYS LOCK

TO SHARE with others the delights of the quiet beauty of the Rideau Waterway is the inevitable desire of all who come to know its locks and winding channels. A sail on its pleasant waters on a day in high summer adds to the joys of boating a feeling of intimacy with the past, with history that still lives in the work of men who were masters of the art of building. Even to visit the locks by land, as can now be done easily by automobile, is an attractive variant from the usual speeding along main highways, since most of the locks are to be found at the end of winding side roads scarcely worth a hair-line on the map. The sound of running water as it tumbles over waste weirs or laps over lock gates, the feel of the smooth surfaced masonry, and the sight of ancient stone houses, clipped hedges, and velvet lawns—all these take one's mind back across the years and give momentary relief from the speed and pressure of today.

Suppose we journey then along the full route of the Canal, looking, not at every detail of its construction, but at its more intriguing spots, and stopping to inquire when there seems a likelihood of local lore. Naturally the full beauty of the Canal is to be seen when sailing its waters but only a very few parts of the route are inaccessible by road and so we can attend to the interests of travellers by land as we go.

Kingston may well be the starting place of the trip. The ancient fortress at the exit of Lake Ontario, to supply which the Rideau Canal was built, is well named the Limestone City because of the many buildings which are given dignity by this handsome grey stone. It was the scene of much martial excitement in days now long past. On the twelfth day of July, 1673, Frontenac, after an adventurous journey up the rapids of the St. Lawrence with four hundred men, founded the fort that was to bear his name. He wrote at the time that he had come through "the most beautiful piece of country that can be imagined." His name is perpetuated in Frontenac County, so that today county administrative matters are carried on under the name of this great adventurer of early Canada. LaSalle in 1676 rebuilt the original little log fort, said to have cost only the modest sum of ten thousand francs, and then set about establishing this outpost of the West as a citadel of New France. He built here four ships and so started the naval shipbuilding which was to be an important part of Kingston's activity in later years. Although much of LaSalle's work was undone by his successors, his is nevertheless regarded as one of the greatest names in the history of Kingston. It, too, is to be found today in daily use, for, among other things, the unsightly bridge across the mouth of the Cataraqui River, which can be the beginning of our cruise up the Canal.

For three-quarters of a century after the arrival of LaSalle, Fort Frontenac continued to be a vital French outpost, its last noted occupant being the great Montcalm who in 1756 sailed from it across the lake to capture Oswego from the British. Two years later, however, the British General Bradstreet landed near the fort with three thousand men and captured it on August 27, 1758, thus ending its service to New France. On its bastions the British flag flew for the first time in New France after Louisburg.

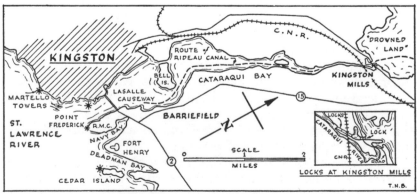

The Kingston end of the Rideau Canal

For twenty-five years the fort lay in ruins, until it was revived as a centre for the settlement of United Empire Loyalists, fleeing across the lake to new homes in Upper Canada. Its strategic importance was obvious, and so as the threat of war moved from the east to the south, fortifications soon began to appear as defensive measures against the United States. Blockhouses built in 1812 did not as it turned out have to be used during the war which started in that year. It was, however, the critical position of Kingston as the main British fortress on Lake Ontario that led the British government to plan extensive additions to the defence works and, correspondingly, to build the Rideau Canal.

New stone barracks, still to be seen, were built in 1824. Fort Henry, constructed as a log fortress in 1812, was rebuilt in stone in 1820. More elaborate plans for six major fortresses were advanced by Sir James Kempt during the construction of the Canal but again cost daunted the authorities and only one of these was built, the replacement of Fort Henry with a much larger and more massive stone structure. It was constructed between 1832 and 1836 and was named not after a royal personage, as is so often casually imagined, but in honour of Sir Henry Hamilton, the Lieutenant-Governor of that time. Today the fortress can be seen restored to its original condition. During the summer months, in the ancient courtyard, sentries dressed in the uniforms of a century ago pace the wall or perform drill in the old style; the colour may be designed for tourists, but this reproduction is also a salutary reminder to Canadians of a vital bit of the history of their own land.

Many legends are told of Fort Henry and some of the true stories about its use are almost as good as legends. One of the legends has it that the Fort was constructed from plans intended for a fortress in Kingston, Jamaica, through the error of a clerk, so that it is oriented the wrong way round! One authenticated incident in its history is that when John Montgomery (whose tavern had been an assembly point for Mackenzie's forces at a critical point in the rebellion of 1837) and fourteen of his friends were imprisoned within its walls in 1830, they escaped by pulling out the mortar from between the stones in their cells; eventually they found refuge in the United States. The mortar used for the Rideau Canal locks was fortunately of superior quality.

There are other reminders of an uneasy past visible from Fort Henry. Navy Bay, on the left as one leaves the fort, was once the scene of shipbuilding for the Great Lakes fleet which had assured the British a vital control of Lake Ontario in the War of 1812. After the Rush-Bagot convention of 1817 had limited the naval force to be maintained by either side on the Lakes, vessels retired or still unfinished mouldered away; the dockyard itself was closed when Fort Henry was being rebuilt, between 1832 and 1836. The Royal Military College now stands adjacent to Fort Frederick, the remains of which can still be seen in its pleasant grounds. Latest of all the Kingston military defences are the four Martello Towers which were built in 1846 at the time of the Oregon boundary crisis to protect Kingston Harbour and to surround the entrance to the Canal. These were the last defence structures to be erected in central Canada for almost a hundred years. They are beautiful both in the symmetry of their design and in the excellence of their workmanship. From our view of these historic sites, the LaSalle Causeway leads us back to the modern city; two ancient cannon at its eastern end are the only obvious links between the past and this utilitarian but singularly ugly structure.

Our journey through the Canal begins at Cataraqui Bay—the mouth of the Cataraqui River which forms a long inlet from Lake Ontario. When the Canal was started, there was no bridge across Cataraqui Bay from the site of the town to Fort Frederick, but in 1827, just as the canal work was beginning, the first steps were taken to provide this connection. For about ninety years, until 1916, this vital link was a wooden bridge one third of a mile long, made up of short (forty-foot) spans resting on masonry piers, and only twenty-five feet wide. It was a toll structure and so was almost universally known as the "Penny Bridge," one penny being the charge for pedestrian crossings. It had a swing span with an initial opening corresponding to some of the limiting dimensions on the Canal. This opening, today crossed by a steel swing span, constitutes the southern gateway to the Rideau Waterway.

If we proceed on our sail up Cataraqui Bay, Barriefield with its ancient church on the hill is to the right, as we round Bells Island. The Bay gradually narrows until, just after passing under the fine bridge carrying Highway 401, we come to the entrance to the rocky gorge which leads to Kingston Mills. At the end of a winding channel is the foot of the first lock of the Canal; to the right of the locks was the old course of the river as it tumbled down what must have been a beautiful waterfall. The site of the fall is now occupied by one of the several little power houses which utilize the flow in both rivers which serve as the Canal, when there is sufficient drop to make power generation economical. The flight of four locks combined with the steep rock cliffs on either side, make this one of the more impressive sights along the Waterway. Three of the locks form a continuous chain, the fourth being separated from the others by a wide bay, one part of which was originally intended to serve as a dock for vessels needing repair. Here is the lockmaster's house, and near by one of the few remaining blockhouses still to be seen along the Canal. This fine old building has been maintained in good condition and is today in active use, although the television aerial on its roof may seem incongruous.

Standing at the upper lock, one can see clearly the magnitude of the work that was necessary to transform this location from its original state, when a small mill stood on the bank of the little river as it tumbled down the waterfall into the gorge. A dam had to be constructed, the central part of stone but with two long wing dams, each over a thousand feet long, built of clay and broken stone, which stretched out on either side to raise the level of the pond thus formed high enough so that it would reach back upstream to the next lock at Lower Brewers Mills, over ten miles away. This dam at Kingston Mills exemplifies one of Colonel By's basic designs for the Canal—how, by building dams at strategic locations, he could drown out rapids and small falls and thus provide smooth water on which to sail up to the next dam. There may still be seen on either side of the main channel, the remains of old tree stumps which were flooded out when the water level was raised by this dam at Kingston Mills. In those early days the stumps gave the area "a most desolate appearance," according to Lieutenant Frome, one of By's assistants.

The site of the mill must have been a busy scene when the canal works started. The old road to Montreal, then only recently completed, crossed the Cataraqui on a wooden bridge near by and a few farms had been developed in the neighbourhood. One of these farms was then owned by John Tuttle whose daughter, Mercy, married a sailor from the Kingston naval yard. This young man, Daniel Walker, had run away from his home in England, and joined the British Navy. He was one of the party of naval officers and men who marched, on snow-shoes, from Fredericton to Quebec, through what was then wilderness, during the winter of 1813. They were sent in haste to Kingston to assist with the building up of the fleet then operating on Lake Ontario. Young Walker was a stone mason by trade, six feet tall and a good singer; as one result of his singing he met his future wife, for they both went to a singing school which had been started in Kingston. No doubt on his visits to the Tuttle farm he heard talk of the building of the locks. At any rate he obtained his discharge from the Navy and then worked on the construction of the Kingston Mill locks. After the Canal was opened, he continued to farm the Tuttle land until his death.

He was but one of the many men recruited for this work by the contractor Robert Drummond. Drummond was a Scotsman who had arrived in Kingston only in 1828; he started work on the locks in the same year. He was followed to Canada by three of his nephews, all of whom became well-known citizens of Kingston and one a Senator. Robert Drummond's niece, Jane Drummond, became the second wife of John Redpath, another of the main masonry contractors of the Canal. The families thus united have been remarkable for the contributions which their members, down to the present, have made to the development of Canada.

Robert Drummond quickly won the respect of Colonel By and was entrusted with the works not only at Kingston Mills but also at both Lower and Upper Brewers Mills. He completed the big job at Kingston Mills without any serious setback, and the stone-work of limestone blocks cut by his masons is that to be seen today. Evidence of the excavation he carried out in order to build the locks has long since been covered up but it was clearly a difficult job for hand drilling, the rock being of an unusually hard variety. An indication of By's feelings for him is given by the fact that one of four silver cups which the Colonel had specially made in England was presented by him to this contractor for the Kingston end of the Canal. Cups were presented also to John Redpath and to Phillips and White, contractors to be mentioned later. The date "21st August 1831" appears on the cups, this being the date on which it was hoped that the Canal would be opened; though the official opening had to be postponed until May 1832, the earlier date was allowed to remain. Two of the four cups are now in Montreal, one in the Château de Ramezay; a third is in the United States. It is known that Colonel By presented these cups to indicate his complete satisfaction with the contractors' work, a gracious and characteristic gesture of the Superintendent.

By also gave, apparently only to Drummond, a silhouette which is now in the possession of one of Robert Drummond's descendants in Ottawa. On the back of the small gold frame is an inscription in By's own handwriting: "Mr. (Robert) Drummond from Lt. Col. By R.E., Rideau Canal, January 1832."

Drummond must have been a strong and aggressive character for he was soon involved not only in lock building but also in ship building. His first boat was 80 feet long with a beam of 15 feet and drew 6 feet; it was equipped with a twelve horsepower engine. We give these technical details because this was also the boat that made the first sail through the Canal, bearing Colonel By and his party on their memorable journey of May 1832. It was used in the first instance, however, for the mundane purpose of pumping out cofferdams (temporary dams built to surround a part of the river bed where masonry had to be built). For this purpose it was fitted with special pumping engines, surely one of the very earliest pieces of floating construction equipment to be used in North America. It took its practical name, the *Pumper*, from this activity.

Another of Drummond's ship-building ventures was not so successful. In 1831 he built a much larger boat, measuring 110 feet long with a 26-foot beam. It was supposed to draw only 3½ feet of water but, when launched, it drew so much more than this that it could not be taken into the Rideau Canal system, and had to be used instead on the St. Lawrence. The discovery must have been especially embarrassing as the boat had been christened the *John By*. Drummond was also interested in commercial navigation on the Canal and attended the first meeting held to discuss this matter, convened in Kingston in the year 1830 on 25th December (so say the records; the Scottish influence must have been early at work).

Kingston Mills today is a peaceful spot except when large express trains roar past, over the bridge which carries the main line of the Canadian National Railways from Montreal to Toronto and Chicago over the third lock. It is possible to see the gorge from the windows of trains, going in both directions, but few speeding passengers suspect, as their train rumbles over the steel girder bridge four miles out of Kingston station, that they are crossing an historic site. The easiest way to reach the locks by road is to take the highway which passes Kingston station: it follows the route of the earliest road from Kingston to Montreal.

Soon after the intersection with the great new arterial highway which now by-passes the city itself, appears the rocky hill adjacent to the locks and then suddenly, round a bend in the road, one comes upon the locks themselves, the blockhouse immediately conspicuous. On a still day, the sound of the water falling over the spillway dam and down the former waterfall encourages contemplation of the old masonry with its graceful curving lines, the varying reflections in the changing waters, and the sharp beauty of the gorge itself clearly seen beneath the railroad bridge which, for once, does not unduly disfigure the scene.

Soon after Kingston Mills, the road joins Highway 15 which then becomes the means of reaching all points on the Canal as far as Smiths Falls. Many travellers on this road do not realize that it runs through a chain of lakes, since almost all of them are hidden just on either side. A glance at the end-paper map will show how the highway parallels the Canal. By using some of its many left-hand side roads, one can manage to visit most of the points on the Canal that deserve notice. To begin with, the road crosses three shallow gullies, filled with water backed up by the Kingston Mills dam. Then it climbs, to such an extent that near Joyceville it offers one of the finest views possible of this part of the country; it is fortunately still so well wooded that it must not be dissimilar to the country seen by Colonel By and his associates well over a century ago.

Little more than a mile along the road, after rounding the big bend at Joyceville, a signpost indicates the first of the several side roads to the left. "Washburns" is the first name on the board, this being an alternative designation for Lower Brewers Mills, the site of one of the very few mills that existed before the Canal was built. Just over a little hill which starts as soon as we leave the main road, and round a sharp bend, is a scene which in summer has a touch of Constable about it. Through a thick screen of foliage a small wooded island can be seen, separating an overflow dam, white with its curtain of water, and a single lock, neat and trim with its surrounding lawns. It is similar in its essentials to most of the single locks which we are going to see along the Rideau Waterway. To this point the dam at Kingston Mills, now ten miles away, has backed up the water along what used to be the channel of the little Cataraqui River. As the water was raised it drowned out two small rapids on the way to Lower Brewers

Mills, rapids which were distinguished because of their unusual names—Jack's Rifts and Billydore's Rifts. (The word "rift" was used in those days to indicate what MacTaggart calls "ripples on the water.") Today, travellers glide over these unusually named spots up and down the lake which, for some strange reason, has never been given a name, being still called on all the maps "Drowned Land."

Our boat will be raised thirteen feet by the lock at Lower Brewers Mills. As we wait for the slow rise of the water, we can examine the site of the old mill adjacent to the overflow dam; we note that the Canal really is a canal here, both above and below the lock. The old course of the Cataraqui River was extremely winding in this vicinity. The builders of the Waterway cut directly across these bends to give an almost straight channel for the next mile and a half to Upper Brewers Mills. Here we find two locks which parallel an overflow channel in a lovely natural valley; a new reinforced concrete bridge carrying a county road connecting with the nearby main road is cleared just before the lock entrance.

This restful scene gives no clue to the drama of the locks' construction and the tragedy of the recurrent fever which took such toll of Robert Drummond's workmen as they laboured at the excavation and the building of the dams, now grass covered and almost indistinguishable as artificial structures. The old mill stood on a narrow stretch of the Cataraqui River which here tumbled its way down the natural gorge now used by the Canal above the locks, flowing out of the great Cranberry Bog, three-quarters of a mile away. A small dam to operate a saw mill had been built at a spot called Round Tail, in order to control the water level in the marsh. Another little dam had been built at the other end, to control the flow from the Bog in the other direction, into Whitefish Lake and so down the Gananoque River. It was these two dams which created such an undesirable condition in the marsh, for the water level, though not high enough to cover up all vegetation, was at the same time just high enough to make travelling through the Bog a grim experience. As we have seen, Colonel By's death almost occurred as a result. By's bold decision was to build an entirely new dam below the mill site, high enough to drown out the Bog entirely and to give the requisite depth of water for navigation along the Waterway. This meant that he would drown out also the two existing little dams, and connect the new Cranberry Lake with Whitefish Lake; the water level in both would be made the same. To prevent the escape of water down the Gananoque River, another dam would be necessary. This was built at what is now Morton. It provides a convenient means of escape for the excess water which flows in the spring-time into the combined lakes from the streams and lakes around.

It was possible for Drummond and his men to build the locks and the great earth dam, today tree-covered, while the little river flowed down its old channel. This is now the tailrace from the small water-power plant which blocks the gorge and deflects the main channel of the Waterway to the locks round a pleasant bend. It must be admitted that none of the modern water mills on the Canal are things of beauty. But they use the water to good effect, generating power for the Gananoque Electric Light and Water Supply Company. This is now one of the very few independent electric power companies in the province of Ontario; it is a local enterprise, managed and operated from the small but most pleasantly situated town of Gananoque on the St. Lawrence. Its origins go back to the earliest days of public electricity supply, the company from which it developed having started operations with a small steam-operated dynamo as early as 1885. As local industry demanded more power, further supplies were sought from the falling water of the Cataraqui River, as controlled by the Rideau Canal. The small plant at Kingston Mills was the company's first plant on the Rideau, built in 1913 and enlarged in 1926. This plant at Brewers Mills was constructed in 1939 and the plant at Washburns in 1948. That at Jones Falls, further up the Canal, was constructed at about the same time, the first unit starting in June 1948 and all four of the generators which the station contains being in service by the end of that year. The four stations are inter-connected by means of high tension transmission lines which also carry the power to Gananoque; the station at Kingston Mills is the control station. The four little "mills" (for so they are, in effect), operated from one of them, provide another of the contrasts between older works and the advances of modern engineering which are so frequent on the Canal.

The rock-lined channel to Cranberry Lake up which we now sail is a peaceful winding stretch of water, trees forming thick curtains along its steep banks. As the open water of the Lake, the first of the Rideau group, comes into view we enter upon what used to be called "The Court of the Duke," a stately name adopted by early travellers after they had noticed that a rocky promontory on the east bank presents an almost perfect profile of a human face, which can be imagined to be that of the Iron Duke himself. The Duke of Wellington never visited Canada and so never saw the Canal but the name of this bit of water is a tribute to his interest in the Canal and in navigation in Canada generally.

We leave the narrow channel at the Round Tail, a smooth rock forming the end of the tail of land which here separates the channel from the Lake. Beneath us are the remains of the old dam which caused the canal builders such trouble. On their journeys, they must have been glad indeed to reach clear running water after navigating the winding channel through the fetid swamp—MacTaggart's "dreadful place." Even so experienced a traveller as John By himself was once lost in the swamp after being separated from his provision canoe and thus stranded with only a little cheese and a few drops of brandy. John MacTaggart tells us that they were too hungry to sleep and so "halloed out as loud as [they] could . . . being sometimes answered by the owl, afar in solitary woods, and the lake bird, called loon, also deigned to reply from the distant waters. . . . [They] frequently loaded the gun with powder and fired it off, the sound reverberating through the forest and rocks. . . ." By the light of the moon, they started paddling again in early morning, fortunately coming across an Indian who was shooting wild duck just as they were despondent of finding their way out of the morass. The Indian guided them to Round Tail rock and so to the safety of the well-travelled gorge of the Cataraqui River.

Studded with islands, its banks gently sloping down from well-wooded ground, with occasional rocky headlands to break up the even shoreline, Cranberry Lake is today a perfect example of Canada's northern scenery. Its water level is such that it now connects also with a larger body of water, Dog Lake. A pleasant detour into this lake (passing on the way through a narrow gap named the "Fiddler's Elbow") leads to Dog Lake Landing, whence a portage road used to run to the small settlement of Battersea. The main channel is clearly marked for us through Cranberry Lake by means of the buoys familiar in all lakes, which are carefully placed in position each spring by the men who maintain the Waterway.

At this point a fisherman is apt to become restless and doubtless want to stop while he casts just one fly. It is hard to deny

him once the steel bridge which crosses the lake at Brass Point
is passed. It is a low-lying structure, sure sign that the water level
of the lake is well controlled, and contains a simple swing span
for the passage of boats. We shall have to signal to have this
opened but the bridge tender has his house so close to the bridge
that he could almost operate it by leaning out of his living-room
window. As we slowly pass through the narrow opening, it is
practically certain that we shall see faithful fishermen using the
centre spans of the bridge as a fishing platform. On even the
coldest mornings in the late fall, as long as any part of the fishing
season is open, ardent rodmen are to be found here, muffled up
against the cold winds which sweep down the lake, their patient
wives often sheltering in their cars. The bridge is easily reached
from the main road (still Highway 15) by a turn one mile south
of Seeleys Bay, and the road to it gives a glorious panoramic
view of the full sweep of Cranberry Lake. I must confess that
no view of the Waterway is to me so moving as this scene on a
calm summer day, the blue waters of the lake fading into the
distance beyond the wooded profile of Beaupré's Island, with its
attendant islets around, cattle grazing on the green fields to the
right, wheat growing in well-tilled fields. For this is a man-made
lake, one of the first so made in North America, dammed up after
a fight in the wilderness against ravaging fever, the rigours of the
Canadian winter, and almost unbelievable difficulties in construction.

The horrors of Cranberry Bog are soon forgotten as we sail
into one of the most fascinating sections of the Waterway; the
channel winds in and out between the many headlands and small
islands which make the traverse of Little Cranberry Lake and
then of Whitefish Lake an exercise in careful navigation but also
a constant delight to the eye. The junction of these two lakes is
formed by a narrows, from which a small bay leads to the village
of Seeleys Bay. Motorists using the main road will likely pass
through this settlement without seeing any sign of water and
must often wonder about its name. A slight diversion from the
main road, however, would bring them to the small wharf which
in times past served for much of the traffic reaching the town.
Today, as with most of the little places which were once lake
ports, the wharf serves only the modest needs of pleasure craft.

A rewarding diversion from the route along the main channel is
a short excursion into Morton Bay which opens off Whitefish

Lake near its northern end. The bay leads to the control dam at the small town of Morton, the flow over the dam forming Morton Creek, the headwaters of the Gananoque River. Canoe travellers coming up the Canal can complete a most profitable circular trip by now descending the Gananoque River and then returning to Kingston along the St. Lawrence. To the right of the narrow entrance into Morton Bay stretches almost a full mile of great rock cliffs, the "High Rock Dunter." Almost five hundred feet high, this magnificent natural wall is decorated by living trees and enlivened by the darting flight of birds in and out of its nooks and crannies—a sight long to be remembered and revealed only to those who travel the Waterway.

The main channel continues through the narrows at the tip of Morton Island, and we follow it as it then swings round to the north, past Hog Island into the little bay which lies at the foot of the great flight of locks which now replace Jones Falls. The scope of this masterpiece of engineering is well hidden as we approach it from the south. It is a place little known even to motorists since it lies almost two miles from the main road, approached only along an exceedingly tortuous side road. The turn into this road is often missed coming as it does at the foot of a rather dangerous hill just to the north of the village of Morton. But all who do know Jones Falls appreciate it as the scene of the greatest of all the achievements of Colonel By and his fellow engineers and builders, a piece of construction which today still evokes the admiration of all who know even the rudiments of the practice of civil engineering.

Fishermen can be left to swap yarns with their brothers of the rod who are always to be found round the Hotel Kenny in summertime, while we explore the locks and see the great arched dam. The main flight contains three of the four locks, built as a continuous series and so forming a giant staircase to lift the water level by forty-five feet to a large pond. At the other side is the fourth lock which completes the rise of full sixty feet and gives access to a rock-bound channel. This waterway leads to the great structure which creates this small lake, about a quarter of a mile beyond the upper lock. We can gain access to the dam, however, by what can only be described as a piece of mountain road, so steep are the gradients on the narrow portage road which leads up from the lower lock, past one of the lockmasters' houses and the small overflow dam, out on to the broad expanse of grass

which has now grown all over the top of the big dam. Up the
Waterway, we see steep rocky cliffs, the actual route of the main
channel through which it is almost impossible to detect, so closely
do the rocky shores surround the bay into which we look. Only
the sight of a marker shows how vessels can wend their way
round one of the steep headlands. High rock banks rise on either
side of the dam, and its curved outline itself gives a remarkable
feeling of strength even to those uninitiated into the ramifica-
tions of engineering design. It is a true arched dam, one of the
first ever to be built in North America.

Constructed of large, neatly cut blocks of the local limestone,
the dam at Jones Falls is 350 feet along its crest and rises to a
height of over 60 feet above the bottom of the rocky gorge which
it spans, and down which a small stream once tumbled. John
MacTaggart described this gorge as he saw it when surveying
for the Canal in 1827: ". . . a narrow ravine scarcely a mile in
length and having a 60-feet fall. The banks of this narrow and
crooked ravine are lofty, averaging 90 feet in height. . . ." Mac-
Taggart had several schemes for getting the Canal up this precipitous defile, based on the earlier ideas of Clowes. It remained,
however, for Colonel By himself to develop a scheme bolder than
any of these suggestions, for a dam more than twice as high as
any that had been built in North America at that time. In the
light of the fact that all the stone was hand cut and hoisted into
place by small winches, in the isolation of the Canadian forest,
the daring and indeed grandeur of his conception seem all the
more remarkable. Luckily he found a contractor capable of carrying out this great pioneer piece of construction work, a man
whose name is a household word across Canada today, John
Redpath. One of the local tales about the building of the dam
recounts how a wandering Scottish mason happened to come to
the works when the Royal Engineers were at a loss to know how
to proceed, and used a mythical British device for some unusual
masonry work. Is this perhaps a version of the coming of John
Redpath to the scene of one of his greatest contract works?

Fortunately, records exist which show how the dam was actually built. A dam of clay and other soils was slowly and laboriously
raised across the bed of the little creek, the flow of the stream
being taken care of in a wooden sluiceway on the north side of
the dam as it exists today. All this soil was placed by hand with
the aid only of wheelbarrows for transport; it shielded the site

The Entrance Locks at Ottawa as they appeared in 1839
(From drawings by W. H. Bartlett, published in London, 1842)

Yesterday: the Rideau Queen *approaching the old turning basin in Ottawa
(From a photograph in the Public Archives, Ottawa)*

Today: the C.P.R. Canadian *transcontinental train leaves the Ottawa
entrance to the Canal on its inaugural run*

of the masonry work which was slowly raised, also by hand power. At intervals, the sluiceway was raised too, in a progression which is technically called "leap-frogging." So the crest of the dam was gradually raised until it reached the desired level, a permanent spillway being built into the masonry work as it advanced, on the south side of the dam. This has now been replaced by a separate little spillway channel on the other side of the rocky hill which we descended when coming over to the dam; the old spillway opening has been used for the construction of a penstock or pipeline which feeds water, under the head created by the dam, to a small concrete power house at the lower end of what is left of the gorge. This is yet another of the modern concrete blockhouses which now use waste water from the canal system to such good effect. Trees are fortunately providing it with a steadily increasing shield. The strength of the old masonry work was well shown when it had to be cut through for the building of the penstock. Some of the workmen would doubtless have welcomed the opportunity of telling the original builders what they thought of their workmanship, judging by what I heard when this work was going ahead.

The chain of three locks is in itself an unusually fine piece of masonry construction, as can best be realized by standing near a gate on one of the upper locks when boats are locking through. The site was a natural one, but a good deal of excavation had to be carried out for the building of the lock masonry up what now looks like a natural staircase. Something of what the site was like when the locks were built can be imagined by looking closely at the upper (fourth) lock, set in its narrow rock channel. Considering all the rock work for locks and dam, the importance of the blacksmith's shop at the time of construction can well be imagined; it is still standing, an old building to the south of the upper lock. Unfortunately the old log blockhouse built here to protect the workers in the first instance and then the works themselves, from the long anticipated further attacks from the south, was removed some years ago.

The immense quantities of stone required for the dam and locks necessitated an unusually large labour force. A construction camp was therefore the first major undertaking, and accommodation for 200 men was provided. When the work was in full swing, there were forty masons employed, most of them in the two special quarries which were opened up in the forests nearby; the most suitable stone was found about six miles away, between Elgin and Phillipsville. The great blocks of carefully hewn stone were hauled by oxen to the edge of the river, transferred to floating scows, and then towed by small tugs to the site of the works. Apart from manpower, there was, of course, for motive power on land only the few oxen which had been brought into the forests for slow haulage jobs. We know that the dreaded swamp fever was especially severe in this construction camp at Jones Falls. One of the old records tells us that at a critical period during the summer of 1828 there was no one able to take even a drink of water to his mates, since everyone in the camp including the doctors had been attacked. Many men died and were buried in a small graveyard set aside near the great dam.

Apart only from the chain of locks at the Ottawa end of the Waterway, the works at Jones Falls constitute the most extensive engineering undertaking at any one location along the Canal. In their complexity, and the daring of their design, they are unrivalled not only on the Rideau system but upon any of the early canals of North America. John Redpath, the Scottish masonry contractor who took on this novel and important part of the work, had already gained valuable experience in the building of the first Lachine Canal. He was a native of Berwickshire who had been trained as a stone mason when he landed in Canada in 1816. His first independent contract was the building of a dairy in Montreal; his stature as a builder is shown by the fact that he won his contract for the Lachine Canal work when only twenty-five, five years after his arrival in Canada. In addition to his work in the Rideau system, he built also Notre Dame Church on Place d'Armes, Montreal (although a good Presbyterian), and many of the notable early buildings of the Canadian metropolis, including some of the first buildings of McGill University.

Redpath made good profits on his contract work, including the Rideau Canal, and invested wisely in Montreal real estate, with the result that he soon extended his business interests in a variety of directions such as banking, railways, shipping, and coal mining. He was one of the original members of the Montreal City Council when it was established in 1832 and served on it for eight successive terms. Quite his most interesting venture, however, was the start in the year 1854 of a sugar refinery, on the banks of the Lachine Canal in Montreal. The new refinery was the largest factory in Montreal; so began a great sugar refining venture, carried on to the present day, although now under the aegis of the Canada and Dominion Sugar Company Limited. John Redpath's "sugar loaf" still appears in the modern trade mark; his name is still one of the prized possessions of the Company as it celebrates the centenary of its original unit, just as this book nears completion. Across the land the words "Let Redpath sweeten it" are well known. When readers of this book next see them, they may remember that it was the profits from building a part of the Rideau Waterway that helped to finance the founding of the Redpath sugar refinery. John Redpath died in March 1869, just after Confederation became a reality. His son, the Peter Redpath whose name adorns so much at McGill University, carried on the business until 1880 when he retired in order to travel and study law. He was admitted to the bar as a member of the Middle Temple, in London, after passing the age of sixty—the Redpath vigour had certainly been inherited in good measure.

Redpath's successful contract work for Colonel By was rewarded by the gift of one of the silver cups mentioned earlier; and his cup is still in the possession of the Redpath family. Many of his old account books, both personal and business, are preserved at McGill University in the McCord Museum and it has been my privilege to examine them. The care with which they were kept, and the character of many of the entries, show how fine a man John Redpath was. There is more than one entry of this nature: "Charity—XX by Mr. R's orders." In one of his own private books I came across a card of admission to a temperance discussion in Montreal, used as a bookmarker. Despite this, the men working at Jones Falls were allowed to have liquor at Mr. Redpath's expense; one item refers to a barrel of brandy, obtained from John Torrance and Company for the sum of £13-0-9 (about $35!). Charged to the Jones Falls account were also such pleasing items as a box of cigars, a bugle, and a fiddle. There are several items listed as "Expenses to Lachine to see the men off," notes which testify once again to the character of the man.

The day books for the job show that the men employed by Mr. Redpath were almost equally divided between Scotsmen and *Canadiens*, a reflection of that happy blending of the two races which has been a distinctive mark of the life of Montreal. Many of the men could not write so that their entries consist only of "X—his mark." There are occasional references to "Esthertown," apparently a name given to the small construction camp which grew up around the dam and locks. The name suggests that it was selected to honour Mrs. By, who would certainly have been known to John Redpath, but these references in the old account books appear to be alone in tendering honour to the woman who was so closely linked with the building of the Waterway. Near these entries I came across some dried maple leaves, so fragile that they could not safely be handled, but presenting their own silent message across the century.

The only sad note struck in all these old records occurs as the entries from the job at Jones Falls near their close. Apparently John McCuaig was left at the site as guardian during the winter of 1831–32, when the works were complete. He wrote a rather pitiful letter to his supervisor, on February 5, 1832, complaining about his poverty, and finished by saying: "I am very lonesome— Pray make haste back." Later in the year, McCuaig, who was still at Jones Falls, was severely reprimanded by John McPhee, his supervisor, for having left the job without permission. His letter of defence makes rather tragic reading for he explains that he had to go and see his family since the entire village in which they lived was in danger of being wiped out by the cholera. So violent was the plague, that he had not been able to wait for permission, but had walked from Jones Falls to Kingston, left his valuables in the office of Robert Drummond, and then walked on to his home village of Hallowells.

The name of the locks commemorates not the builders who laboured in the wilderness but the original owner of the land around the rapids and of the little mill which first utilized the power here in these falls of the Cataraqui, the Honourable Charles Jones of Brockville. Mr. Jones had planned a small townsite around his mill and had intended to call it Charleston, after himself, but his suggestion disappeared with the eclipse of his mill by the Rideau Canal works. Although no town has developed around this set of locks, the great dam has for many years been a favourite picnic ground during the summer for residents from all the countryside around. Before the days of the automobile, when courting was often done in the course of country walks, there was a local tradition that any girl visiting the Jones Falls dam in a new white summer dress on the twenty-fourth of May and being there courted by a young man would be married within the year. Many residents of Leeds County have a warm spot in their hearts for the quiet beauty of Jones Falls.

But we must continue our journey for there is still much of the Rideau Waterway to explore. As the boat moves up the flight of locks we have a final opportunity to admire the trimness of the masonry before the upper gates release us into the rock-bound approach channel. This has to be navigated carefully but we shall soon find ourselves moving past the crest of the great dam which we have just visited on foot. From the water, however, it is difficult to see the dam at full value. The route to the open waters of Sand Lake passes through an unusually winding series of channels, bounded by high rock cliffs. One of the first of these, on the right, carries the unusual name "The Quarters." This, an abbreviation of "The Officers' Quarters," designates the site of the small camp for the officers of the Royal Engineers who supervised the building of the dam and locks. The outlook would have enabled the officers to keep a watchful eye on progress, even when in camp, but the main reason for the choice of this location was probably its situation high above the bog which used to be on this side of the old rocky gorge, and the presence of a spring of clear cold water. This spring is still used by those who choose this spot for camping or for a pause to admire the view.

A sharp turn brings us into Eel Bay, a beautiful little stretch of water almost completely surrounded by high banks; we leave it around another sharp bend, the point on our port side being known as "Saint's Rest." We round Cordwood Island, the name of which shows how this tiny rock has served to catch driftwood floating out of the lake, into which we have now entered. A leisurely sail along its south shore will bring us to another single lock, now known as Davis Lock, but formerly called Fosters. This quiet place, remote from all but a side road off a side road, has gardens which are always a joy to see. Beyond this lock is the lake with the lovely Indian name, Opinicon. Its old designation, Mosquito Lake, used during the building of the Canal, tells its own story. The lake also carried the name of Davis at one time. Mr. Davis was one of the first settlers in this part of the Rideau country, having established his mill at the site of the lock which now bears his name around the turn of the last century.

Opinicon Lake is a strangely formed body of water, with a narrow channel from the clear water of the part which must have been the original lake into the "drowned land" which forms the upstream section. A number of old tree stumps are still to be seen in the shallower parts of this upper section, away from the main channel. For almost the first time in our trip, we see signs of extensive settlement around the shores, mostly summer residences, large and small.

More serious in purpose is the establishment of the Biological

Research Station of Queen's University, first set up on Opinicon
Lake in 1944. The location proved to be so suitable that a
permanent site of 65 acres was acquired in 1946; this has been in
use since that time as a field research station for Queen's biological students. They have found out much about the lake itself
and the fish and plant life with which it abounds. Since the lake
is a shallow one—its maximum depth is only 35 feet and more than
half of its area is less than 15 feet—the game fish which inhabit
it are limited to those species which can live in relatively warm
water. The largemouth bass and the northern pike are pre-
dominant, although some smallmouth bass are also found. The
locks at the two exits from the lake make it truly a landlocked
stretch of water so that it provides an ideal place for a detailed
study of fish life. Its importance is indicated by the fact that the
Ontario Department of Lands and Forests, through its Wildlife
Division, has established sanctuaries (205 and 35 acres in area)
at the northeast and southwest corners of the lake, where fishing
is prohibited at all times.

Aquatic vegetation is abundant, in part as a result of the flooding of much shore land when the Canal was built. This adds to
the biological interest of the lake and also improves the fishing.
The workers at the Research Station in their investigations of the
fish population have even gone so far as to mark with small metal
tags many of the fish they have caught, all in the interests of
science. They can prove, beyond the shadow of a doubt, that bass
weighing more than six pounds have been caught in the lake.
The average size of fish is more likely to be about two and a half
pounds, however, and even that is a fair sized fish, especially for
the novice. The tagging of fish, and subsequent catching of tagged
fish, has enabled the station staff to trace the movements of fish
in the lake. Possibly the most surprising of their many findings
is that the average "cruising distance" of bass is only about one
mile. One of their tagged fish was caught twice, at the same
location, within two weeks.

Back in the main channel we follow a zig-zag course across
the second part of Opinicon, heading for a corner from which
there would seem to be no exit through the high sloping banks.
Buoys, however, mark a wooded headland named Squaw Point,
and a very sharp turn discloses another set of lock gates, flanked
by a smooth-running mill-race. This lock, called Chaffeys, so
snugly fitted into the narrow wooded valley is, at least in my
opinion, the loveliest lock of all.

Cruising the Rideau Lakes

CHAFFEYS LOCK TO POONAMALIE

CHAFFEYS always seems to me to be more remote from everyday bustle than any other of the locks on the Waterway. It may be the effect of the stand of trees which surround the lock and its winding approach channel, possibly of the graciously sloping lawns of the nearby hotel or the well-kept grounds around the lock itself. Whatever the cause, the peaceful character of the surroundings cannot long be resisted. A rest at the water's edge to watch the shoals of fingerlings darting about in the crystal-clear water in their unending search for food, a silent swim in the cool of the headpond on a broiling day in late summer, or a lazy half-hour on the high bank following the slow progress of a trim cruiser up through Lake Opinicon will drive time out of mind in real enjoyment.

On such a lovely day, I once watched a solitary sailor manoeuvre his slim craft, with its raucous outboard motor, alongside the wharf by the lock. We passed the time of day and both turned together to watch a small and rather nondescript spaniel slowly lift himself off the pile of camping equipment in the bow of the canoe. My surprise must have shown itself, for the sailor explained that the little dog had been through a bad time on the trip from Ottawa. He had been persistently sea-sick. I suppose that there is no real reason why an animal should not be sea-sick but until that summer's day I had never thought of it. So pitiful did the little dog look as it limped ashore and slowly rolled itself in the cool grass that I never visit Chaffeys without thinking of its misery on the Lakes and its evident relief when once it set foot ashore.

Chaffeys is a place of many other memories—of a first miraculous bass caught in the Rideau country; of the sudden discomfiture of a distinguished man of letters from a Canadian university when he fell into the turbulent water as a group of canoes were locked up, and of his subsequent chagrin at his bedraggled appearance before the ladies of his party; of evening sorties by canoe up into Indian Lake and down the broad waters of Opinicon when song and sunset combined in a harmony of sound and colour.

In the dark interior of the Mill a more remote past seems to crowd upon one's mind. The stately old building was purchased some years ago by a well-known Canadian. With simple furnishings, he has converted the bare interior into a pleasing summer home with a character all its own, in which the immense working floor of the old Mill now serves as living room, kitchen, storage space, and general reception area. The great handhewn ash beams which carry the upper floor are sturdy reminders of the timber which was once available in this land, and of the skill with which it was worked; the like of it cannot now be found in all of eastern Canada. Sitting at the breakfast table of this unusual residence, it is literally possible to cast a line into the mill-race below through an opening in the floor, and even to catch one's breakfast in the swift-flowing water, if one is lucky. Upstairs a writer's den looks upon a view of Lake Opinicon and the woods which has undoubtedly helped to stimulate the thoughtful commentaries which Canadians from coast to coast used often to hear, through the medium of the radio, from the owner of the Mill.

The name of this lock is that of the owner of the original Mill which was displaced by the building of the Canal, Samuel Chaffey. "A very extensive establishment, consisting of saw, grist, and fulling-mills, carding machines, stores, barns, distillery etc., filling up the whole river, and not to be estimated at a less expense than £5,000": this was the settlement which John MacTaggart saw during the course of his survey in 1827. He found great difficulty in suggesting in his report to Colonel By how the Canal could be fitted into the narrow gorge. Samuel Chaffey died of the usual swamp fever only a few days after obtaining a promise of a contract for work on the Waterway. Colonel By, when submitting in 1830 an official statement of the money which would have to be spent in acquiring property that was to be affected by the canal works, made a strong plea, with his customary kindliness, for the award of a life pension to Mrs. Chaffey. He based

this suggestion on the fact that the Mill brought in, so he had
been informed, an annual income of £300, even though the Mill
buildings were valued at only £2,000. The records do not show
whether his request was granted, but if the Commissary General
took his usual position it is unlikely that Mrs. Chaffey got a penny
more than had to be paid for the Mill itself.

But the Chaffeys were of good Somerset stock, and unusually
resourceful, so that it is unlikely that Mrs. Chaffey actually suf-
fered. One member of the family had already won renown in
England by his invention of the Chaffey Travelling Crane or
Derrick. It was not long before the Chaffeys of the Lock were
applying their nimble minds to problems of this continent. One
of the nephews, after working on the Great Lakes and inventing
a new type of propeller, travelled as far west as California. While
there, he saw an irrigation project at Riverside and was so taken
with the idea that he formed a partnership with his brother who
was a horticultural expert and knowledgeable with regard to land
use. Out of their joint real estate venture came the model irrigation scheme at Ontario, California, which was for long known
as the outstanding project of the state. Eventually they returned
to Canada but the Dominion government bought the mill rights
at Chaffeys in 1886; shortly after this the famous brothers left
Canada for Australia. Here they put their knowledge of irrigation
once more to good use and soon built irrigation canals in the
now-famous Murray Valley; this proved to be the foundation of
the remarkable development of intensive fruit cultivation in that
area, the products of which are known today throughout the
world.

Not long after the Canal was completed, Chaffeys was the
scene of the only serious military activity which the Waterway
was ever to witness (at least as far as I have been able to discover). This was at the time of the rebellion in Upper Canada of
1837–38 when all citizens were subject to call by the government
to assist in the defence of the realm. An old document discovered
in 1931 lists the names of "loyal men who turned out to defend
the locks and other works" at Chaffeys in July 1838. In the old
graveyard beyond the lock are tombstones of many of the men
whose names are to be found in this list of the 1838 defenders,
and here too is a stone raised in memory of "Mary Ann Chaffey
and her first husband Samuel Chaffey."

Links with other lands such as those created by the Chaffeys

have been and still are maintained by the fishermen from all over
North America who go out from Chaffeys to adjacent lakes. Harry
Keys, a cartoonist from the Columbus Ohio *Sunday Dispatch*,
spent a summer vacation at Chaffeys in 1936 and was so im-
pressed by all that he saw during his visit that he made the Canal
the subject of one of his vivid cartoons. He depicted a number
of well-known figures of the Rideau Lakes district and showed the
route he had followed. As a caption to an amusing sketch of a
battle for a really big fish, he lamented: "It's too bad the Duke
of Wellington couldn't live to witness the Battles of the Rideau."
His main caption contained more serious words: "The war of
1812 left a bitterness that poisoned the relations of Canada and
the United States . . . [but] the Waterway that was built to keep
Americans from invading Canada has become a magnet to draw
them northward in quest of vacations on the beautiful lakes surrounded by pine forests and dotted with islands—and there
Canadians, who were once afraid we'd come, are now glad to
have us."

The Hotel Opinicon, often better known to Americans than to
Canadians, has a remarkable collection of stuffed fish, beautifully
mounted in glass cases, and the size of these trophies from the
Rideau Lakes must be the cause of endless arguments among its
guests. Are such displays meant to be an encouragement to the
novice, or a vivid challenge to the tellers of tall tales? I can never
quite decide. In any case, the Hotel Opinicon has its full quota
of fishing yarns. There is the story about the young farmer who
lived near Chaffeys and who became the proud father of a baby
boy. He determined that as soon as his wife was well enough to
walk, the baby's superiority would be demonstrated on the
famous scales used by the Hotel for checking the actual weights
of fish caught in the lakes around. On the great day father,
mother, and baby, and two admiring grandmothers, took the
woodland walk from their farm to the Hotel. The baby was
solemnly placed in the scales and one of the grandmothers was
allowed the privilege of being the first to observe the figure recorded. She promptly fainted before saying a word as to what
she had seen. When she was questioned later she replied, acidly,
that it was the first time she had seen a newborn baby turn the
scales at twenty-two pounds.

I heard this story for the first time from the president of a
great Canadian university, in the course of a discussion of rela-

tivity in the little Community Hall at Chaffeys Lock. The hall provides a convenient meeting place for the small conferences which are sometimes held in this secluded spot. But I have heard other stories about fishing at Chaffeys, and about the Hotel Opinicon, deep in the woods of Pennsylvania. Possibly because the ancient Commonwealth is the home of so many lovers of the out-of-doors, it is the state which seems to have peculiarly close links with the Rideau Lakes. I cannot remember a single summer visit to Chaffeys without seeing at least one automobile with the Pennsylvania marker plate upon it.

Chaffeys is, as we have discovered, a gateway for the lakes beyond. Above its single lock our boat moves through a long winding channel, along which are homes and many boat houses. The last turn in the channel passes under a high railroad bridge. This particular bridge deserves notice for it is a link with the great days of railway building in Canada. It now carries what appears to be a very minor branch line of the Canadian National Railways served only by one daily passenger train each way. The line is, however, the main C.N.R. line from Ottawa to Toronto, and is still the most direct railway link between these two major cities. It was built by the Canadian Northern Railway and was extensively used until the nineteen-thirties when it fell into its present secondary place as a result of the "pooling" system of the C.N.R. and C.P.R. trains between Ottawa and Toronto which was introduced as an economy measure in 1932. The scenic beauty of this single line which passes through the heart of the Rideau Lakes, and its convenience as a short route, make many regular railway travellers regret that it cannot today be used for main line service, and that the only through trains upon it pass such a lovely spot as Chaffeys in the middle of the night.

Beyond the high girders of the bridge, we come suddenly to the waters of Indian Lake, the first of the large connected lakes which are usually grouped together as the Rideau Lakes. Ahead of us is an unusually large island, Scott Island, around which is a perfect chain of small lakes, each with its own special features. If we sailed to the left, we would pass through Benson, and through Mosquito and Loon Lakes—again the familiar names of the north country. The main channel of the Waterway veers to the right, however, and passes through a very narrow channel between Scott Island and the mainland. This may be crossed by an ancient and singularly frail looking chain-operated ferry scow.

Despite its appearance, the barge is safe enough to transport small passenger cars, to the merriment and surprise of new visitors. The channel leads into Clear Lake, a symmetrical body of water about one mile long; its clear water, well-wooded sides, and the picturesque islands breaking its surface lead some admirers to call it the loveliest of the Rideau Lakes. I would hesitate myself to choose among so many welcoming candidates.

At the far side of Clear Lake is another winding channel, and here we see to best advantage one of the details which give special novelty to a sail through the Waterway. This is the use of standard-sized highway direction signs to indicate the windings of the channel, some fixed on to points of land and some attached to posts standing in the water. Momentarily, one might think that one was at the wheel of a car as the familiar square white sign indicates a sharp curve! Sharp the curves are indeed, in this channel named "The Elbow"; it has to be treated with due respect by navigators of even the smallest craft.

It leads into Newboro Lake, once inappropriately called Mud Lake. There are ninety islands on this one lake alone, varying from small rock knolls to areas which may properly be called small estates and are the sites of extensive and sometimes beautiful summer residences. The names of the islands provide a study in themselves; they range from Whitehall to Fingerboard, with a fair scattering of family names, including the simplicity of Sarah. A devious but well-marked course takes us to Newboro Lock past the fishermen we are certain to see on this lake notable for the sport. The lock's normal rise of seven and a half feet brings us up to the level of Upper (or Little) Rideau Lake, the summit level of our journey. The fourteen locks through which we have come have raised us 162 feet above the level of Lake Ontario at Kingston. We have still to pass through thirty-three locks before we get down to the level of the Ottawa River.

Newboro Lock has now been electrified since it is the busiest of all; it leads to a winding channel about one mile long. Its banks are today covered with lush vegetation, trees in many sections coming to the water's edge and shielding almost completely the small town of Newboro which grew up at this point following the building of the Canal. This channel, unlike many we have already traversed, is an artificial one; every bit of it was excavated by hand in the dense forest. The land which it penetrates is the Isthmus, another scene of devastating attacks of the swamp fever at the time of construction. This is the location, mentioned earlier, where Colonel By ordered a wide clearing to be made through the forest in an attempt to get a breeze to blow from one lake to the other which would clear out the fetid swamp air and also, it was thought, the fever. The old records contain many tales of the hardships experienced here, which have the quality of nightmare when we hear them at this now tranquil location. The beauty of the channel is spoiled only by a really ugly high-level highway bridge, built recently to replace an old steel truss structure which, although no less ugly, had at least the merit of being unobtrusive. What looks at first like yet another bridge suddenly appears ahead of our boat but it proves to be merely two approach embankments to what was once a bridge. The bridge girders were removed from the actual crossing of the Canal in 1953, about a year after Canadian National Railways had decided to close down their Brockville to Westport branch line.

This incident of the railroad history of Canada turns out to be related to the history of the Rideau Waterway. Only a few years after the Canal had been completed and had opened up for settlement the Rideau Lakes country, meetings were held at Farmersville (now known as Athens) at which grandiose plans were discussed for a new railroad to connect the St. Lawrence River and Lake Huron, through the Rideau Lakes country. These meetings led eventually, after many years of discussion, to the securing of a charter for the construction of the Brockville, Westport, and Sault Ste Marie Railway, which was to connect the Grand Trunk Railway at Brockville with the Northern Pacific Railway at the Soo. That such a difficult and unpromising route should ever have been contemplated is a wonder but the charter was issued, and construction of the B.W. and S.S.M. Railway commenced. The railway was completed as far as Westport and the first train operated on March 4, 1888. The initials invited parody; not long after the line started to operate they came to indicate the "Bad Wages and Seldom See Your Money" line. The slogan proved, unfortunately, to be all too true for the line was never extended beyond Westport and was never a paying proposition. In its final six years of operation by Canadian National Railways, a loss of almost half a million dollars was sustained. On August 30, 1952, the last train puffed its way from Brockville to Westport and back, and all traffic was then suspended. The line was dismantled shortly after and even the bridges have now been taken down.

It was the Canal which enabled construction of the railway to be completed when it was, for the first locomotive used on the railway was brought up from Kingston on a canal barge. It was landed at a spot near the end of the channel through the Newboro Isthmus, and run on a temporary track until it reached the railway itself which was being constructed by a large gang of workers, mainly Italian. The little engine then shuttled back and forth on the piece of line which had been completed, gradually extending it to its terminus at Westport, and southwards to meet the section being constructed from the Brockville end. The railway repaid its debt to the Canal many times over for in its early days much of its summer traffic consisted of visitors, campers and fishermen included, to the Rideau Lakes country. This was long before the days of even good county roads, let alone convenient modern highways, and Brockville thus became an important junction from which ran many special trains to take Canadians and Americans to the beauties of the Rideau country by the short rail journey. Better roads and the automobile soon ended this service of the railway to the Waterway and all that now remains, beyond the memories of old-timers, is a grass-grown track through the woods and the gaunt remains of bridges and other structures such as the one in the Newboro channel.

The Westport which was served by the railway is at the west end of Upper Rideau Lake. It is a happy community of less than one thousand people, with a settled look about its pleasantly grouped buildings which fit well against the wooded hillside to the north. Almost every building in the town has a view of the water. Its churches especially stand out. The attractive Roman Catholic church was built almost a century ago under the active direction of Father J. V. Foley whose name is still remembered appreciatively and its building was distinguished by the fact that residents of all faiths assisted gladly in its construction. Considering the often bitter religious feelings of those early years in Upper Canada, such co-operation, which is reflected in other records of this part of Ontario, is worthy of note.

The equally pleasing Anglican Church was built some years later and has recently been skillfully renovated. Those interested in the inter-relations of politics and religion will find special interest in a marble stone in this church. It is related that an ardent church worker at the time St. Paul's was built was the owner of the marble works then operated at Westport. This man was a great admirer of Sir John A. Macdonald, and after Sir John's death in 1891 he made formal acknowledgment of his admiration by erecting a marble reredos behind the altar of the church in his memory. On the marble base was inscribed: "To the Glory of God and in memory of Sir J. A. Macdonald, K.C.B., Premier of Canada. Died June 6th, 1891." When the Bishop of those days (whose political affiliations, if any, are not now known) saw this stone, he strongly disapproved of the wording and ordered the base of the cross removed to the corner of the sanctuary; there it has remained until this day.

At least one large private residence in Westport will attract the visitor. It is occupied by a Canadian architect who has shown that it is not necessary for the professional man to reside in a large city if he wishes his work to become well known. From his office in this apparently "isolated" country town have come designs which have been translated into most acceptable buildings throughout all of eastern Ontario, and indeed beyond. This is but one way in which towns such as Westport, developed under the impetus of the timber trade which has now disappeared, are adjusting themselves to a new lease of useful life. Such a possibility is not open to all city dwellers but on first seeing Westport especially at the height of summer, many must wish that their vocations would enable them to forsake the crowded streets of cities for such quiet rural living.

At Westport has been located since 1951 one of the fish hatcheries of the Ontario Department of Lands and Forests. The town is on the small stream flowing out of Wolff Lake and those which connect with it, and this stream flow, which is part of the essential water supply to the Rideau Lakes system, makes it a natural and convenient location for a fish hatchery. Largemouth black bass are distributed at the appropriate times of the year for the restocking of the Rideau Lakes system and other waters of eastern Ontario. The Hatchery is also used for the "wintering" of speckled trout and Kamloops trout, types of rainbow trout, which are similarly distributed in the spring. Another small fish hatchery at Glenora provides pickerel fry and lake trout fingerlings to Rideau waters and some restocking of bass is also carried out from the White Lake bass ponds near Sharbot Lake, which lies to the west of Perth. About three million pickerel eggs and seventy thousand bass and trout fingerlings were placed in the waters of the Canal and the associated lakes in 1954. Large though these numbers may appear to be, they represent a relatively minor fish restocking programme. Fortunately for the eminently desirable policy of conservation now being maintained by provincial wildlife officials, the waters of the Rideau system have such a satisfactory natural reproduction of the warm water species of fish, for which they are chiefly famous, that artificial restocking on any very extensive scale is not really necessary.

Perhaps this is a good opportunity to say something of the catch that fishermen can hope to obtain in the Rideau Lakes. Bass fishing takes pride of place throughout the entire Rideau system, largemouth bass being found in the stretches of shallower and more weedy water and the smallmouth bass along rocky shorelines and shoals. Pike are found similarly in all parts of the Waterway. Lake trout constitute the prize fishing of Big Rideau Lake and for those who regard the masquinonge as their ideal fish, the lower stretches of the Rideau River itself provide fine sport in the appropriate season. Yellow pickerel are also found throughout the entire Waterway. Perhaps I should explain that the fish Canadians call the yellow pickerel is known in the United States as the wall-eyed pike. And we shall find that some American fishermen refer to our small pike as pickerel! With such confusion in terminology, is it any wonder that fishermen can generate such heated arguments about their catch?

But confusion seems worse confounded in the names of some of the common pan fish which are also to be found in most parts of the Canal. Take the ordinary bullheads. This name is generally used to describe the Northern black bullhead—*Ameiurus melas melas* (*Rafinesque*) is its full title—but the amateur angler will use the same name to describe the Northern brown bullhead—*Ameiurus nebulosus nebulosus* (*Rafinesque*). In Kemptville, bullheads are known as mudpouts, and in the province of Quebec as barbot. I was first introduced to this terminological jungle when sympathizing with a fisherman who was bemoaning his bad luck. He explained that he was catching some wonderful pickerel but was having to throw them all back as the season had closed the day before. I noticed that my disconsolate companion had a single fish in his can, one new in appearance to me: he told me that it was "the fish with twelve names." Apparently its most common name is the black crappie; it is another of the types of pan fish which are common throughout the Waterway. To biologists it is known as *Pomoxis nigromaculatus* (*Le Sueur*) but that is not one of the twelve names I heard on that fall day, as we sheltered from one of the first winds of oncoming winter. Strawberry bass, strawberry fish, moon fish, moon bass, and calico bass are some of those I did hear that morning, and of which I have since been courteously reminded by officers of the provincial Fish and Wildlife Service; the other six names went with the wind. Perhaps one day I shall again meet my piscatorial puzzler and have my curiosity finally satisfied.

From Westport the route of the Canal and of our journey follows the beautiful wooded north shore of Upper Rideau Lake for five and a half miles to the Narrows Lock, and again we have a view of a variety of residences, most of them for summer use only in this typical "Shield" country. To the far north, the Shield is bare and rugged but here the mantling green foliage softens its harshness. The eastern end of the Lake is dammed by an embankment crossing the narrow gap between the two approaching shores of the mainland. It is broken only by the Narrows Lock which drops us a mere four feet to Lower (or Big) Rideau Lake. This simple structure which today blends so well into the surrounding landscape as to appear almost a natural formation is one of the most persuasive examples of By's genius in designing the Canal works. Before the Waterway was built, Rideau Lake was one sheet of water, a narrow channel at this location connecting its two parts. Early plans for the Canal merely showed a deepening of this natural channel. Colonel By, however, realized that by building a lock here, and thus raising the level of the upper part of the Lake by a few feet, he would not need to excavate the channel through the Isthmus to such a great depth. Today, with our intimate knowledge of the lakes and connecting streams, with our maps and our aerial photographs, such a procedure appears to be a very logical solution, but Colonel By had to work out his scheme on the basis only of what he could see from the ground and from the water.

Big Rideau Lake, well named, is nearly twenty miles long and within its boundaries are over three hundred islands of every shape and size up to Big Island which is almost three quarters of a mile long. Summer cottages, summer mansions, summer hotels and even summer communities are to be found around its shores and on many of the islands; days can be most pleasantly spent cruising around this one lake, enjoying life in the open air and camping at the many spots which can promise sleep beneath tall spruce trees to the murmur of the lake waters against the shore. And still the camper would be close to main roads and main railway lines, and within easy distance of large towns.

Rideau Lake was in use as a trafficway for some time before the Canal was constructed. A rough road through the forest led from the St. Lawrence at Brockville to the most easterly point on this part of Rideau Lake, which was then called The Bay. We know from early records that the first settlers in the town of Perth, the original military settlement of eastern Ontario, travelled to their new homes by this forest route, either by foot, or in rough carts. At The Bay they boarded scows and sailed down the lake to Olivers Ferry (which we shall reach later), transferring there to ox-drawn sleds which followed another rough trail through the forest in order to get around Pike Falls on what is now the River Tay. They then boarded scows again for their final sail to the little group of log cabins which constituted the beginnings of Perth, first town of the Rideau country. It was natural that a settlement should be established near the transfer point from the road to Rideau Lake. Portland is the name which was given to this little town, after William Henry Cavendish Bentinck, Duke of Portland, a prominent public figure in Great Britain.

From the earliest days of the Canal a branch channel has existed, leading from the main channel which follows the west shore of the lake, down six miles to The Bay and Portland-on-the-Rideau. Originally a busy transfer point for traffic for the Waterway, its snug harbour is now a haven for pleasure craft of every description during the summer months, and a storage place for them during the winter. The quiet village of today has one major lumber mill as a reminder of the great timber trade of the past. Highway 15 runs through the village, however, and this has restored some of its importance as a transfer point. Now summer vacationers pass from road to lake instead of settlers on their way to prospective homes in the forest. This is the first point along the highway from which the waters which form the Rideau Waterway can actually be seen since we left the Drowned Land near Kingston Mills, even though the road and Waterway have never been far apart. The construction of a greatly improved highway through the village and beyond may, however, make motorists even less liable to take notice of this pioneer settlement, as they dash through on their way to either Kingston or Smiths Falls.

Like so many other villages in rural Ontario, however, Portland has its stories of unusual hardihood and strange adventures to tell. The first permanent settler was Herman Chipman. When he built his little log cabin, his nearest neighbour was four miles away. The first tree in the necessary clearing of the forest was cut by his eldest son, Ami Chipman, in January 1837. In that same year, Mormon missionaries (one of whom may have been Joseph Smith) travelled through the forest tracks of this part of Upper Canada. They must have been persuasive members of their faith since later that year Ami Chipman, with his wife, his mother, and two children and with ten other men left the clearing in order to join the Mormon brethren at their newly founded settlement in the far mid-west of the United States. Some of the men drove their cattle along the forest roads all the way to Cleveland, Ohio. The main party went by boat, down the Canal, and crossed the St. Lawrence at Cole's Ferry. They joined forces at Cleveland, where they hired a team to take the women and children as far as the Ohio River. There they boarded a steamboat which took them as far as St. Louis. At St. Louis they transferred again and sailed 400 miles up the Missouri River to Richmond in Colwell County. There they landed, and proceeded inland to the El Dorado of the Mormons at Fairwest; here they met Brigham Young. The last lap of their journey brought them to Grand River, and a meeting with others who had come to form this idealistic Mormon settlement.

Within three weeks Ami Chipman and his little group had seen all they wanted to of the Mormon way of life. With others, they escaped and got as far as Quincy. They were followed, however, and were forced to return to Fairwest where the leaders of the insurgent group surrendered to the Mormon authority. All new-comers to the encampment were closely watched and Ami Chipman and his family and friends had to participate in the new life. They were still dissatisfied, however, and managed to build a log canoe in secret. Eventually, two years after their arrival, Chipman contrived an escape in this frail craft with his family. They sailed the 350 miles to St. Louis alone and there they were able to arrange for transportation back to Canada. Eventually, they all got safely back to Portland, walking much of the way.

Their adventure must surely rank among the strangest of the stories associated with the start of the Mormon movement.

Portland's location in Bastard Township may well prompt readers to wonder about this unusual use of a somewhat special word when studying maps of the Rideau country. There are many tales told to explain it but the simplest is probably the correct one. It is recorded that the township was to have been called Stevenstown, after the first settler who had been granted land within its boundaries. At the registry office, when land divisions were being arranged, the clerk called for the name of this particular area when its turn came in the official proceedings. Old Mr. Stevens must have been a shy man for it is said that he hesitated to suggest his own name. The clerk, impatient to get on with his work, exclaimed that since this township did not appear to have a father, it must be a bastard township.

All country dwellers will know that the townships of old Ontario are still very real and often very lively political subdivisions, serving many useful purposes. This particular township has a claim to fame quite apart from its unique name. On June 10, 1828, Dr. Peter Schofield gave a public lecture on temperance to the settlers of Bastard Township, the first such lecture ever to be given in Canada—and deserving of mention here if only to counterbalance the frequent references to distilleries and their products which the habits of those times have made inevitable. Dr. Schofield's lecture must have been unusually effective for it led to the setting up of the first Temperance Society in Canada. At least a part of the text of the lecture was recorded, fortunately for posterity, for it includes what claims to be an eyewitness account of the spontaneous combustion of an early Canadian who had been guilty of drinking some of the singularly potent liquor which the pioneers managed to concoct.

Courtesy demands that we should mention also the County of Leeds of which Bastard Township forms a part. This is one of the historic counties of southern Ontario, stretching from the banks of the St. Lawrence as far as Smiths Falls and including the route of the Canal all the way from Seeleys Bay. Leeds County was one of the areas set aside for settlement by the United Empire Loyalists who flocked across the border in the closing years of the eighteenth century. Theirs are the names still attached to many of the locks on the Waterway. Grants of land were made by means of certificates of ownership for lots of one or two hundred acres. The recipients usually had no knowledge of the ground in question and inevitably some had no personal interest in the land itself; as a result the certificates were widely used as articles of barter. In one case a certificate for two hundred acres in Bastard Township not far from Portland was offered for a pair of rough boots. The offer was refused: these acres form today one of the best farms in the district. Storekeepers would take the certificates in payment for goods. In one recorded case, a certificate was given in exchange for a calico dress and the storekeeper then proceeded to sell the land for from two to four dollars an acre. That calico dress, however, no doubt had a special value in the hard life of the pioneer women. Deer skin was the most common material used for dress, for example, many being clad completely in garments made from it. Even after the first difficult years, it was common for women to be dressed in homespun dresses, with deerskin petticoats, dyed blue with the bark of the soft maple. Headgear was most commonly rabbitskin bonnets, a severe limitation for even the most ingenious milliner.

The land of Leeds County was fertile when first cleared, especially on the clay flats between the knobs of the Precambrian rock which are a feature of the landscape in its western part. The county is known as "Leeds the Lovely": its lakes and the forests which still remain provide some of the most picturesque scenery of eastern Ontario. This is a transition region, for the junction between the old Precambrian rocks and the more recent sedimentary rocks follows an uneven course to the north along the western border of the county. Portland itself is a good point from which to observe these geological features. From the water, as we approach the harbour, the land around is gently rolling and for the most part arable. As we sail away, towards the northern end of the lake, we shall see a gradual change back to the more usual Precambrian scenery. The Rideau Lakes themselves reflect this geological arrangement, in the deep water which is to be found along the rugged northwest shores of the two main lakes, as compared with the shallower water at Portland and other similarly situated points on the south and east shores.

Our course from Portland lies to the north, along a channel which wends its way around seemingly innumerable islands, some of them intriguingly named, others—Cow, Turnip, and Jerry—suggesting perhaps a domestic incident now forgotten. A steady seven-mile sail past these islands encourages that favourite pastime of vacationing travellers when on the water: scrutiny of the establishments large and small that summer residents have devised for a variety of unusual sites. At the end of the sail we find ourselves at another constriction of the lake, this time not blocked by an embankment and lock, as at The Narrows, but just a narrow rock-bound channel, "Rocky Narrows." Past the narrows, which presents no difficulties with navigation, we come into the "Middle Expanse" of Big Rideau Lake with ahead an uninterrupted sail of five miles to the next narrows. There are fewer islands here, the lake being little more than a mile at the widest section of this Expanse, but the shoreline can be enjoyed here to the full, even by the navigator whose attention is not now claimed by islands as it was on the previous "Upper Expanse." In due course, the shores close in on us again and we are soon able to make out clearly another low-lying steel bridge, as unsightly as usual, with its essential swing span.

This is the Rideau Ferry Bridge, on the road from Lombardy to Perth, and thus easily reached from Highway 15. The location used to be known as Olivers Ferry and it is so shown on the maps of the Royal Engineers, prepared when the Canal was built. This is one of the few cases in which the name of one of the early settlers has been lost to us by the substitution of a local or regional name. The location is well known to all residents of the east of Ontario who love the water for near here is held each year the famous Rideau Ferry Regatta, a water festival which brings together a collection of pleasure craft surprising in its size and variety. So large are the Rideau Lakes themselves, and so many their inter-connections, that it is only on the occasion of such gatherings as the Regatta that one realizes how many pleasure vessels do now sail on even this central part of the Rideau Waterway.

From the bridge we can proceed into the "Lower Expanse" and the final stage of the passage down Big Rideau Lake. Instead of taking the direct route to the lower end, however, we can veer off to the left and proceed slowly and carefully to the approach channel to the Beveridge Lock. On the right is Stonehouse Island where the first distillery of the Rideau country was built, but the stone building which gave its name to the island is no longer to be seen. The two Beveridge Locks up which we must now be lifted are not on the main canal route and were not built to the direction of Colonel By. They were a project of the federal government of Canada, in 1886. The little canal into which they lead, however, is contemporaneous with the main canal, its distinction being that it was constructed by a private company formed by citizens of the town of Perth. They were anxious to have their new settlement connected with the Waterway and set up their company with the liveliest hopes. They had to build four small locks and do a certain amount of dredging but since their original capital was only $15,000, it can be seen that their undertaking was a minor venture compared with any part of the Rideau Canal itself. The Tay Branch was finished about 1835, and it is up this waterway that we sail for six miles, through flat but wooded country, in order to reach the old town of Perth. Larger craft cannot go this far; only canoes can make the final part of the sail since the channel has not been maintained and in the vicinity of Perth are swing bridges that swing no more.

Perth, the second largest town on this route from Kingston to Ottawa, is today the county town for Lanark County, with a population of about 5,000 and an unusually diversified group of small industries which give it a settled economy remarkable for a rural centre. Something of its individuality is suggested by the skyline which gradually comes into view around the turns of the narrow channel as it leads through the weeds towards the turning basin in the heart of the town. A necessary but ugly steel water tank, emblazoned with the name of Perth, stands out but the slender spire of St. James' Church provides a first suggestion of the European atmosphere which continues to pervade the town despite its industries. St. James' is one of the few churches in the whole of Canada which is of a Royal foundation. At the basin a traveller up the Tay Branch may well feel he has moored in the Old World. Old stone buildings with overhanging balconies rise from the water's edge to characterize a scene reminiscent of many a canal in Europe.

Two streams enter the still pool of the basin, branches of the River Tay which separate near the other side of the town forming an island on which stand the town hall and other buildings. A park has been created between the two streams and was given to the town in memory of John A. Stewart by his widow. Complete even to its children's bathing pool, it might well be the envy of many much larger cities. As the main street leads away from the basin, it crosses a nondescript bridge which has replaced a well-proportioned old stone arch originally built here to span the main branch of the Tay. Modern store fronts face the broad roadway of the street; but above them the eye traces out with pleasure the fine lines of grey stone buildings reminiscent of Scottish architecture of the last century at its best. The elegance of the building now used by the Canadian Legion, for instance, would be typical of many of the older buildings, if only their modern trappings were stripped clean. This roadway was also once flanked on both sides by mighty trees; their trunks have been cut flush with the ground in an act of vandalism which must surely be unequalled in eastern Canada, committed in order that gaunt electric light standards might be erected. The genuine character and flavour of the past which have nevertheless survived all these unfortunate modernisms suggest that Perth, if reconstructed, might well be the Williamsburg of Canada—if only we could find a Canadian John D. Rockefeller! Its old buildings may not go back as far in history as do those of eighteenth-century Williamsburg, but the taste which created them is worthy of perpetuation.

The few buildings which are preserved in their original state encourage one to think that this suggestion could be more than an idle fancy. The town hall, built in 1862, five years before Confederation, at a cost of only $12,000 has, for example, a clock installed in 1874 which has faithfully struck the quarter-hours for the townspeople ever since. The fine hall on the second storey, a room forty-five by seventy-five feet, still keeps its original simple dignity. Around the town may be seen many a noteworthy old house, some spoiled by modern additions or changes, but others looking just as they did when they were built. One house in particular, set in its own large garden, was built in 1836 and its comfortable and gracious interior has been mercifully preserved almost exactly as it was.

Standing in this house, as I have been privileged to do, one feels inevitably closer to the early settlers. The first several hundred Scottish settlers arrived in 1816 after wintering in Quebec City, and making their arduous way up from the St. Lawrence by way of Brockville. Their first minister arrived the year following, the Reverend William Bell, an austere man whose strength of character must have heartened many a doubting newcomer to these Canadian forests. The Scottish influence has always been strong in Perth, starting with the original military settlers: one of the principal land subdivision lines is known to this day as the

"Scotch Line." For its first decade, the settlement was known as the "Perth Military Settlement" and was in charge of retired military officers on half pay. They kept up rigid standards of gracious living, far removed though they were from civilization, so far indeed that it is related that on going out to dinner it was usual for officers and their ladies to be accompanied by a servant carrying their chairs. Furniture might be in very short supply but they dined at tables set with linen, glass, and china which would have adorned a well-furnished city house.

For many years Perth was the military, judicial, political, and social centre not only for its own county but for a large part of the Ottawa Valley, including the fledgling settlement of Bytown. Eventually, Bytown came into its own and long before it changed its name to Ottawa it had given up its dependence upon Perth. The Scottish settlement continued its steady progress, however, and made its own contribution to the life of eastern Ontario. Possibly the most unusual item in this contribution was the production of "The Big Cheese" by the local cheesemakers for the Chicago World's Fair of 1892, in order to demonstrate Canada's potentialities in dairy products. The cheese weighed eleven tons and measured six feet high and nine feet in diameter. So much attention did it attract that a concrete replica of it was made; this now stands near the railway station, surely a public monument without an equal.

It is in the life of its people, however, that Perth has excelled. From Perth have come many famous Canadian jurists, including one member of the present Supreme Court of Canada. A member of the federal cabinet in office as this book is written is a Perth man, interest in politics being another continuing Perth tradition. The liveliness of its menfolk may even be seen in the fact that Perth was the scene of one of the last duels to be fought on Canadian soil. On the morning of June 13, 1833, two young law students decided to settle in that way their differences over the hand of a young lady. One, Robert Lyon, was killed; he is buried in an old cemetery where his tombstone is still to be seen. His opponent lived to become a Superior Court judge at London, Ontario; he married the lady in question.

The town's earliest political battles were in connection with the Rideau Waterway. A link with Perth was not a part of Colonel By's original plan, for this was not necessary considering the military objective of the Canal. Residents of Perth, however, were determined to have access to the Canal and so, under the guidance of their first outstanding political figure, the Hon. William Morris, they set up the Tay Navigation Company. This step was taken in 1830, only fourteen years after the establishment of the settlement in the forest, and so it is not surprising that the Directors of the Company had the greatest difficulty in raising the capital necessary for their simple canal works. They made repeated requests to the government of Upper Canada; their persistence was finally rewarded: in January 1832, the government did make a grant which raised the available capital to $10,000. A number of streets were laid out with access to the waterfront. On April 27, a public land sale was held and a further sum of $1,500 was realized. Echoes of this sale may be heard in Perth today, for it is still held that some of the land then sold was a part of an intended "green Belt" for the town. Any such accusation made at the time would have been the least of the promoters' worries! Those who thought of purchasing lots around the proposed turning basin—the one in use today—would not do so until excavation had actually begun. The promoters, in the end, had to arrange to obtain a loan of $5,000 from the Bank of Upper Canada; with this it was possible to start construction of the basin in the summer of 1832.

In comparison with the main Canal works, the construction of the Tay Navigation was a very small undertaking. A minor amount of excavation was involved, and the building of four small wooden locks, three of them close together and of such a size that one man could operate all three. They were designed by a Perth builder named John Jackson; two were completed in 1831, but the finishing of the other two was just one more of the worries of 1832. To cap it all, the fall of that year was a very wet one and so little progress was made with the work at the turning basin. Since this was in the centre of the town, the difficult position of those responsible for the Company was only too obvious.

Hon. William Morris was one of the two sitting members of the Legislature for the Perth district; his fellow member was Donald Fraser, an early resident of the county, and a bitter political opponent of Mr. Morris. In October 1832, Mr. Fraser wrote to the Executive Council of the province of Upper Canada complaining about the way in which the Tay directors had disposed of Cockburn's Island (part of the land they sold to raise money for the navigation works), and suggesting that they had benefited personally by the sale. Mr. Morris made a most spirited reply and the battle was on. The Executive Council investigated and eventually reported in a way which exonerated the Company. One cannot disassociate from this bitter controversy the fact that on November 30 of the same year, two voters submitted a petition to the House of Assembly suggesting that Donald Fraser was ineligible to hold a seat in the House since he did not have the necessary freehold qualification. A trial was held and Fraser was officially unseated, one of the very few such cases in Canadian political history. He contested the next election, however, and was again returned following an election campaign even the printed record of which is exciting reading. The little canal which is now so tranquil a feeder of the Rideau Waterway was far from tranquil then.

More difficulties were encountered. The navigation works were still incomplete in 1834, for in that year another petition for a further grant was addressed to the government. It must have been passed for the works were finished that year, and a little steamer, the *Enterprise*, was built at Perth in order to provide a regular service between Perth, Bytown, and Kingston. It was commanded by Captain William Richards and if ever a character sailed the Rideau waters, Richards was that man. A native of Ireland, orphaned at the age of twelve by the piking of his parents, a sailor in the British Navy through the War of 1812, then a free trader to the West Indies, survivor of many fights with pirates and the wreck of his own boat in a typhoon, he finally settled on land in New Brunswick, and then moved to Perth. Even under his capable command, however, the little steamer was not a success, the Tay Navigation being really too shallow for the operation of a steamboat. The little pioneer craft was broken up a few years after it had been built but traffic continued on the Navigation, carried now on barges. In great measure this feeder canal was used for the transport of squared timber down to the Rideau Lakes and it was largely upon commercial ventures in this field that the economy of Perth was founded. Tolls on the Navigation, however, were not sufficient to keep it in proper repair with the result that it steadily deteriorated, and another round of appeals to the government became necessary.

By this time it was the federal government of Canada which

had to be appealed to. The time came when Perth was represented in the federal cabinet by one of her most noted sons, the Hon. John G. Haggart. He eventually held the portfolio of Railways and Canals; for forty-three years he was a staunch supporter of Sir John A. Macdonald. It is, perhaps, not without political significance that while Mr. Haggart was its Minister, the Department of Railways and Canals took over from the Tay Navigation Company the little feeder canal and embarked upon an ambitious programme of reconstruction. The old arch bridge to Cockburn's Island was demolished—another continued grievance in Perth today and apparently one well justified. The wooden locks were replaced by the new stone locks at Beveridge's, near the mouth of the Tay, and the entire channel was dredged to give a depth of five feet. It was immediately christened "Haggart's Ditch" and Haggart's Ditch it has remained to this day.

Down this Ditch we must now paddle, away from the turning basin in the centre of Perth, manoeuvring under and around the old bridges and past the wide clearing marking the old "Scotch Line" of the early settlers. The tree-lined channel, no longer an occasion of frustration and debate, takes us peacefully down to the locks, and so to our larger boat on the main channel. Ahead to the east is the lock with the strangest name of all, Poonamalie.

Down the Rideau

POONAMALIE TO OTTAWA

AT POONAMALIE, a name to excite the imagination, the Waterway has reached the Rideau River. This steady stream, fed by the Rideau Lakes, is to form most of the Rideau Waterway for the remainder of the route to Ottawa. A narrowing channel takes us from Lower Rideau Lake to a fork, the river going off to the left, and the marked route of the Waterway veering to the right. At the turn, we can just see the dam across the river which gives the necessary water level in the lake for navigation of this artificial canal. Just past the entrance are stop-log grooves in the two sides, for use if an emergency ever requires this part of the Canal to be drained for repairs to the lock. But our attention is soon diverted from the water to the trees which line the Canal, one of the finest stretches of cedars in eastern Ontario. The delicate scent of the cedars will gradually become noticeable as we glide with engines cut down towards the lock. Here is what can only be described as a "Cedar garden," enhanced by well-kept lawns around the lock buildings which are even more velvet-like than elsewhere on the Canal. The right bank especially attracts admiring attention: it bears a solid screen of cedar foliage, so dense that it conceals the road which runs through the trees as through a tunnel. This is the approach road to the lock, at the end of an insignificant side road which leaves Highway 15 about two miles southwest of Smiths Falls.

A walk through this scented forest tunnel, on a day when the heat is oppressive, gives pleasing testimony to the rightness of such phrases as "the cool of the garden." Those who know India are reminded by it of similar roads on the other side of the world, the shadows cast by the closely planted cedars being an almost exact replica of the patterns to be seen on Indian roads through plantations of Tiger Bamboo (so called since they provide excellent natural protection for stalking tigers). It was just such memories of another land, accompanied no doubt by an appreciation of the contrast between the rough pioneer conditions under which the Canal was built and the stately official life of India a century ago, that led one of the officers of the Royal Engineers to bestow the name Poonamalie (Poon-a-malee in pronunciation), on this isolated little lock.

All the early records show it merely as the lock at the First Rapids of the Rideau; the mile and a quarter canal was excavated, using a natural depression as a start, to circumvent a swift-running part of the Rideau River. Immediately opposite the lock, on the other side of the artificial island created by the little canal, Cockburn Creek joins the main river from the west. This little tributary rises very close to the headwaters of the Mississippi River—the Canadian Mississippi, of course, itself one of the main tributaries of the Ottawa River upstream of the Rideau. Soon after the Rideau Canal was built, there was talk of connecting the Rideau with the Mississippi by way of Cockburn Creek. This was, however, just another example of the grandiose schemes for inland waterways which were promoted at the height of the canal-building era, most of which became no more than pipe dreams as the railway gradually displaced the canal. Poonamalie has therefore had to remain the melodious name of a quiet backwater still guarding the outlet from the Rideau Lakes; through its lock gates we continue our journey along the Waterway as it descends the Rideau River.

We may well allow this strange link with India to remind us of the services rendered in the building of the Canal, and so of Canada, by the young officers of the Royal Engineers who acted as Colonel By's assistants. We know some of their names—Boteler, Briscoe, Denison, Frome, Pooley, and Victor—but otherwise singularly little about them, with one notable exception. The army lists give us details of their military careers but nothing to tell us what manner of men they were. We know that Lieutenant Briscoe was in charge of much of the work at Jones Falls, and that Lieutenant Pooley was placed in direct charge of the building of the locks and dams at Smiths Falls. There can be very little doubt that they constituted an unusually able group of young engineers, and equally that they gained much by working under John By. Most of them came out directly from England, to work in virgin bush with few amenities for decent living, and even fewer facilities for carrying out engineering work in the accepted manner. Their achievement in supervising the detailed engineering required for the building of the Canal must therefore call forth high praise. In all the records which I have examined, I have encountered only one reference to a mistake in the engineering work on the Canal, this being a slip in the levels at Clowes Lock. There is information to be secured, however, which suggests that these young officers were not only good engineers with a high sense of their responsibilities, but also men of many parts. We shall see something of their other interests when we come to consider the influence of the Canal upon the city of Ottawa.

The later career of Lieutenant William Denison is proof of the leadership given to his young assistants by the Superintending Engineer. Denison returned to England just before the completion of the Rideau Canal. He was the sponsor and original editor of one of the first sets of professional publications in the field of civil engineering. The first of four volumes of *Papers on Subjects connected with the Duties of the Corps of Royal Engineers* was published in London in 1837 by J. Crane, a printer of Crane Court off Fleet Street. Denison's Introduction shows that he viewed these duties as productive of many benefits beyond material ones: "There is pleasure in the mere exercise of the intellectual faculties; there is pleasure in the acquisition of knowledge for its own sake; but when knowledge is combined with utility, when it is available for the benefit of others, the pleasure is infinitely increased. . . . but this study and labour brings with it its own reward, not only as it enables [engineers] to perform their duties efficiently, but as it is the stepping stone to the cultivation of those sciences which open a wider range to the intellect, extend their sphere of usefulness, and which, by occupying the mind and improving the faculties, tend eventually to make them better officers and better men." John By had died when those words were written but they harmonize so well with what we know of his own approach to his profession that it is surely just to see behind them, at least in part, the lessons which he had instilled into his young assistants. It is, therefore, most unfortunate that Denison did not leave for us any record of Colonel By.

Denison's own contributions to the *Papers* show that he was a keen observer while in Canada. His notebooks must have been well kept for, even after the interval of some years, he was able to describe in detail parts of the Rideau Canal works with which he was concerned. Again, under Colonel By's direction, he carried out experiments into the strength of timber at Bytown and described his results in what must be one of the first, if not the first, Canadian scientific paper. It was published by the newly founded Institution of Civil Engineers and won for its author one of the first awards of the famous Telford Silver Medal. Denison describes how he used to get sappers to cut down any new specimen of tree which he saw in the course of his work in the forests along the Canal. From these he had small specimens of wood cut which he proceeded to test in a simple testing machine, made for him in the blacksmith's shop at Bytown. His paper contains the detailed results of over seventy tests, all carried out in this simple way but most carefully made; the results are of significance even today. His one regret was that he had to return to England before he had time to repeat his tests upon dried specimens cut from the same trees. Clearly, building research is not a development of the last few years.

Denison's future career was distinguished and in following it we move again far from rural Ontario. After service in a number of military posts in England, he was selected in 1846 as one of the first governors of Van Diemen's Land (now Tasmania), then proceeded in 1854 to occupy the same post in New South Wales with the title of Governor-General of Australia; he became Governor of Madras in 1861, and finally, for a short period, Governor-General of India. He had been knighted in 1846. Through all the civil and military preoccupations of these appointments and indeed until his death in East Sheen, England, on January 19, 1871, Sir William continued the interest in public works which he had early shown with the Rideau Canal.

Little more than a mile down the river below Poonamalie, whose name has lured us for an interval in distant lands, is the first of the four locks at Smiths Falls. Just ahead of it as we approach is an unusual type of rolling lift bridge; it carries the Canadian National line which we saw last at Chaffeys Lock. But it is as a divisional point on the Canadian Pacific Railway that Smiths Falls has become well known, at least by name. That name is peculiar since it came from a man who originally owned but never lived at the Falls and does not follow his spelling!

The town is named after Major Thomas Smyth, another United Empire Loyalist and one of the first to settle on the St. Lawrence, at Crosby near Brockville. In 1786 he secured a grant of four hundred acres, in the fourth concession of Elmsley Township of Leeds County. It is more than probable that Smyth did not know that his grant included a notable waterfall for he had done nothing with the land by 1810 and there is no record of his having even visited it up to that time. In that year, he became short of money and so mortgaged his four hundred acres to a man in Boston for the unusual sum of £233-11-3, using his certificate of ownership in the manner of the time almost as if it were currency. The money was apparently never paid to Major Smyth and he must have assumed that the land remained his to use as he wished. In 1823, he finally gave it some attention: with a small group of men he built a simple dam and saw mill at the Falls. There were still no settlers there, despite the attraction which waterfalls naturally had for the pioneers. Within a year, however, Smyth was brought up to court at York (now Toronto) and lost his land. He must have been a man with a certain kind of foresight, for he had removed the equipment from the mill before the court rendered its judgment. The land was then disposed of for £105 at a sheriff's sale in Brockville in 1825, to the Honourable Charles Jones whom we have met as a Rideau landowner before. Within a few months, Mr. Jones had displayed once again his business acumen, for he sold the land to Abel Russell Ward for £600. And it was Ward who was really the founder of the town. Indeed, the early settlement was known for a time as Wardsville but the name was soon changed to Smyths Falls, and eventually to that by which it is known today.

Abel Ward reconstructed the old mill of Major Smyth and had it operating again by the summer of 1827, only to learn almost immediately that it had to be demolished to permit the construction of the canal works. He claimed the sum of £5,000 as damages but Colonel By was able to settle with him for £1,500. This sum suggests that the mill must have been a substantial establishment, for this was almost the largest settlement made with any of the mill owners along the route of the Canal. The famous falls were considered by MacTaggart to be "as appalling an object as any that is to be met with; they fall over beds of hard bastard marble rock, 36 feet in less than one quarter of a mile. At this place there are numbers of islands formed by snies winding around the Falls. . . ." The Clerk of Works may have been slightly influenced in his judgment of the Falls for he called one of the backwaters Hornet's Snie, naming it so "from the trouble these insects gave us; while patiently measuring and surveying it we were severely stung."

Despite the rugged character of the Falls, construction of the Canal at this point did not prove too difficult, for a natural depression was available for building the main flight of three locks; the rocky ravine occupied by the Rideau was left relatively untouched, apart from the dam which was built across its head. James Simpson was the contractor, a young Irishman from Londonderry who came to Upper Canada after a stay at Lockport, New York, where he may have acquired some interest in canal work. He first demolished the old mill to Colonel By's directions, and then built access roads to connect the Falls with the existing road through the forest from Brockville. Building of the dams and the locks then started, troubled mainly by the many springs in the rock foundations. The construction of the upper single lock was a relatively easy operation since it was founded completely on rock, although "easy" is certainly a relative term: no unexpected difficulties arose, but the hand drilling and the slow laborious blasting and removal of the rock must be remembered. It is this lock which we approach just after we pass under the C.N.R. bridge. On some old maps it is called Jones Lock, presumably after the Honourable Charles, but in the official records of today it is merely designated as Smiths Falls Detached Lock No. 37. It is to be regretted that all the locks could not have been left with more personal names, if only as an historical record of the early pioneers.

In the basin just upstream of the upper lock gates is the largest assembly of boat houses we have seen on our trip so far, structures not distinguished architecturally—indeed some of them look as though a slight breeze would demolish them. After locking through, we move slowly across another basin with the main part of the town immediately to the left and fine little civic parks along both banks. A swing bridge carries the main street of the town over the head of the flight of locks which now lie ahead of us. It also carries Highway 15, which has been our companion all the way from Kingston, over from our right bank to the left, whence it runs through the town and away round to the west in order to link Perth with Ottawa. We shall not be near it again until we reach the heart of Ottawa: access from the land to the remainder of the Waterway is by way of county roads until we reach Highway 16 near Kemptville.

Progress of a boat through the three locks, which provide a drop of 25 feet to the main river channel, offers an opportunity for some of its passengers to walk away from the swing bridge straight up the main street of Smiths Falls. Here used to be the large factory building of the Frost and Wood Manufacturing Company, a company which had its origins in the small machine shop set up by Ebenezer Frost on Gould Island in 1839. He formed his partnership with Alexander Wood, of Glengarry, in 1846 so that for over one hundred years the names of Frost and Wood were closely associated with the industries which have made Smiths Falls a busy centre, quite apart from its importance to the railway. Closed in 1955, this famous old plant has had its site used by a modern hotel. The main street is unusually wide, flanked by the buildings typical of many eastern Canadian towns, with two hotels standing out prominently; they are busy, but the activity of today is far different from that of the country hostelries which used to be a vital part of the life of rural Canada before the automobile changed the character of their business for all time.

From the locks the route of our craft continues within the boundaries of the town, past the inevitable signs of modern housing development on both banks. In the background, on the left bank, are usually traces of smoke, betraying the location of the great junction of Canadian Pacific Railway routes. A mile from the foot of the flight of locks, we approach another lock with an overflow dam clearly in view some distance to the right of the lock entrance. As we tie up, ready for the lockmaster to open the gates, we find that we have come to a pair of locks bearing the quaint name of Old Slys. Again, there has been a change in name through the years for although the original records use the modern name, some maps of the early twentieth century call these locks McCrearys. Although the locks are only a few hundred feet from one of the main streets of the town, they have all the characteristics which travellers on the Waterway come to expect—beautifully kept lawns, well-appointed buildings to house the lockmaster and his stores, and masonry so well maintained that it is difficult to imagine that it has been in service for much more than a century, and has been subjected to all the rigours of the Canadian climate. The builders of the Waterway as we have found elsewhere knew their masonry and selected their stone well.

The locks are located in the old river channel, and their construction had the effect of flooding the little log house which had been built here by Old Sly—such was the accepted name of the original settler. He was paid £50 in compensation. The building of the locks could not have been carried out without some method of controlling the flow of the Rideau during construction. This was done by means of a special channel in the rock of the south bank; a cut sixty feet wide was laboriously excavated through the hard limestone, and fitted with the necessary control structure. This is the channel which now looks so normal a river bed with a "natural" falls; it can be inspected a few hundred feet to the south of the locks. Erosion of the rock strata in the many years since the channel was excavated has eradicated all traces of the original cutting, so that few people ever imagine that they are looking at the handiwork of contractors as they admire the beauty of the small falls. And there are many visitors, since this is naturally a favourite picnic spot, not only for residents of Smiths Falls but for many others who travel the busy modern highways which serve the two banks of the river. A high railway bridge spans both locks and the falls; this carries a line of the Canadian Pacific Railway but surprisingly still not the main line, merely a branch line to Brockville. We shall not see the main line until Merrickville, thirteen miles away.

The river channel in the two miles after Old Slys is singularly crooked, and our navigator will have to give constant attention to the wheel. The Rideau is not wide here and the presence of several islands adds further complications. A straight channel, however, enables an easy approach to the next lock, another one with a tangled history of names. The level of the river has been raised, to the elevation which it has at the foot of the lower lock at Old Slys, by a low arched dam built right across the original river bed. The dam not only serves to retain the water at the proper level but acts also as an overflow dam, the whole flow of the stream going over the top of the dam in a beautiful curved curtain of water. Several dams on the Rideau River perform this double function; it necessitates a firm foundation below the dam, so that the constant fall of water will not erode the material on to which it falls. The south end of this dam acts almost as a guide wall into the lock, one with no unusual features, its normal lift being about nine feet. Now called Edmunds Lock, it has also been called Edmons' and is even marked on some old maps as Mills Lock. Edmunds Lock would seem the appropriate name for it is built near the side of the house of one of the earliest settlers in this part of the Rideau Valley, James Edmunds.

Another three miles of winding channel, along a stretch of the river which widens out into what is almost a lake a mile across, deceptive only in the shallowness of its water, brings us to another attractive spot and another favourite haunt of the discerning fisherman, Kilmarnock Lock, originally known as Maitlands Rapids. This part of the Rideau River always reminds me of the English fen country with its low banks, the flat and fertile fields around, the many trees overhanging the quiet waters. The lock itself is located in a small artificial canal, little more than one quarter of a mile long. The lift of this lock is sometimes only two feet, so that the whole establishment gives the impression of being a large model of some of the other locks. The garden which surrounds the lock is one of outstanding charm. It is, perhaps, dangerous to make any distinction in such matters but if ever there were a competition for the loveliest garden along the Canal, that at Kilmarnock would be a strong challenger for the leading place.

A walk from Kilmarnock Lock, long but profitable, can be taken to examine a canal structure that is almost unknown, visited only by the occasional hunter or by those who like us are students of the Waterway. As our journey can be an unhurried one, suppose we tie up the cruiser and follow the road which crosses the lock by one of the standard wooden swing bridges. About a mile to the south, the road swings to the east and crosses a wide stream on a substantial bridge which is a reminder that we have been walking on an island: it is quite a large one, well over a mile across. We do not cross the bridge but turn aside along a narrow lane which ends at an isolated farm house. Now comes a stile and then the pleasure of walking on a thick carpet of leaves through an extensive and well-kept woodlot. On the outskirts of the wood we can see water again through the tangled bushes and finally the trail ends at a low-lying embankment. A

mound of earth, with a cattle guard at its centre, and thick weeds
and rushes hiding much of the water around, may seem unex-
citing. This is, however, no ordinary mound of earth but one of
the control dams of the Waterway. You will be able to see the
difference in water level between the two sides, a difference
which equals the head on the lock at Kilmarnock. We are now
on the opposite side of the island to the lock; this dam had to
be built in order to cut off any possible flow of water round this
side of the island when the control dam on the main channel of
the river was built. Although now remote from any habitation,
this dam lies almost exactly where one of the earliest bridges in
this part of Upper Canada was constructed. It was known, then,
as the "corduroy bridge," and formed part of one of the pioneer
roads through the forest, leading to the ferry operated by Mr.
Maitland close to the rapids to which he gave his name. The
woodland country is a physical reminder of the tribulations of
the men who in surveying for the old earth dam had to run their
levels with cumbersome levelling instruments through the thick
bush.

We journey in the contrasting comfort of a modern cruiser, an
uninterrupted sail now of about six miles down the river from
Kilmarnock Lock, following a fairly easy channel, to the next
stop, Merrickville. The bridge which we saw in our walk is
visible soon after we leave Kilmarnock, but of more significance
is the second waterway which we see on our starboard bow, not
quite two miles from the starting point. This is Irish Creek, flowing into the Rideau from Irish Lake, the route first selected for
a part of the course of the Canal. It is difficult today to imagine
that any alternative could have been seriously considered but, as
has been said before, full details of every part of the land are
now available whereas the early surveyors knew only what they
could see from the banks of the streams upon which they travelled
in their canoes. The flow of Irish Creek was also, in all probability,
much greater a century ago than it is today, such is the effect of
our "development" of the land. It never was used as any part of
the Waterway and remains today just another of the minor
tributaries of the Rideau, unknown and unnoticed by all save
those who live near its banks.

The early attention given to Irish Creek is more fully explained
by the fact that it lay in one of the areas first settled by the more
venturesome of the United Empire Loyalists who decided to come

up from the St. Lawrence into the forest and live upon the lands which they had been granted. The district on the south bank of the Rideau just downstream of Irish Creek was known in the early days as the Upper Rideau Settlement, that immediately downstream of Merrickville as the Lower Rideau Settlement. Both areas were comparatively well settled when the building of the Canal started. If this seems strange a glance at a map of eastern Ontario will give an explanation. Despite the length of our voyage from Kingston, changing directions have brought us to a point only twenty-five miles from Brockville, and so from the St. Lawrence. The mouth of Irish Creek is actually the point on the Rideau which is closest to the St. Lawrence; our course starts to swing to the north, heading for Ottawa, soon after we pass the creek. It was therefore natural that the first settlers to venture inland from the Brockville area should select land for settlement on the nearest main waterway that they could find. The falls at what is now Merrickville provided a natural focus for such settlement. William Merrick, a millwright from Massachusetts, built his first log house at the falls which now bear his name as early as 1796, and Merricks Mills was therefore a well-established little community when the building of the Canal started.

A long approach channel, which calls for a slower cruising speed, leads to the locks at Merrickville; it diverts from the main river channel almost half a mile upstream of the locks. Once again, Colonel By used a natural low-lying piece of land in which to excavate an artificial channel leading to his locks which he could then build "in the dry," that is, without having to trouble about diverting the flow of the river from the site of the works. One of the earliest plans for the locks at Merrickville did show them in the river bed but I have a definite feeling that it was the engineering intuition of Colonel By which led to the orderly layout of the works as they exist today. As our boat noses into the upper lock this arrangement is spread out before us. The flight of three locks seems much more graceful than any other of the corresponding groups of locks on the Canal, since it has the added interest of the rounded lines of a pleasant basin between each pair. On the left is a group of buildings, easily distinguishable as old mill buildings, and clearly still in use or at least in good state of repair. Beyond them is the bridge which crosses the main river channel, with more mill buildings on the far bank.

And a little way up the hill can be made out the oldest house in Merrickville, still in use and in fine condition, even though it was built in 1821 by William Merrick, well before the Canal was undertaken.

On our immediate right, however, is a building which takes the attention first: another of the original blockhouses, fortunately preserved in splendid condition. The blockhouse was built at the same time as the locks, as part of the military programme. Its presence at this location is explained by the relative proximity to the "frontier"—the word used in all the old records to describe the international border running along the St. Lawrence. There was a road running from Brockville to Merricks Falls, where it crossed the Rideau River on one of the earliest bridges of the region. When the locks were built, this "road to the frontier" was carried on a rolling bridge over the head of the top lock, and then ran over Mr. Merrick's dam which existed approximately where the present control structure stands. The old blockhouse, then, was strategically placed for the defence of the locks against possible invasion from the south. Never needed for defence, at one time it was used as a residence for the lockmaster and for a short period even as a church, but it is now used as a museum and as headquarters for the local historical society. The whitewashed stone walls, the overhanging wooden upper storey, the massive doorway, and the great wooden beams which support the upper floor make it possible to forget such phenomena as motor lawn mowers and imagine the sappers about their business, presided over by a red-coated officer of the Royal Engineers.

The same atmosphere of the past is created in the town by dignified homes, built of massive masonry in well-ordered proportions. At the top of the hill, along the main street, is the mansion built in 1845 for Aaron Merrick by Samuel Langford who served as an apprentice mason on the canal works, and who built several of the stone houses to be seen along this part of the Waterway. The house is still in use, the residence of a prominent Merrickville figure; its pride is a magnificent staircase extending from the first floor to the third. Just along the street is William Merrick's house, with an unusually fine doorway; Stephen Hedger Merrick's is not far away. All three of these Merrick houses were built by the sons of the original settlers. The graves of many of the pioneers are to be seen in what remains of the original village churchyard; here on the tombstones is given an account of the century and a half during which this little town has served as a centre for the district around and given several generations of pioneer stock who have left their mark on many branches of Canadian life.

A study of the town's history will show what an active community it has been. It has had a public library, for example, for almost exactly a century, founded by Aaron Merrick. The first troop of Boy Scouts in Canada is said to have been formed in Merrickville. And the town has had electricity, generated by the fall of the river water, since 1895. Long before such modern developments, however, Merrickville had supported a number of local industries which gave it an enviable stability through the years. There have been small foundries here for more than one hundred years and the mills down by the Canal have been in constant operation since the turn of the eighteenth century. The original Merrick mills were started in 1793, to saw lumber and grind grain, but their scope was steadily increased. In 1848, William Merrick built a new section of the mill for the carding of wool. Later he sold it to Thomas Henry Watchorn and it has remained in the Watchorn family up to the present time; Thomas's grandson is the present owner. It operated without a break for 106 years, producing handsome tweeds, blankets, and rugs, but on October 31, 1954, it was forced to cease operations during a crisis in the industry which affected over a score of Canadian woolen mills in addition to this, the oldest in Ontario. The mill is in good shape and is naturally being maintained and it is to be hoped that the bell which is an unusual and distinctive feature of the old building will ring its call to work again. Even though electricity has long been used to drive its machinery, the Mill has always been closely associated with the Rideau Canal and its closing seems to be another break in the economic history of the Waterway.

In the large bay formed by the Rideau River at the foot of the Merrickville locks we start up our engines again. Ahead can be seen another high railway bridge clearly silhouetted against the sky. The trains which cross it are most often hauled by modern Diesel locomotives, for this is at last the main line of the Canadian Pacific Railway with two busy tracks linking Montreal with all the west by way of the junction at Smiths Falls. Two miles further on we come to Clowes Lock; this stretch of the river has banks with well-kept farms in view for most of the way,

whose established appearance points to the early settlement of
this part of the Rideau Valley. The lock is on the left bank of the
river and presents the usual trim appearance. The associated dam
is another graceful arched structure which serves also as an
overflow. The hand-cut blocks of stone (limestone in this case)
which form this dam are particularly fine and merit especially
careful study as our boat is locked through and we recall again
that all the quarrying, transporting, and final setting in place,
were done by hand. Contrary to general belief, this lock is not
named after Samuel Clowes, the surveyor who made the first
detailed report upon the proposed canal, but after James Clowes
who owned a small quarry near the lock, long since grown over.
There is no record of any compensation being paid to Clowes who
probably provided much of the stone needed for this lock and the
next, but Colonel By's records show that he did have to pay £600
to a Mr. Lukes for the flooding of a part of his distillery. This
further addition to our growing list of such enterprises served
the thirsty pioneers of the Lower Rideau Settlement.

Past Clowes Lock the course crosses over to the right bank in
order to enter the approach canal to the next pair of locks,
Nicholsons. It has to be admitted that this crossing of the river
immediately above the next dam was apparently due to a mistake,
an error in the necessary levelling for this part of the works. The
channel is well marked, however, so that with ordinary care a
boat can cross to the right bank without getting caught in the
sweep of water as it speeds up prior to tumbling over yet another
low arched dam—this one raises the water level sufficiently to
get us into the approach channel to Nicholsons. Many years ago
a barge became separated from the tug that was hauling it just
at this critical location and was carried over the dam on to the
rocks below. A woman and a little girl were alone on the barge
but, most fortunately, escaped with only a complete soaking. For
many years the remains of the barge persisted as a caution to
travellers until the last of it was finally washed away.

The approach to Nicholsons Locks is a narrow cut through
solid rock about two-thirds of a mile long, the locks being located
at the two ends. Here again we shall tie up, for another side trip.
A short walk away from Nicholsons along the county road
(which here hugs the right bank) back in the direction of Clowes
Lock, will bring us to another of the stone houses whose clean
lines are a distinguishing feature of this relatively remote part of

eastern Ontario. Almost all of these stone houses are in use; most
of them are well preserved; some have been restored to their
original simplicity by the removal of such later additions as
porches and extensions. Usually rectangular in original plan, they
reflected the architectural traditions of the Old World rather
than the New, their severely plain lines being reminiscent of
some phases of Scottish house design. A frequent distinguishing
feature, in addition to the beautifully cut limestone blocks, is an
elaborately designed wooden fan-light frame as a part of the
front door. Few of the houses retain their original interior arrangement but those that do have a very spare lay-out consistent
with simple living and heating by fireplaces and stoves. The particular stone house near Nicholsons Locks was known as the
"Kelly Place." It is now occupied by a farmer, and with his
permission we can turn off the road through an orchard in order
to reach a grassy hillock, topped by a gaunt giant of a tree. Here,
in disordered array, are gravestones of the pioneers.

This is McGuigan's Cemetery, one of the earliest burying
grounds in this part of what used to be Upper Canada; that it is
in such a sad state of neglect is an unfortunate reflection upon our
corporate sense of the past. The site overlooks a magnificent
sweep of country, typical of the Rideau Valley at its best; over
the trees below flash reflections of the sun from the waters of
the river. This is the land that the early pioneers came to think
of as their homeland, after years of hard work and the struggles
with nature which characterized the building of the Canal. Some
of the builders of the Canal are buried here with the early settlers.
One grave has a lovely child's head to mark its carved stone, even
here in what was then the limit of settlement in the forest; it
commemorates a small girl who was drowned at Clowes Lock
during its building. Her mother and father are buried on each
side of her—both had died soon after the child's drowning. As
always, the inscriptions on such stones, plain or ornate, stress to
those who read them how all projects such as the building of the
Canal are carried on to the accompaniment of the labour, the
heartache, and the joy of individual lives.

It was within sight of "McGuigan's" that the Battle of Merrickville was fought. This is the name still given to a rowdy fight
which occurred during the building of the Waterway but I have
been assured by an old man, whose grandmother was a child at
the time, that it actually took place at Clowes Lock and not at

Merrickville. During the work at this lock, some timber was cut on the farm of a Mr. Mosher but was not paid for as promptly as he wished. He therefore summoned the Sheriff from Brockville, a Mr. Sherwood, to come and arrest the men on a charge of trespass. Mr. Sherwood came to the lock and looked things over but decided that discretion was the better part of valour and returned to Brockville to get some necessary assistance. He swore in about a dozen deputy sheriffs there and came back to make his arrests. He was met by a large gang of the navvies working on the Canal, all Irishmen, whose dander had been aroused by this legalistic action. Armed with pick handles and clubs, they were successful in putting the sheriff and his men to complete rout. Captain Burritt, from Burritts Rapids, was then called out with a company of the Grenville militia. They came up the river and managed to make the necessary arrests. The whole gang of workers were then taken to Brockville under guard, and brought up in court to answer for their actions, but, with the loyalty which you might expect from aroused Irishmen, none would testify against his fellow. It was impossible to get any evidence of the trespass and the case had therefore to be thrown out of court. The navvies then celebrated with a few bottles of "mountain dew" and returned to their camp at Clowes Lock in extremely good spirits.

This is one of the many incidents told me about the Canal by Norman Walsh who served forty-five years on its maintenance staff, for many years as Foreman Carpenter; he is in his seventy-fifth year as this book is written. He can retell incidents which he heard from his grandmother, who was a little girl of eight when she stood and watched the *Pumper* make its first trip through the Canal. Mr. Walsh's great-grandfather, on his mother's side, was the McGuigan whose name is perpetuated in the cemetery. An Irishman from County Tyrone, he came to Canada in 1814 with his regiment, the Loyal Lincoln Volunteers, and was stationed at Kingston. On his discharge he received a grant of one hundred acres and was well settled in his new home when the great excitement of the building of the Canal commenced.

It was after Mr. Walsh's great uncle, Robert Nicholson, that Nicholsons Locks were named. Nicholson's father was a United Empire Loyalist of undisputed patriotism, who was living in Albany County, New York, when the Revolutionary War broke out. Because he would not join the rebels, he was thrown into Albany Gaol and later sent to a prison ship on the Hudson River.

From this he managed to escape, and joined Jessop's Rangers as a scout and sharpshooter; his original squirrel rifle is still in Mr. Walsh's possession. Robert Nicholson is mentioned in General Haldimand's famous certificate as one of the band of Loyalists who came up the St. Lawrence in 1784, settling in Augusta Township of Leeds County, that sanctuary of so many U.E.L. families. Such family links with events which, to most Canadians, are "just history" lend special interest to the talks which one may still have with Loyalist families in the Lower Rideau Settlement, as this part of the valley is still known to the very old.

Again we must return to our craft on the Canal. The way back takes us over bare rock, for the country limestone near Nicholsons Locks is very close to the surface. It may be that this position of the rock has resulted in special conditions for growth here. Whatever the reason, this spot is known to the discerning few as a place where splendid bittersweet can be gathered at the right time of the year. We may see some of it as we sail slowly down the narrow channel between the locks, admiring the neat appearance of the ground around, despite the outcropping of rock. Ducks are almost certain to add a finishing touch to the rural scene. The lower lock leads directly to the main river channel, whose well-wooded banks blaze out in the fall of the year from the leaves of the many hard maples.

Within little more than a mile comes another division of the river; markers point to the channel on the right, another dam across the main river being clearly seen at the head of what is now a long island. An easy passage along a canal, a mile and a quarter long, leads to the single lock of Burritts Rapids. This canal required little excavation when the Waterway was built, since it is a natural hollow which was used by the high water in the spring as a sort of floodway, supplementing the main river channel which is here somewhat restricted. The rapids have long since lost their original character and it takes a real effort of imagination to gain some idea of what the river was like when first seen by the earliest settlers. There is no old building to assist, for the mill in the village (at the utilitarian bridge which brings the county road over from the west bank) is now dilapidated.

Burritts Rapids as we see it today is a tiny place but it, too, could fill its own page of history. The Burritt family in North America goes back more than 350 years; during the Revolutionary War it, too, was Loyalist and gave up holdings in the United

States to come up to Canada. The family name will be known to students of early American history: the "learned blacksmith" of Longfellow's poem, Elihu Burritt, was the cousin of the man after whom Burritts Rapids was named. The latter was Colonel Stephen Burritt who served for seven years in the famous Rogers' Rangers. Eventually, towards the close of the eighteenth century, Stephen Burritt came up from the St. Lawrence to the Rideau Settlements, made a raft in Cox's Bay (near Nicholsons Rapids), and floated down the Rideau until he saw a location that appealed to him for his home. This was near the rapids which were henceforward to bear his name. He built himself a log house in a clearing which was close to the Anglican church of today, and there the first white child in this district was born on December 8, 1793. The baby grew up to be Colonel Edmund Burritt, the military tradition in the family being of long standing. The Burritts were responsible for many of the firsts in this newly developing part of Upper Canada. Christ Church, still in use as the Anglican place of worship, was built in 1831, before the Canal had been opened. It is well worth a visit from all who are interested in early church architecture, its "bull's eye" windows being unique in this part of Canada. The first Masonic Lodge meeting in the district was held in Colonel Stephen Burritt's house on May 22, 1815.

The record of Burritts Rapids might never have lengthened beyond its opening had it not been for timely help given its first settler. Very soon after Stephen Burritt had constructed his log house in the forest and settled down with his young wife, he was attacked by a severe case of ague and fever. His wife was similarly afflicted; both were so seriously ill that neither one could help the other and for three days they lay helpless in bed without fire or food of any kind. On this third day, a band of Indians arrived at the rapids. When they disembarked for the portage, they sensed from the unnatural quiet that something was wrong. Entering the cabin they found the two white people in their critical state. The Indians busied themselves immediately; the squaws prepared medicine and food and the braves got fuel and soon had the cabin warm again. The Indians waited until husband and wife had recovered sufficiently to look after themselves, even going so far as to gather up and store the corn from a small field for the sick man. The lives of the Burritts were saved by this kindly action; from that day on, their house was always open to any Indian traveller. It is told that it was no uncommon thing

for visitors in later years to awaken in the morning and find that
a number of Indians had come in for shelter during the night,
making themselves comfortable, as they knew they could, in the
lower parts of the big house that the Burritts eventually built.
When proceeding up river in the spring, it was customary for the
Indians to leave some of their things with the Colonel for safe
keeping. On their return in the fall, they usually left some token
of their well wishing for their white friend, often in the form of
especially valuable furs.

Burritts Rapids was soon outstripped by its neighbouring settlement of Merrickville, to some extent because of the coming of
the railway. Even with the steady growth of road transport,
Burritts has still remained almost in a backwater, for the main
roads of the district run some miles on both sides of it. The only
development of any note has been the establishment by the
Ontario government of the Industrial Farm near by but since this
is not the sort of place to attract the ordinary traveller, Burritts
remains a quiet kindly little centre for the farms around, a place
in which even an unfamiliar automobile is looked at with interest;
in some ways it could be eastern Canada's nearest equivalent to
the English village.

Burritts is the last settlement that we shall see until we are
near Ottawa; now we start down the "Long Reach"—a stretch of
level water unbroken for almost twenty-six miles. There is navigating still to be done but there are few really sharp turns to
make and only two bridges to pass. One of these is a new high-
level highway bridge which carries Highway 16 across the Rideau,
on its way from Ottawa to Prescott. The old bridge at this location, a few piers of which remain, was known as Becketts Landing
bridge, taking its name from the ferry that preceded the bridge.
The construction of the new bridge removed the necessity for
any attendant and so the little settlement has all but disappeared.
The second bridge, a modern reinforced concrete structure, with
ample clearance given through high approach embankments, is
located close to Kars. Wellington was the original name of this
settlement. There has never been a Wellington Post Office listed
officially, but Wellington was the name by which the village was
generally known as recently as 1904. There is no agreement as
to when the designation was changed. The name Kars is taken
from a stronghold of the Crimean War. The settlement was
founded a few years before the building of the Canal started

(one record states in 1820), the junction of a small creek with the Rideau River making the location of some importance for lumbering. Its development followed the usual pattern of these forest outposts of the United Empire Loyalists. Lumbering was responsible for its start and early growth; mills were then established; farming followed and led to the building of a grist mill and cheese factory; and the settlement then changed but slowly as the agricultural character of Carleton County has gradually developed. That it contributed to the busier days of the Waterway is indicated by the fact that one of the early boats used regularly on the Canal was built near here, at the mouth of Stevens Creek.

Slightly less than two miles after the high-level bridge at Becketts Landing we should catch sight of the entrance to Kemptville Creek on our right. This creek used to be navigable for six miles by all vessels using the Canal, as far as the centre of Kemptville. Regular sailings were in effect from Bytown to Kemptville even before the official opening of the Canal, but navigation up the creek today is not too easy and only the smallest pleasure craft can venture up it with safety. Kemptville is another important railway junction and the seat of a number of rural offices for the area. The Agricultural College for eastern Ontario is here and associated with it are offices such as that of the District Wildlife Officer for the Department of Lands and Forests.

The banks of the Long Reach are generally low enough to permit us to see something of the way in which this part of eastern Ontario is developing. It is obviously very different in character from the countryside we saw between Kingston and the Rideau Lakes. The flat limestone at Nicholsons, near the little building on the right bank at the upper lock, gives us the clue to the character of this countryside. For most of its sixty-two mile course, the Rideau River flows through country which is the largest unbroken tract of shallow soil overlying limestone to be found anywhere in southern Ontario. This area extends for about 1,400 square miles, including Smiths Falls, and comes very close to Ottawa. The rock which is exposed is called by geologists the Beekmantown formation; in places it contains a great variety of fossils. The Rideau River itself flows in its own valley-plain which contains some good soil, as can be seen from the farm lands along the banks, but once the river is left, the land is generally not too suitable for agriculture. When the first settlers came in to it, it was almost completely covered with forest, largely hardwoods, oak and pine being much more common then than they are at present in the small woodlots which still remain. Much of the land should have been left under forest—but in saying this we are, of course, being wise after the event. Despite all the back-breaking labour which went into its clearing, some of the land in this district has now been abandoned. Only 40 per cent of the area is farmed, according to a survey made by two good friends of mine who know Ontario well. Almost as much again is used only for pasture and is otherwise unimproved. The average size of the farms is about 200 acres, almost twice the normal size of farms on good clay soil, and the size is slowly increasing as the farming population decreases. A little progress has been made with reforestation and it is to be hoped that this trend will increase, for the land is suitable for tree cultivation. Even today, it has the greatest concentration of maple groves in Ontario, and maple sugaring is a general farming activity in the spring of the year. A portion of the best ground is to be found on the small areas of higher land which can sometimes be seen from the Waterway. Some of these are raised beaches, survivals from the era when this entire area was covered by the sea. The bones of a whale were found in one of these beaches near Smiths Falls. Other hills are what the geologists called drumlins, unusual formations of mixed soils caused by the passage of glaciers when the ice, which once also covered this land, retreated.

Our passage down the Long Reach will also enable the vigilant passenger to see a few examples, even from the river, of all the main stages of farmhouse development that are to be found here in old Ontario. There are even log cabins, roughly built of untrimmed logs without much finish to their construction. Today these original buildings are used as storage sheds but later buildings, made of squared logs with plastered chinks and shingle roofs, are still in use as farmhouses; a few of these are in very good condition, the result of the care with which they were built many years ago. On the older log buildings, one can occasionally see the original settlers' type of roof, made of cedar "scoops," hollowed cedar logs split down the middle and used as large shingles. One can also see fine examples of the next stage in the use of logs: a type of construction which included a simple frame for the house, this being filled in with short cedar logs, arranged faggot-like across the wall, and the spaces between the blocks of cedar being chinked with lime mortar. Houses thus built are very warm and, if well constructed, economical to build and pleasing in appearance. So successful has this type of building proved to be that it is in use even today, where there is an adequate supply of cedar logs. There is one good example of this type of "cedar block construction" a little way down the river from the bridge at Kars. It is on the right bank but is rather difficult to distinguish since the bank is well lined with small cottages—the advance guard of the scores of summer residences which surround Ottawa.

We are still twenty miles from the capital, however, with much to see before the end of the journey. Between Kars bridge and Long Island lies some of the well-developed countryside which has just been described and the good soil along the river banks has helped to create the fine herds of dairy cattle which are to be found within what is colloquially called the Ottawa "milkshed." Traffic on the highway which runs along the right bank is another indication of proximity to an urban area. Past the next locks there will be a steadily increasing number of cars and trucks on the roads along both banks.

These next locks are reached by one of the longest approach channels which we have yet used. It is another natural one, being the original right-hand river channel around Long Island. The three miles of the island completely shield from view the little village of Manotick, the name of which was adopted from an Indian term meaning Long Island. Although situated at the dam which blocks off the left-hand channel of the river, and complete with the usual old mill building at the dam, Manotick is a relatively recent settlement. When reviewing the history of the Canal and its use, we noted that it was founded in 1859 by M. K. Dickinson, the "King of the Rideau," in connection with the mills which he built at the falls on the river. By 1879 there was a population of about four hundred here and a group of mills were busily operating. One of these had the distinction of being one of the only two bung mills in Canada, the bungs being made from the basswood which was then in plentiful supply in the Rideau Valley. The bungs made here at Manotick were shipped to all parts of the country and even overseas; Scotland, for instance, was an important market. The main water mill is still operating today, up to 1,800 horse power being developed in the original mill building. Possibly the most remarkable thing about the village, and it may even make it unique, as its participation in four townships, since it is located exactly at the junction of four of the old township division lines.

Past the village we cannot see, we continue slowly down the channel, nearing the end of the Long Reach. The channel widens out as it approaches the Long Island dam and locks, located about half a mile from the narrow downstream point of the island. Even from the small wharf at which we pull up at the head of the upper lock, the dam, to the left, seems to be a structure of some magnitude. It is another arched masonry dam, 31 feet high and over 700 feet long, a really noble pile of cut stone. The original intention was to use it as an overflow dam and the curtain of water thus formed would have soon become one of the sights of Bytown. But such an attraction was not to be: the erosion at the toe of the dam when it had been raised to a height of only twelve feet was so serious that plans had quickly to be formed for an entirely new method of bypassing the normal flow of the river. It was fortunate that the island was so narrow at this point, for Colonel By was able to arrange for an overflow channel to be excavated right across the island, using a natural depression which lay near the west end of the dam. A timber dam was hurriedly constructed at the entrance to the overflow channel and fitted with the necessary controls. Although it was after all finished in good time to permit of the opening of this lower section of the Canal during the year 1831, the dam failed in the spring flood of 1836.

This great wash-out took place on June 8, 1836, just as the busy season for traffic on the Canal was starting. The Superintending Engineer was then Major Bolton, also of the Royal Engineers. He quickly drew up plans for a new timber dam, with a rather better foundation design, got a large crew of men at work by June 23, even as plans were being completed, and had the new dam in operation—and so the Canal in use again—by August 1. This would have been a remarkable achievement even if carried out with all the aids of modern mechanized construction equipment; to have had the Canal in operation after only a six weeks' delay in the year 1836 was an outstanding feat. Major Bolton found time not only to direct the work but to keep reasonably full notes, from which he compiled a paper some years later, so that we have a good knowledge of how he designed the work and carried it out. The same channel is in use today, although more modern piers have replaced the timber cribwork of a century ago.

This is the first occasion on which it has been necessary to mention anything in the way of a failure during the construction of the Rideau Canal. The success was so notable that it is only fitting to stress once again that the Royal Engineers designed all forty-seven locks and associated dams without benefit of modern methods of site investigation; even the proportioning of the sizes of dams, lock walls, and other water-retaining structures was based on experience rather than upon theory. The quality of the technical achievement of the Royal Engineers comes more clearly into focus when it is remembered too that all the works so designed had to be constructed in virgin country without any modern aids to construction. This wash-out of the overflow dam at Long Island was a small thing in itself, similar to many a failure on much greater works which have been built in the intervening years. It was clearly due to imperfect foundation conditions and is certainly no reflection upon the integrity or workmanship of the contractors for this part of the works. The plural noun is used since the Long Island dam and locks were built by Messrs. Phillips and White, two Montreal men who in partnership were responsible for a good deal of early building in eastern Canada. We know little of Andrew White, who seems to have been the sleeping partner of the pair, but Thomas Phillips was rated by Colonel By one of the very best masons he had at work "on the line of the Canal," as he so often expresses it in his letters.

This partnership of Phillips and Andrew White was a link in a more extensive co-operative arrangement. One of the papers in the private collection of books and records of John Redpath, now in McGill University, proved to be a long legal dissolution of a partnership which included not only Phillips and White but also John Redpath and Thomas McKay. We have described Redpath's great work at Jones Falls; earlier in the book there was a brief mention of the work of McKay in the vicinity of Bytown and more will be said about him in the next chapter. These four prominent contractors made a private partnership, presumably to share any possible losses which could not be foreseen in the carrying out of the canal works in the unknown country of the Rideau. They dissolved their partnership on March 27, 1831, since all their canal contract work was then complete, apart only from the dam at Jones Falls which is specifically excluded in the document of dissolution. Apparently, they had pooled their finances for the job, since in 1831 they divided the total profits in four equal parts, each part a sizable sum of money for those days, and each proving to be the foundation of a fortune some evidence of which is to be seen even today. What makes this quadruple partnership so interesting, however, is that it is an exact duplicate of another North American "invention" of the last two decades, the joint venture project, through which a number of large contracting companies combine their resources and share their losses and gains on projects which involve unusual risk or are of such a size that no one firm could tackle them alone. The Hoover (Boulder) Dam was one of the first modern structures to be built in this way, a group of big construction companies combining to form Six Companies Inc., in exactly the same way as these four pioneer "companies" combined to build much of the Rideau. Once again, when history is examined, the building of the Rideau Canal is seen to have set an example of good construction practice which was rediscovered only a full century later.

The standing of Thomas Phillips as a masonry contractor is well shown by the fact that the government of the time tried hard to persuade him to undertake a contract for completing masonry work at the Grenville Locks on the Ottawa River. As already explained, these were built under the Royal Staff Corps, the officers of which do not seem to have had the same wide experience and therefore the same skills in construction, as the officers of the Corps of Royal Engineers. No amount of persuasion would influence Phillips to undertake this additional work, even though he had offered to work with Colonel By on some lock work which was then contemplated for Montreal. In explaining this refusal to Colonel Durnford in Quebec City, Colonel By said that Phillips had told him that ". . . the officers of the Royal Staff Corps had not been accustomed to conduct work on a large scale and that he [Phillips] felt confident that he would be interfered with more than he would like. Mr. Phillips [added By] is an excellent workman . . . but I have observed that he has a very peculiar temper and cannot at all times agree with his own partner, Mr. White." Apparently Phillips elected to use his profits from his contracting work by investing in Montreal real estate. It is certainly on record that he donated to the city the land now known by his name, Phillips Square, in the heart of uptown Montreal; there is thus yet another link between that city and the Rideau Waterway. It is of interest to note that the head office of the Canada Cement Company is located on Phillips Square, since the Company has a great plant at the site of the quarry from which came the cement used in the building of the Canal.

Before we continue our journey towards Ottawa, we should take a closer look at the three Long Island locks clinging closely to the right bank, surrounded by a curtain of foliage which makes them blend into their surroundings in contrast to other locks that stand out from the landscape. They have a total rise of just over twenty-five feet, three feet more than the drop in the rapids now drowned out by the dam; the rapids are still to be seen, in part, in the left-hand channel on the west side of Long Island. When the Canal was built, the island and all the land around was almost uninhabited, and there was only the "paltry" saw mill to which we have referred before, at the foot of the rapids. MacTaggart exclaimed: "A piece of rougher wilderness could with difficulty be found in Canada; a road opened through it would greatly benefit the progress of the works." Today the dam, the locks, and the island are used all through the summer months by picnickers, swimmers, and fishermen who need only make a relatively short drive from Ottawa to enjoy the recreation they offer.

Just after leaving the tip of Long Island we come to the inconspicuous mouth of the Jock River. The name is almost certainly a derivative of Jacques; it has been spelled in a variety of ways through the years. Today, except when in spring flood, the Jock is almost a minor stream even though its bed widens out in some places to give it the appearance of a small river. At the time of the building of the Canal, however, it must have been an appreciable size, since it was much used for floating logs down from the forest on their way to the Ottawa. It was used also for floating sawn lumber up to the military settlement of Richmond, much of this coming in very early years from the pioneer saw mill at Merrickville, down the Rideau River with all its rapids, and then up the Jock. The pleasant but sluggish waters of the Jock today are a graphic example of the effect upon watercourses and stream flow of the resolute clearing of the land, the destruction of forests, and the consequent depletion of groundwater reserves upon which steady river flow completely depends.

But the Rideau River, with the natural reservoirs provided for it by the Rideau Lakes, still flows steadily down to its junction

with the Ottawa. On the four-mile sail down river from the end
of Long Island to the next lock at Black Rapids, the last lock
before we reach the civic boundaries of Ottawa, we shall probably
see many canoes, some driven by paddles, others by noisy outboard motors. The country is fertile and wooded, at least along
the river itself. The lock and dam we shall find to be very similar
to those at Clowes, the lock again on the west side of the river,
the dam again a long overflow structure; the only difference is
in the great length of the dam at Black Rapids. This was not all
by design, for the eastern end of the dam has had repeatedly to
be rebuilt as erosion of the river bank at this end has taken place
at times of high flood. The dam is now stabilized, but we can
clearly see the effect which the sandy character of the bank has
had upon this particular structure. Being only nine miles from
the heart of Ottawa, Black Rapids is an even more popular swimming place than Long Island. The group of buildings around the
lockmaster's house includes even the ubiquitous hot-dog stand,
a certain reminder of the proximity of all the wonders of civilization. The peace and quiet of the lock, however, seem to induce
respect for the lawns around on the part of the many city visitors
and it is rarely that one sees tell-tale rubbish on the carpet of
grass which provides such an agreeable resting place after a swim
in the pool below the lock.

The final lap of our voyage to Ottawa proceeds on a singularly
beautiful stretch of the river, the east shore a high bank, with sand
so clean and well graded that it was widely used for building
purposes in the Ottawa area; one location on this bank is actually
known as the "Sand-Pits." For many years, sand was loaded into
barges by means of long chutes, for transport to Ottawa. This
interesting local feature has long been overshadowed by the
steady development of Uplands Airport which reaches almost to
the top of the high bank just below Black Rapids. Originally
quite a small field, Uplands has now been developed as an experimental and training centre for jet planes for the Royal Canadian
Air Force and so has been planned with the longest runway in
North America. Now that this has been constructed, Canada is in a
good position to argue with a certain Texan city as to which
centre has the largest runway in the world! The aircraft which
will almost certainly pass above us, and our vessel, representing
the slow but steady travel on the Waterway down the years, set
past and present in a striking opposition. As we approach the

limits of the great modern city of Ottawa, however, it will gradually become almost impossible to keep any perspective with regard to time and its passage, so completely intermingled are the ancient and the modern along the Canal.

We do not have to proceed very far before we are theoretically within the limits of Ottawa, for the annexation by the city in 1950 of large outlying areas brought its boundary line to the centre of the Rideau River just a few hundred yards below the dam at Black Rapids. Sailing now, then, inside the metropolitan area, about two miles below the lock at Black Rapids we pass under another high railroad bridge which carries the transcontinental line of Canadian National Railways on its way to the west. Round a great bend, finishing with a very sharp turn, we finally come to the crest of the great Hog's Back Dam. The dam, now a centre for recreational facilities of unusual appeal to Ottawa citizens, is located at the site of what used to be the finest waterfall on the entire Rideau River system. Control of this waterfall involved the greatest fight with the forces of nature that Colonel By had to make and it was the scene of an accident which almost took the life of the builder of the Rideau Canal.

The Canal in Ottawa

AT HOG'S BACK the twin Rideau waterways, the river and the canal, separate. Hog's Back is therefore a cardinal point in the layout of Ottawa. It is also, in its own right, a place of history and of drama.

A glance at a map of the city from Hog's Back to the Ottawa River at the foot of the great final flight of locks will make the last stage of our journey along the Rideau Waterway clearer. The city is clustered about the Chaudière Falls on the Ottawa River, but stretches far to the west, past the Remic and the Deschenes Rapids to the southern tip of Lac Deschenes. To the north across the river lies the neighbouring town of Hull, bounded by the Ottawa and by the Gatineau coming in from the northern hills. Almost immediately opposite the mouth of the Gatineau are the Falls of the Rideau, over which the Rideau River plunges as it joins the Ottawa. The Rideau swings round from the southwest in a great sweep, made up of small rapids and bends and placid slack-waters, which extend about six miles from the Hog's Back to the Falls. Hog's Back is, however, a little less than two miles from the Chaudière Falls and almost due south of them. Within the triangle thus formed is the heart of the city of today.

Between the level of the Ottawa River and that of the water now impounded by the Hog's Back Dam is a drop of 115 feet. It was this drop, in so short a distance, climaxed by a final 35 feet down the Rideau Falls themselves, that necessitated some route other than the Rideau River for the whole distance between Hog's Back and the Ottawa. The Canal, now really an artificial waterway, separates from the Rideau at Hog's Back, and flows roughly parallel to it until Dows Lake is approached. From this shallow artificial lake, the Canal turns east to run parallel again with the river, and but a third of a mile away from it at one point. For its final stretch, the Canal makes a sharp turn in order to flow almost northwest to the head of the flight of locks which finally bring it to the Ottawa River at the head of the little bay, known long ago as Entrance Bay, today a quiet backwater at the foot of Parliament Hill.

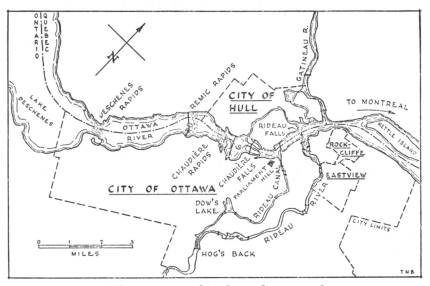

The Ottawa end of the Rideau Canal

So well shielded are the Falls of the Rideau by the utilitarian stop-log dams which straddle their dual crests, and so over-shadowed by the National Research Council's building on Sussex Street, that many visitors to Ottawa fail to realize that a pair of beautiful waterfalls is to be found close to the centre of the city. The falls can best be seen on land from Hull on the opposite shore of the Ottawa. But they were first noticed, and for almost two centuries were repeatedly admired, by travellers on the Ottawa River; all the *voyageurs* passed them on their way to and from the West. In like manner, they can be most fully observed today from the Ottawa, and this is now possible with a resumption of public boating services during summer months. Sailing close to them, one can appreciate better the famous description recorded by Samuel de Champlain: "At its mouth [the Rideau's] there is a wonderful waterfall; for, from a height of twenty or twenty-five fathoms, it falls with such impetuosity that it forms an archway nearly four hundred yards in width. The Indians, for the fun of it, pass underneath this without getting wet, except for the spray made by the falling water." Champlain got his dimensions a little wrong, but we can easily recognize the falls from his description, despite the decrease in the flow of water over them in summer time. To see them in all the majesty of the spring flood, however, is to see them as did Champlain so many years ago. The name "Rideau" was not given by Champlain, as some think, but at a later date by Canadian *voyageurs* who likened the falls to a pair of curtains; the name soon came to be used generally to describe the river behind the falls, which ran back into the forest and was used only by the Indians. But even the Indians did not attempt to canoe up the turbulent and tortuous first few miles: they regularly portaged from the Ottawa River up to the still-water above the great falls at Hog's Back, taking the shorter two-mile journey to these falls from their landing place at the foot of the Chaudière Falls.

To find a way of taking the Rideau Canal through a forbidding piece of country, and thus to circumvent the great drop in water level from the Hog's Back to the Ottawa, was the first and most immediate problem which Colonel By had to face when he arrived at Hull in the late summer of 1826. With Lord Dalhousie, he selected the little bay as the most desirable location for the start of the Canal. Earlier surveys had shown the necessity of a bold scheme for an artificial waterway for the first few miles of the Canal, no matter what route was selected. To investigate possible routes for these first few critical miles was the task assigned to John MacTaggart when he arrived to assist Colonel By in October 1826. Fortunately, he has left for us an account of this first surveying experience of his in the forests of Upper Canada, an account so revealing of the difficulties experienced even in survey work for the Canal that it will be quoted at some length. Today it takes only a few minutes to drive from Confederation Square, at the head of the flight of locks, to the Hog's Back Dam, making every allowance for modern traffic delays— here is MacTaggart making the same journey over a century ago:

Having procured three faithful men to assist me to explore, as many axe-men, and two to carry provisions, we sallied out into the woods in the beginning of November 1826. The axe-men continually cutting down a line through the underwood, we were enabled to take, what is called in survey-ing, a flying level, which is a rough guess to a foot, more or less, of the rise or fall of the country above any fixed data. Having continued at this fagging employment for three days, my assistants keeping in the neighbourhood, returning nightly and giving information respecting swamps, gullies, streams, mountains, &c. I at last came upon the famous Rideau, at a distance of between four and five miles from the above beautiful bay.

Taking a level of this extent in England would not have occupied more than a day; but in a dark dense wood the subject is quite altered, and a surveyor has to change his home system altogether: for instance, if we get upon a hill or other eminence in Britain, we may see the natural lead of the land; but in Canada, owing to the wilderness, you have to grope for this like blind men. On coming out on the river, I found it to be forty-five feet above the level of the Ottawa, and that if a cut were to be made from thence to the valley which descended into the bay, a rocky ridge would have to be broken through, nearly two miles long, and about sixty feet deep to the bottom of the canal. To attempt such a work would have been madness: the thing is by no means impracticable, but it would devour an enormous sum of money. Finding this, we left behind our various scientific instruments, and ascended the river. Having penetrated about three miles, we came upon foaming rapids, where the river was narrow in width and the banks high. Here was the famous Hog's Back, and here we proposed to raise the river by a dam, so that the water might be brought on a level with the head of the Entrance Valley above alluded to, which was eighty feet above the Ottawa. But the question arose again, if the river could be raised here to the required level, was it possible for us to retain that level through the wilderness—a distance, we supposed, of seven miles?

To ascertain this, now became the object of research, and we set to work accordingly; but meeting with various gullies, and huge swamps, to get through which (they being full of water) became almost impossible, we waded, and were often obliged to crawl on our hands and knees under the brush-wood, and this in water. Finding, therefore, we could make no good job of surveying then, until the swamps froze, we wended our weary way back to the Ottawa as best we could, and there awaited the coming of the frost, which did not happen sufficiently for our purpose until the 20th of December, and then it was accompanied by a foot-depth of snow.

The "wilderness" which is being described is the district known today as The Glebe and Ottawa South! The Clerk of Works goes on to tell how he spent Christmas of 1826 in these dismaying conditions:

No matter; we started again, cut holes through the thickets of these dismal swamps, directed a person to go about half a mile before, and wind a horn, keeping to one place, until those behind came up; so that by the compass and the sound, there being no sun, we might better grope out our course. For in the woods you have not only to keep a course, but you have also to discover what that course is; not as on sea, where the course is known, before the ship starts, that one port bears from another; but in the wilderness the relative position of places is not known,—a cause which improves the instinct of the Indian, making it so superior to that of a European. We had this matter to study deeply; and we had likewise to seek for that track where we could best preserve our level, in the shortest possible distance. This compelled us frequently to diverge from the direct course; a ridge of rocks or a deep swamp, the one much above, the other beneath, the required level, had necessarily to be shunned as much as possible. . . .

I mention these things out of no vain boast, but as curiosities in science, and must own that the subject perplexed me not a little. Placed in thick and dark snow-covered woods, where, unless the axe-men cut holes, a prospect of five yards could not be obtained; doubtful what kind of land lay on either side, or directly before; calculating at the same time, the nature of canal-making in such places, the depths to dig, or the banks to raise, so that the level might be kept from one sheet of water to another, the former eighty feet above the latter; while the weather was extremely cold, and the screws of the theodolite would scarcely move: these things all considered, were teasing enough to overcome, and required a little patience. When night drew on, two of the axe-men were sent off to rig the wigwam *shanty* by the side of a swamp. This was done for two reasons, or say three: first because water could be had in the swamps to drink and cook with, if the ice were broken to get at it: secondly, the boughs of the hemlock grow more bushy in such places, and are so far more easily obtained to cover the shanty; and thirdly, there are generally dry cedar-trees found there, which make excellent firewood, and the bark of dry cedar is the best thing in the world for lighting a fire with. When the party got to the place, there was a very comfortable house set out, a blazing fire with a maple back log, ranging along for a length of twenty or thirty feet. There, on the bushy hemlock would we lie down; roast pork before the fire on wooden prongs, each man roasting for himself; while plenty of tea was thrown into a large kettle of boiling water, the tin mug was turned out, the only tea-cup, which being filled, went round until all had drunk; then it was filled again, and so on; while each with his bush-knife cut toasted pork on a shive of bread, ever using the thumb-piece to protect the thumb from being burned; a *tot* or two round of weak grog finished the feast, when some would fall asleep,— others to sleep and snore; and after having lain an hour or so on one side some would cry *Spoon!*—the order to turn to the other—which was often an agreeable order, if a spike of tree-root or such substance stuck up between the ribs. Reclining thus, like a parcel of spoons, our feet to the fire, we have found the hair of our heads often frozen to the place where we lay. For many days together did we lie in these wild places, before we could satisfy ourselves with a solution of the problem already posed represented. In Dow's great swamp, one of the most dismal places in the wilderness, did five Irishmen, two Englishmen, two Americans, one French Canadian, and one Scotchman, hold their merry Christmas of 1826—or rather forgot to hold it at all.

It is not easy to link this account of hardships in the bush with the Ottawa of today, so great have been the changes through the years. And yet there are still views of the Rideau River within the city limits which enable one to forget momentarily the city around and to imagine the river as it was when first seen by Mac-Taggart. One such view is to be obtained near Billings Bridge, and very appropriately so since Bradish Billings, after whom the bridge is named and who lived close to the south end of the bridge site, was one of the two settlers on the Rideau when the Hog's Back Dam was built. Billings was the son of one of the first Loyalist settlers in the Brockville district; he came up the Ottawa early in the century and, after working for Philemon Wright, obtained land of his own on the banks of the Rideau and built a log cabin here in 1812. He then married a remarkable young woman, Lamira Day, the school teacher at Merrickville, and they settled down to a long and happy life together on this first estate of the Rideau country. There are many tales told about the Billings, especially about Mrs. Billings who lived to a great age, watching the metamorphosis of the construction camp of Bytown into the capital city of the Dominion. One anecdote only, however, is relevant to our story of the Waterway. In 1814, Mr. and Mrs. Billings, with their young daughter Sabra, the first child to be born in Gloucester Township, were returning from a canoe trip to Merrickville. They came to the portage around the falls at Hog's Back and there met Philemon Wright who was also canoeing on the river. They talked before disembarking and became so interested in their discussion that nobody noticed that the Billings' canoe was edging towards the current which swept over the falls. Too late, Philemon Wright shouted his warning but the frail craft with the Billings family in it was caught in the swift water and carried over the falls before the eyes of Wright's horrified party. Wright rushed around the short portage road, expecting to find battered bodies and a wrecked canoe. Instead he found the canoe afloat and Bradish Billings still in control of it, his wife safe with the baby quiet in her arms. This is believed to have been the only occasion on which a canoe shot the Hog's Back Falls; even the most experienced Indian travellers would never attempt the feat. It is a measure of the character and skill of Bradish Billings as a woodsman that he was able to save his family by his handling of the canoe in this emergency. He prospered in his lumber business and eventually built a fine house near the site of his original cabin. The chimney only of this mansion stands today, clearly to be seen from Billings Bridge, but neglected and unknown to almost all passers-by.

The Hog's Back Falls, in their original state, must have presented a wonderful sight, the most spectacular of all the falls and rapids on the Rideau. Their crest was approximately where the modern dam stands. It was on the shores of the still-water pool immediately above the falls that the other early settler had built his home in the woods. Captain Andrew Wilson was a retired officer of the British Navy who served under Nelson in the Battle of the Nile and had been an officer on H.M.S. *Victory* at the battle of Trafalgar. He was one of the many retired naval personnel who came to Canada with the usual grant of land for good service. It was Captain Wilson's luck to be given an area in the untouched forest land of the Rideau. Unlike many other early landowners, he came up the Ottawa and penetrated into the bush in order to settle upon his grant. The fact that he called his log cabin Ossian Hall, that he brought with him "the best library that ever was taken into the wilderness," and that he was the author of a three-volume naval history and a life of St. Paul is provocative indication that he was a character of whom one would like to know much more. From his clearing in the forest, he watched the building of the Hog's Back Dam, and as a Notary Public and a Justice of the Peace, he was very closely associated with Colonel By in the maintenance of good order in Bytown and at the great dam itself. We have some record of his salty conversation, his tall tales of the sea, and know that he was an occasional visitor to the cheerful bar of the Columbia Inn at Hull.

MacTaggart recommended to Colonel By a dam some distance downstream of the present one at Hog's Back. Again, however, he was overruled by the Superintending Engineer who, with his greater engineering skill, saw that only by a dam constructed at the falls themselves, high enough to back up the Rideau as far as Black Rapids, could he be sure of achieving the convenience in lay-out that would enable him to develop a simple navigation system from the flight locks into the main stream of the river itself. This meant a dam which would retain water to a height of almost fifty feet. It was regarded by many as a most foolhardy proposal for the dam had to be constructed right across the swift-flowing river. Nothing like it, nothing half as high, had ever been attempted before, even in the United States which in those early days was naturally ahead of Canada in its engineering achievements. But John By persisted and finally had his plans approved. So speedily were these prepared that a contract for the construction of the dam was awarded early in 1827 to Mr. Fenelon. The agreed price for the masonry—the dam had been designed as the usual structure of cut stone blocks with a heavy upstream earth embankment—was 1s 10d per cubic yard. This gave a total price for the complete dam of £4,595-0-8, or about $12,000! Lieutenant Denison of the Royal Engineers, who spent much time at Hog's Back during his service on the Rideau Canal, has left us an account of the progress of the work, and from this we know that Mr. Fenelon constructed a small railway to bring stone from the quarry which he opened on the west bank, a quarry which may still be seen today. It is entirely probable that this was the first railway in Canada; it certainly antedated the line from Laprairie to St. John's, in Lower Canada, which is usually stated to be Canada's first railway.

It required rather more than the ingenuity displayed in building a little railway, however, to tame the waters of the Rideau. Although Mr. Fenelon made preparations for the handling of the waters of the spring flood, a sudden rise in the level of the river in February 1828 caught him unprepared and much of the work he had done was swept away. This resulted in the termination of his contract. In view of the obvious complexity of the work, and the dangers inherent in this battle with the river, no other contract was awarded; Colonel By decided to build the dam himself, with the men of the Royal Sappers and Miners whom he could spare for this work (men of the 7th and the 15th Companies had now arrived at Bytown). But the completion of the dam was to become an ever increasing worry and it almost, as we have said, took the life of its builder. To begin with, before much more work could be done in this early spring of 1828, the main spring flood arrived and caused a further failure on April 1st. The great difficulty was, of course, to control the flow of the river while building the dam across the original bed. Once a river gets "out of control," as engineers describe it, it is extremely difficult to master it again and this was certainly Colonel By's experience. He had stout aid, however, from Philemon Wright who added building to his many other achievements. He had already contracted to build the dam and lock at Burritts Rapids. Now he agreed to close the gap created by the uncontrolled flood in the

start of the Hog's Back dam, for the sum of only £300. For this
critical task he employed some of his most skilled woodsmen; their
timber cribwork and the rock fill placed in it eventually finished
the job but it took until November 1829 to complete this essential
step in the over-all scheme of construction.

Work was possible on the main dam concurrent with this work
by Philemon Wright, and it was prosecuted vigorously, much of
it under Colonel By's immediate direction. By the middle of
March 1829, the dam had risen to such an extent that the water
level had been raised by 37 feet. Work had gone on right through
an unusually severe winter, with very low temperatures. This
must have been one of the first occasions when a major earthwork
was constructed in freezing weather so that it is perhaps not to
be wondered at that no precautions were taken against the effect
of freezing on the clay used for the fill in the dam. No real trouble
was suspected by those on the job when the water level started
to rise again at the end of March 1829. When leaks began to
develop under the new work, however, Colonel By was summoned from his home at Bytown and took personal command of
the measures which were put in hand to control them. Even he
was unprepared for the final failure for he tells us in one of his
letters that he "was standing on it [the dam] with forty men
employed in trying to stop the leak when I felt a motion like an
earthquake and instantly ordered the men to run, the Stones
falling from under my feet as I moved off." William Denison who
was also there with his chief tells of "the whole mass of earth
above the level of the water remaining suspended for about five
minutes after the key-work had given way, forming an arch of at
least fifty feet span, under which the river roared and foamed,
and over which several people passed safely; in a short time,
however, the action of the water widening the breach, carried
away the abutments of this arch, and the whole was precipitated
into the river."

The disappointment which this failure meant to Colonel By,
with the water as close as four feet to its final intended level, can
well be imagined. It is all too evident in his letters about the
disaster. The dam went out on April 3rd. On the next day, Colonel
By prepared in his own hand, back in his headquarters at Bytown,
an account of what had happened, and sent it directly to his
highest commandant, General Mann, the Master General of the
Ordnance. He refers to the prevailing sickness but says that,

despite this, he will immediately investigate other possible sites for the Hog's Back Dam. He notes quite frankly that he is not optimistic about the possibility of finding another. And it is a measure of the man that he explains that he thinks that the failure was due to the non-recognition of frozen soil in the fill used for the dam. Later in the same month, after he had had time to examine the site carefully, following the drop in the water level above the dam, he wrote a long, detailed letter to Colonel Couper, the Military Secretary to the Governor at Quebec, describing the whole operation with singular clarity. The letter even includes a pen and ink sketch of the dam, showing how the failure occurred, with the water line indicated in blue pencil. An actual handling

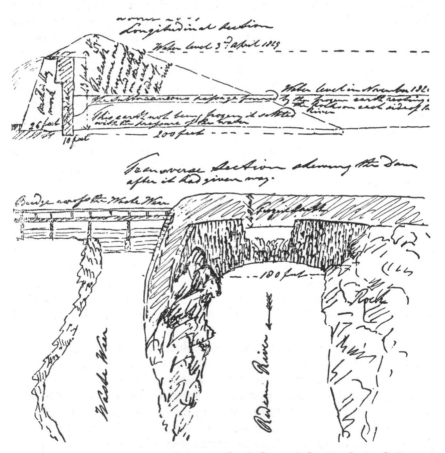

Colonel By's diagram to illustrate the failure of the Hog's Back Dam

of this letter makes real the many hours which Colonel By must have devoted to it in his office down by the flight locks, and its firm handwriting seems to reflect the resolve of the writer, in his closing words, to rebuild the dam at no matter what expenditure of energy. Even at such a critical time, Colonel By's sense of humour did not desert him. He was, somewhat naturally, reprimanded, though mildly, by those in authority. In his reply to the letter which he received from Sir James Kempt, we can sense the careful, and amused, composition: "I feel much obliged by your Excellency's calling my attention to the necessity of constructing the Dams perfectly impervious to water, and I beg to state on that principle I have acted from the commencement of the work." We may hope that the Governor was as diverted by these words as we are today. But the strain of the period, and probably the after effects of his close contact with death, had an unhappy consequence, and John By had his first serious illness later in the summer of 1829.

His resolve, however, was unimpaired. He changed his designs for the dam, finally deciding to abandon his original intention of building it as a massive cut stone structure. He instructed Captain Victor to extend the cribwork of Philemon Wright, which had successfully withstood the flood, across the full width of the river. This was done and earth fill was placed upstream of the gigantic wooden crib thus constructed, with massive rock fill on the downstream side. A waste weir for the handling of the flow of the river under the control of logs in sluiceways was also completed, so that by the end of the year 1829, despite all the disappointments of the work, the dam was ready and the water was raised to its full height. This structure served virtually unchanged for just over a century. The overflow part of the dam was then rebuilt and other improvements made but much of the original fill material remains in the dam which straddles Hog's Back today, though the area is now so well finished off with roads and parking grounds that many visitors probably do not realize that they are on a dam at all.

The boldness of Colonel By's original conception can best be appreciated if one climbs down the left bank of the original river bed to the foot of the falls, and then looks up towards the dam. The idea of damming the entire river up there at the head of the falls, with so great a drop immediately below, and of perching the canal on the side of the hill which formed the left bank of the river, again many feet immediately above the narrow valley in which the river continues to flow, would be regarded as daring even today. And yet there is nothing whatsoever to remind the modern visitor to Hog's Back of the man personally responsible for creating in the dense forest what is now a summer playground. Possibly he would have wished it so. Certainly John By had no idea of the way in which Hog's Back would be developed. He was concerned only with its defence against possible attack from the Americans, and was repeatedly disappointed when he could get no financial allowance for the defence works which he regarded as imperative.

In this, fortunately, he was worrying unnecessarily but his concern about the land around the works at the dam proved ultimately to be more constructive. Some of this was owned by a Mr. Fraser who went so far as to plan a small town, surely one of the first examples of town planning in Upper Canada. Mr. Fraser's motives may possibly have been tinged by financial considerations —unlike modern plans for land subdivisions, of course! Colonel By eventually arranged to purchase from him two lots of 45 acres in area, for £400, after it had been found that Mr. Fraser was charging all the labourers 2/6d for every tree they cut down, "hundreds of which are taken slyly . . . but the stumps remain!" Since a visitor to the works at the time said that the trees at Hog's Back were so thick that he could not see what the land was like, Mr. Fraser might well have become wealthy had not Colonel By intervened.

With the dam completed, the level of the water in the Rideau River was raised to a height such that a canal could be led from it by a route of its own to join the Ottawa River at Entrance Bay. The locks which give access to this final section of the Rideau Canal, the only long stretch which is an artificial waterway, were located at the east end of the Hog's Back Dam. The original river bank here was steep and high so that a good deal of excavation was necessary before the locks could be built. This was carried out while the dam was being built. When it was finished, the masonry work proceeded, and the locks were ready for use shortly after the dam itself. There are two locks but one is really in the nature of a guard lock, since the total drop is only 13½ feet. They lead to a channel about one mile long which is more than likely to strike us, while our cruiser moves along it, as similar in appearance, and in its use, to the older canals of Europe, the road alongside almost giving the appearance of the towpath familiar in the Old World. Towpaths along the Rideau Canal were mentioned and indeed proposed in the early reports but Colonel By abandoned the idea after he had seen the sort of country through which he had to build, and in view of what he foresaw about steamboat navigation. The channel leads to two more locks, those at Hartwells, which together give a further drop of 21½ feet, to the level of Dows Lake; this level is maintained throughout the course of the Canal in the centre of Ottawa, all the way to the head of the flight locks. The concrete wall now to be seen along the narrow channel in the vicinity of Hartwells, which was built between 1921 and 1923, gives no clue to the vast amount of excavation which had to be removed here in order to build these locks and the channels on either side. It was, however, this audacious design which enabled Colonel By to get the Waterway up to the requisite level for it to join with the Rideau River above the Hog's Back Falls.

Hartwells Locks and the associated buildings, we discover, form a pleasant rural scene, unexpected close to a busy city. But, although the locks seem so solid now, more difficulties with foundation conditions were experienced at Hartwells than at any other lock on the Canal. It was probably for this reason that Colonel By included in the original design a waste weir so arranged that through it the entire channel up to the Hog's Back locks could be drained if necessary. The waste weir is still in service but its exact function must often puzzle those who stop to watch some activity at these locks. This may be the locking through of pleasure boats: the locks at Hartwells and Hog's Back are amongst the busiest on the entire Waterway. It may be something connected with the maintenance work on the Canal, Hartwells being a frequent stopping place for the service vessels of the Department of Transport. Close to the lockmaster's house is a basin in which may regularly be seen the large timbers used for the repair of lock gates, kept in water in order to season them for use. On rare occasions, the visitor may find some of the maintenance workmen busy with these timbers, using their adzes in a manner which will make all amateur woodworkers envious; their operations will quickly remind the bystander of all the other handwork which has gone into the building and maintenance of the Canal over many years. The lockmaster's house will also be a reminder of past history; it is of special interest since it was really built as the blockhouse for the defence of the locks. There are many tales told of Hartwells—one of the more amusing anecdotes tells of the vow made by a recent lockmaster who was repeatedly disappointed in his attempts to have his house connected to a public electrical supply: he swore that if ever he did get electricity he would jump into the Canal fully clothed. He did so in due course, to the great delight of his friends who kept him to his wager. There are tales, too, of buried treasure here in the form of coins used for payments to those at work on the Canal; some were indeed found near Smiths Falls but no finds in the Ottawa area are yet on record.

A short run from Hartwells, and a passage through a narrow gap, once the site of a railway swing bridge, the C.P.R. line that used it being now located in a tunnel beneath the Canal, brings us into the smooth waters of Dows Lake, now one of the great delights of Ottawa in the summer, surrounded by gardens and ideal for boating, its boathouse the haven for a fine collection of cruisers, dinghies, and canoes. Looking over it on a summer day, when its waters are seemingly filled with small sailboats, and a few lads are taking a surreptitious swim in its waters despite the strict prohibition against swimming in this part of the Canal, it is difficult to think of its original state as "Dows Great Swamp." It was named after one of the very early settlers and lay right across the only possible route for the Waterway to take up to its junction with the river at Hog's Back. How to cross it must have been a question exercising many minds in the winter of 1826 and the spring of 1827. With his usual vigour MacTaggart developed a solution of his own, though he admitted that in advancing it he might "incur a little ridicule":

The plan, so far as I am aware, is new, and has never been tried before; but the situation of the place, and many other circumstances, justify the method proposed. At first view, one would suppose that a mound of earth might be formed to carry the canal over, or that an embankment of thirty-four feet, with another smaller one at the ridge of the swamp, of sixteen feet, would answer well, and form an extensive sheet of water for boats to rest and pass one another between them; but, after considering a little, we find, that to raise such embankments would be no easy matter, and would consume much money. An aqueduct of wood would be much better, and an aqueduct of wood I propose. Instead, however, of supporting it on piles or arches, as is the case commonly, I propose that the heads of the cedar-trees, which grow as thickly in the swamp as they possibly can grow, and average fourteen inches thick, and seventy feet high, be sawn off to the proper level, in the route of the canal, so as to form props for the bottom, sides, and towing-path. Upon this foundation, with clay, puddle, and planking, I consider there can be little difficulty in carrying the canal over, as is shown in the design. A cedar-tree, when cut down, will remain fresh fifty years; and surely, a tree standing on, and fixed by its roots, is a stronger and steadier support for an aqueduct, than any pile of the height requisite, let it be driven in the best manner possible. Nevertheless, the idea of carrying a canal over the trees in Canada may raise the laugh against us. However, it seems the best plan I can suggest, though you may probably devise something better still when you see the place—a place which cost us much trouble to explore, owing to the cold weather, thick brush-wood, and the waters in the swamp not being strong enough to bear a person properly.

Most fortunately, Colonel By did have a better solution than this brain-child of his Clerk of Works. But we must do full justice to the inventor for in his report to Colonel By he tried to think of all possible objections to his fantastic scheme, even the danger of forest fires which were not unknown in those early days. "As this aqueduct is embosomed in the wood, it will be endangered by fire; and to insure it against the casual flames of the forest, we propose that the wood shall be cut back from it on each side for the distance of four chains, and that this wood be appropriated for constructing the aqueduct."

John MacTaggart has been a frequent companion on our journey; unfortunately very little is known about him except that he did write a book, the only book ever written about the Rideau Canal so far as can be ascertained. He had been recommended for the position of Clerk of Works to Colonel By by no less a man than John Rennie, one of the earliest of the great civil engineers of England. He had arrived at Bytown in the late fall of 1826 and continued at his post until he became so seriously ill with the prevalent swamp fever that he had to return to England at the end of 1828. His book includes a letter of commendation from Colonel By to the Master General of the Ordnance but I am forced to wonder if his departure for England was not rather a welcome relief to the Superintending Engineer. In one or two letters he refers to MacTaggart's "dismissal," and on several occasions points out that MacTaggart had taken actions which were not duly authorized.

MacTaggart's book is called *Three Years in Canada* and the title-page goes on to describe it as *An Account of the Actual State of the Country in 1826-7-8 comprehending its resources, productions, improvements, and capabilities, and including Sketches of*

the State of Society, Advice to Emigrants, &c. It was published
in London by Henry Colburn of New Burlington Street in 1829,
in two volumes. The long title, in keeping with the tradition of
the time, really does describe the wide variety of topics touched
upon by the author. Colonel By says in a letter of commendation
which is quoted in the book that MacTaggart was "fond of research, and of exploring this untracked country" and this would
seem to be well justified by the record in the two volumes. They
contain what purport to be eye-witness accounts of visits to the
Missouri River, the banks of the Wabash, the Rocky Mountains,
Lake "Winnipeck," Moose Factory, Hudson Bay, and the Peace
River (in that order), in addition to the small towns of the east,
York, Kingston, Montreal, and Quebec. How MacTaggart managed to do all this in addition to serving zealously on the Rideau
Canal it is difficult to imagine; perhaps he was using information
gained during an earlier visit to Canada or, on the other hand,
just incorporating in his own record information which he obtained from other travellers. Quite apart from these travel notes,
however, the volumes contain enough personal observations on
the natural history of Upper and Lower Canada, and upon some
aspects of the social life of the time, to demonstrate beyond all
doubt that MacTaggart was a most acute observer. It is to be
hoped that copies of his book may one day be made available for
modern readers. For one thing, they might well be intrigued by
his sharp and eager eye for the girls of the time. "The ladies dress
very well, and seem to have a considerable quantity of conceit;
their dresses here are not so plain and so elegant as with you; they
have too great a profusion of flounces, feathers, and ruffles; few
of them are to be met with very good-looking; the climate robs
their complexions of all the beautiful colours, leaving behind the
sallow, dun and yellow; no pure red and white in Canada, and
dimples and smiles are rare. I endeavoured to fall in love once
or twice, and flung my old heart quite open to the little archer;
but the frost, or something or other, would not allow the arrows
to penetrate."

But we must leave such dalliance and return to MacTaggart as
proponent of the grandiose scheme for crossing Dows Great
Swamp on the tops of cedar trees. It is an idea worth recalling as
we examine the way in which the swamp was finally crossed in
a more orthodox manner by means of embankments which contained its waters and provided the "extensive sheet of water"
envisioned by MacTaggart. Their construction proved to be a

difficult matter; founding embankments on swampy ground is a precarious business even in modern engineering. But the contract for the building of the main embankment was awarded to our old friend Philemon Wright after some work had been done by a Mr. Henderson who abandoned his original contract; in Wright's hands, its completion was assured, despite serious subsidences which developed during construction. This is the embankment which forms the south shore of Dows Lake. Upon it runs the road to Hog's Back and the top is so wide that few of those who use it for travel or for parking to enjoy the lake, realize that they are taking advantage of the top of one of the dams built over a century ago.

The second embankment which was necessary to transform the swamp into an artificial lake was constructed about half a mile north of the main embankment, the contractor being Jean St. Louis. It is a pleasure thus to record the participation of a French-speaking Canadian contractor on the Rideau Canal, surely one of the first of the many *entrepreneurs canadiens* who have made so great a contribution to the building of Canada. There are few comments upon the work of St. Louis in the records from which we may safely gather that his work was satisfactory. The need for this further enbankment ceased when the area around the swamp was cleared of forest, and its grading and filling started, preparatory to its use first as an extensive lumber yard and, in more recent years, as a part of the Federal District Commission's Driveway and gardens.

The two embankments, then, provided a waterway across the old swamp. The canal route had next to be led through higher ground to connect with the natural depressions which could then be followed to the head of the flight locks. Running across the east side of the swamp was a high ridge of ground, very well wooded, known to the early travellers as the "Mountains of Nepean"—admittedly a somewhat grandiose use of the word mountain. It explains, however, the name then given to a depression in the ridge which provided a convenient location for the excavation of a deep cut. It was known as the "Notch of the Mountain," and through this notch the Canal was taken after a major task of excavation. This particular stretch of the Waterway, between the new bridge at Bronson Avenue and the high reinforced concrete arched bridge at Bank Street, is one of singular beauty at all times of the year but perhaps particularly in the early summer when the flower beds on either side are aglow with

colour and the trees which still distinguish this part of the Driveway system have all their new greenery. Lovely though this little
area is, the cynosure of all visitors, it has no well recognized name
today. Perhaps the City of Ottawa and the Federal District Commission might restore to it its romantic original title—the Notch
of the Mountain.

The approach to the Bank Street bridge offers for our admiration as we slowly sail on, many a well-kept garden, and a lovely
water garden on the left, in what used to be Brown's Inlet. The
gradually widening channel with its trim sides and well-wooded
banks provides an impressive entrance to the real centre of Ottawa
for as we swing round the great bend at the Exhibition Grounds
into what is almost another small lake, we can see over the trees
ahead to our left the top of the Peace Tower of the Parliament
Buildings of Canada. Our journey is nearly over. Along this quiet
waterway, on a sparkling fall day in 1951, cutters of the Royal
Canadian Navy gave welcome as part of the escort to a lovely
young princess and her sailor husband, Their Royal Highnesses
the Princess Elizabeth and the Duke of Edinburgh, as they made
their triumphal drive into Ottawa along the full length of the
west Driveway. Soon it came to be her capital city, and again
this part of the Waterway was a scene of special rejoicing. On it
sailed what is probably the largest flotilla of boats ever to assemble
anywhere on the Rideau Waterway, as part of the finale to the
loyal celebrations of the City of Ottawa of the Coronation of Queen
Elizabeth II. It was an impressive spectacle as the slow and
uniform movement of vessels, large and small, on the peaceful
Waterway gave a graceful climax to the evening twilight of a
perfect June day.

The word "slow" has special relevance here since there is a
speed limit of six miles per hour on the Canal within the city
limits of Ottawa. This used to be controlled by a special officer
of the old Ottawa Improvement Commission but since the Driveway system was completed by the Federal District Commission,
regulation of speed on the Rideau Canal has been added to the
diverse duties of the Royal Canadian Mounted Police. And within
recent years, at least one conviction has been obtained in the
Ottawa courts against a reckless motorboat owner who was found
guilty of travelling at a great deal more than six miles per hour.
Regulation is a very necessary precaution for the protection of
canoe users, since the wash of a large motor vessel proceeding

even at six miles per hour between the rigid limits of the concrete walls of this part of the Canal is serious enough to get a small craft into trouble. At the same time the sight of an R.C.M.P. constable solemnly "clocking" a motor boat from his modern steed, a motor cycle, might well tempt the pen of a James Thurber.

The broad reach beyond the Bank Street bridge gives us continuing sights of lovely gardens on our right, and on our left the gaunt and ungainly buildings of the Central Canada Exhibition. Many older residents of Ottawa remember this part of the Waterway when the banks were still slopes of bush-covered soil running down to the water's edge, with a motley collection of old buildings at various strategic points. The fine concrete walls which now confine the Canal between Dows Lake and the final narrow stretch were built from 1927 to 1930. It was only in 1953 that the last remains of the old wharves at the Canoe Club were removed from the sharp corner in the left-hand bank which we shall soon see, as the Canal begins to narrow again. Navigation is awkward for the next mile, but we should be able to notice within the next few hundred yards two small concrete steps on either side of the Canal which indicate where a small wooden foot bridge is erected every winter, when the Canal is drained, to provide a short cut for pedestrians between Ottawa East and the roads bordering on the Driveway. The regular erection of such an "annual bridge" may seem unusual but far more so was the small ferry which for seventy-five years took the place of the bridge in the summer time. Passengers crossed the narrow channel for the sum of ten cents—and this within little more than a mile of the centre of the nation's capital. The pity of it was that, although the row-boat could always be seen there, tied up and waiting for passengers, the automobile age had so weaned the citizens of Ottawa from this convenient means of travel that business grew very poor. The ferry had to be given up in 1950. Strangely enough, its main traffic in its final years was in the fall when it took fanatical followers of the Ottawa rugby games from the eastern shore to the bank adjacent to the football ground—because parking of automobiles in the vicinity of the stadium had become so congested.

The usual triple blast on our siren will bring an answering wave from the tender of an odd-looking bridge which we now approach, and the whole central part of the bridge, roadway and all, will then rise gradually into the air. It is one of the very few examples in Canada of a Strauss lift bridge, its name—the Pretoria Bridge —being merely an indication that it serves Pretoria Avenue, and itself. Immediately following is another large reinforced concrete bridge that carries the Queensway, a fine modern highway that runs without a break right through the city connecting with main roads to the east and west. The Queensway was constructed using the right-of-way previously used by the crosstown tracks of Canadian National Railways, a legacy of the industrial era when town planning was something to be dreamed of in the future. Many Ottawa motorists can remember all too well the tiresome traffic congestion caused whenever a freight train used the old line. It was displaced as a part of major re-planning of most the freight railway lines in the Ottawa area. The old line had served well and even in its last years saw an occasional passenger train. The old bridge was not a thing of beauty. Even this utilitarian structure has its strange tales. Possibly the most interesting concerns a small freight locomotive, which was driven up to the bridge in error when it was open. Fortunately, the Canal is not deep and so the locomotive buried its nose in the mud, from which undignified position it was eventually rescued to the great relief of railway personnel and canal traffic. In the salvage, the bell of the locomotive was removed and somehow found its way into the possession of the little Anglican Church of the Ascension which we have just passed on our starboard bow. There must have been many Ottawa residents who used to wonder why this church persisted in calling its parishioners to worship by a bell which was so unmusical. Actually this was rather an appropriate use of such a bell since this church has always served the concentration of railway people who have lived in Ottawa East in order to be close to the C.N.R. round-house. Indeed there are too few such departures from the normal to enliven a world becoming more and more conventional. Unfortunately, the old bell has now been displaced by a modern electronic chime . . . but the bell still rings. It was given to a small mission church in the country, but a church with no railway connections so that the old links have been quite broken.

Another short stretch of the Canal follows after the swing bridge, again between parallel concrete walls. All this last mile is a part of the Canal which required little excavation of a natural depression. Then comes the sharpest turn in the whole route of the Waterway, a true right-angled bend. There used to be a low brick building on the right bank here just before the bend was

reached but it was demolished in the sixties to make way for the
new Driveway. The building was the last of the many warehouses
that used to serve the heavy bulk freight traffic on the Canal. They
were used in their last years as storage buildings for the Department of Transport but even then it was possible to imagine them
as busy repositories for the cargoes discharged from the cheese
boats and other more general cargo-carrying canal boats.

Before the Canal was built, the natural depression which was
used for this last stretch continued straight ahead, and a small
stream ran down it which eventually reached the Rideau River.
But construction has so completely changed the entire landscape
in this locality that little is to be gained by even trying to imagine
the land as it used to be. The Canal is now a very narrow channel
indeed, bounded on the right-hand side by the wide approach
to what used to be a fine railway station, and on the other by a
steeply sloping bank, graced once again with garden plots. The
steep bank is the only reminder today that we are passing through
the part which used to be known as The Deep Cut, the name being
descriptive of the heavy excavation which had here to be carried
out in treacherous clay. Slides in these clay banks, during construction, are often mentioned in the records, and they caused
Colonel By much worry, but the banks have been stable and well
behaved now for many years. Soon we see the noble sky line
provided by the Parliament Buildings, the Peace Tower, and the
gables of the Château Laurier. We approach them under two
bridges in close proximity to one another, one carrying Laurier
Avenue and the wider, newer one bearing the name of the late
Mackenzie King.

It is just here that possibly the greatest changes of all in the
original land form have occurred. When the final flight of locks
was built, the channel which was excavated immediately above
them led directly to a beautiful beaver meadow of twelve acres.
A small stream flowed out of the meadow; its route lay along
the modern streets called Mosgrove and George as far as Dalhousie; it then turned and passed near the corner of York and
Cumberland Streets, then flowed along York Street to King Edward and down the latter as far as St. Andrew Street, thence
discharging into the Ottawa. The only remaining indication of
the stream is the unusual width of King Edward Street, a direct
result of the route of the old stream. The slight flow which remained when the stream was dammed up by the building of the

Canal was diverted down through the locks. Much of the beaver meadow was excavated to form a very necessary turning basin and this large pool of water remained a dominant feature of the central part of Ottawa until it was eventually filled in about 1910. It was a scene of great activity in the days of freighting on the Canal, surrounded as it was with warehouses and other buildings which served the busy water transport system. Many a famous traveller on the Waterway embarked or disembarked at its small wharves. It was located roughly between the lines of the modern Slater and Albert Streets and so the new Mackenzie King Bridge runs almost directly over it. This central city area and a large beaver meadow seem today quite incompatible, and yet, as recently as June 13, 1954, great excitement was aroused around the lockmaster's house at the head of the flight locks when a beaver was found swimming merrily in Lock No. 2! It must have come unnoticed into the lower locks after a leisurely swim down the Ottawa River from its home near the Chaudière Falls. The lock had to be drained before the lively little animal could be rescued by a Conservation Officer, who duly returned him to more familiar surroundings on Victoria Island.

Hemmed in between the great pile of the station building, a high steep bank, and the cover of a third bridge under which we must sail, is the head of the great final flight of eight locks. While the boat is locked down, there will be time to study the broad expanse of the Ottawa River which now lies below us, and we can admire the way in which the staircase of the locks fits snugly into the valley which separates the great hill on which the Parliament Buildings now stand and the rock cliff which appears beneath the Château Laurier. The eight locks have a total lift of just over eighty feet, from the Ottawa River up to the water level which persists all the way through the city as far as Hartwells Locks. The greater part of the total rise in the level of the canal to Hog's Back thus takes place in this set of locks. They constitute the outstanding single work on the whole Waterway. The dam and locks at Jones Falls are greater in magnitude, more significant perhaps in that they were built in the depth of the forest far removed from any settlement, but the Ottawa flight locks involved more complexities in construction especially in the masonry connections between adjacent locks. Here, if anywhere, Colonel By needed an expert masonry contractor; here, most fortunately, he again had the right man available, Thomas McKay, one of the four famous partners whose success we have described in an earlier chapter. Another young Scottish immigrant to Canada, born in Perth in 1792, McKay had been a partner with John Redpath on the building of the Lachine Canal; Thomas Phillips and Andrew White, their future partners, had also been engaged on the same works. The fact that McKay had worked on the Lachine Canal gives the lie to one of the many stories about him which have come down through the years—that he was selected personally by John By from amongst the penniless young men working on the Union Bridge as a result of a particularly good bit of individual work noticed by Colonel By on one of his visits to the job.

There was nothing spectacular about the building of the flight of locks, apart only from their size and the complexity of the masonry work. The excavation for the locks was not difficult, although complicated by many springs; it was carried out by a Mr. Pennyfather. The locks were located close to the two wharves at which boats delivered goods from Montreal and were surrounded by the yards and workshops erected by the Royal Engineers to serve the full extent of the canal works. It is said that Thomas McKay's original contract price was based on the use of stone to be quarried at Hull but that, after the work had started, he got permission to use the limestone found in the cliffs adjacent to the locks. That this was the stone he used can readily be seen by an examination, preferably near the level of the Ottawa River, of any of the original stonework and the rock in the cliffs nearby. The sand for mortar came from the mouth of the Gatineau River and the cement from the limestone quarry which was opened up for this purpose in the forest behind the little settlement of Hull. Initially, the cut stones were set together in a dry state but it was soon found that some form of mortar connection was essential and so the stones in place were "grouted" together, again in a manner which has many modern applications, using a long grouting tube into which a slurry of cement, sand, and water was poured. No difficulties were apparently encountered on this part of the work for the locks were completed by the year 1830, well in advance of the remainder of the Canal. Colonel By was so pleased by this good progress that he gave a great banquet and ball in Bytown in honour of McKay and his workmen. It is reported of the evening that "An ox, properly prepared and roasted whole, was fixed in a standing posture. The guests then proceeded

to study its anatomy in a very practical manner, after which singing and dancing completed the celebration." It is reassuring to
know that such a convivial function cheered the labour of By and
his associates.

We know of at least one other notable occasion in connection
with the building of the locks, the memory of which, in contrast,
must have been tinged with tragedy for those who participated.
This was the visit to the works of the young explorer, Captain
John Franklin, who was to disappear in the Arctic wastes in 1845.
This final voyage was made soon after he had returned to England
after serving from 1837 to 1843 as Governor of Van Diemen's
Land (now Tasmania), a post, incidentally, which he occupied
for the term next before that of Sir William Denison. He may well
have met Denison during his visit to Bytown since Colonel By
would certainly have had his chief assistants with him.

Franklin's explorations had started, however, at a much earlier
date. He spent two full years, from 1825 to 1827, in Arctic seas. It
was on his return journey from this long spell in the North that
Franklin came down the Ottawa River by canoe from the West.
He reached Bytown on the evening of August 15, 1827, and spent
the night at the headquarters of the 71st Regiment which was
then in barracks at the little construction camp. A letter, written
at the time, tells us that "Colonel By decided to celebrate his
return to the regions of hospitality and civilisation by identifying
his presence with that grand undertaking so highly beneficial to
the continent on which he has spent so much time and labour,
and to do this by arranging for him to lay the first stone of the
locks of the Rideau Canal. The high stage of popularity on which
the colonel so justifiably stands makes his desires and their
accomplishments almost coeval. This morning all was bustle, with
the result that at 4 p.m., the stone weighing about 1¾ tons was
brought to its bed as Colonel By and Captain Franklin arrived
at the spot, when Captain Franklin gave the final knock in due
form." The writer of the letter notes that despite the short notice,
there was "as large and respectable a gathering of spectators as
had ever been witnessed at this place." There are grounds for
the general belief that the stone which Franklin laid was in the
third lock up from the Ottawa River but diligent searches have
failed to reveal any specially marked stone.

I like to think of Thomas McKay as a prominent member of

the little group, with Franklin at its centre, coming down the hill for the stone-laying ceremony, for McKay proved himself to be a great man with many varied and public-spirited interests, in addition to being an unusually good masonry contractor. Alone of all the major contractors on the Canal, he stayed on in the Bytown district. For some years he lived in a house at the corner of Charles Street and Stanley Avenue in the district still known as New Edinburgh but in 1838 he moved into a magnificent stone mansion which he built for himself with his most skilled masons. Derisively called by the local inhabitants McKay's Castle, it nevertheless soon became known as the home of a large and gifted family, a centre of gracious living and hospitality. It stands today and is familiar now by the original name given to it by McKay, clearly as an indication of his close association with the Waterway —Rideau Hall. The residence of Canada's Governor-General is yet another legacy of the Rideau Canal to Canada. The original house has been greatly enlarged since its purchase for use as a vice-regal mansion in 1868, but the original structure still remains. Its distinguished residents, through the years of Canada's history, will all have known the history of their Canadian home but one wonders how many Canadians today realize that the first home of the country was once the residence of a Rideau Canal contractor, that its main fabric was built by masons who laboured on the Canal and, in all probability, on the building of the locks which are so familiar a sight to all Ottawa residents and to visitors to the capital.

Thomas McKay's affection for the district around Bytown is evident in the fact that all his main investments were centred around his big house. With some of the profits from his contracting work, he purchased eleven hundred acres of wild bush land to the east of the settlement. He built his house on the western edge of this forest land, which soon came to be known as "McKay's Bush." One hesitates to mention such a crude name since, under the guidance of Thomas Coltrin Keefer, who married McKay's last remaining daughter, the "Bush" was gradually developed as a special residential district, and was given a new name, Rockcliffe. The engineering significance of the original planning of the roads of this tree-shaded village cannot, however, escape the notice of the residents: such Spanish names as Buena Vista, Acacia, and Mariposa are a direct result of Keefer's engineering work in Mexico. With the other main group of Rockcliffe street names, those of previous Governors-General, they make a strange mixture.

For some years after the completion of the Rideau Canal Thomas McKay continued his work as a masonry contractor. One of his best-known structures was the first Court House for Bytown. This was completed in 1842. The escape of some prisoners, some years after the Court House and associated jail were put into use, led to a further contract for the building of the great stone wall which was for long an unusual feature of this part of Ottawa. It had to be sacrificed when modern town planning resulted in the construction of the Mackenzie King Bridge. Amongst McKay's other varied interests were the big mills which he both built and purchased at the Falls of the Rideau. The last remnants of some of the old buildings still remain as these words are written but they will soon disappear; the Falls will then revert to something like their original unimpaired beauty, although the flow is so greatly decreased. McKay's Mills achieved great fame, blankets made there winning a gold medal in world competition at the Great Exhibition of 1851. McKay was responsible, too, for the bringing of the first railway to Ottawa, or rather to New Edinburgh, for he saw to it that the first line to the Ottawa area came in to a station on Sussex Street. Into this little terminal the first train steamed on Christmas Day, 1854, even though it had to run its last few miles on rails made of maple scantlings since the funds necessary for iron rails had been exhausted. McKay remained, to all older residents of the time, as the man who had done so much in the building of the Rideau Canal, but his public interests steadily extended. He was elected as representative of Russell County in the Legislative Assembly of Upper Canada and served from 1834 to 1841. Following the Act of Union, he was appointed to the Legislative Council of the united Canadas and served there with distinction from 1841 until his death on October 9, 1855.

This grand old man, then, was the builder of the last critical section of the Waterway which has brought us from the St. Lawrence in the wake of the innumerable company who have made the same trip over the century. Shall we now complete that journey by descending the final flight of locks? Being passed down the eighty feet, through the seven locks into the final guard lock, is an unusual experience. It is a slow process, even with the best will in the world on the part of the lockmaster and his men. But time must be forgotten in travel on the Rideau Waterway, and this is not the least of the joys of the journey. There is leisure aplenty to observe again the towers and spires of the Château Laurier and to appreciate anew the stately beauty of the Parliament Buildings, which can be seen from a number of interesting angles as our boat moves on down the locks. We can not expect to see, as once was possible, a train on the C.P.R. coming from the man-made tunnel seemingly in the basement of the Château Laurier, on its way to cross the Interprovincial Bridge into Hull. Major's Hill Park with its splendid rocky look-out, is visible, perched high above the Ottawa at the end of the bridge. But the journey through the locks is soon over. We move slowly out into the waters of the river, our voyage through the Rideau Waterway completed, after more than 120 miles of pleasant wandering through beautiful country, and passage through forty-seven locks, which have lifted us to Upper Rideau Lake and then brought us safely down to the level of the Ottawa.

May I suggest now a further conclusion to the long voyage, which will be a quiet contrast to the dramatic landscape at the end of our passage, but which will bestow a final and fitting memory of the human effort that created the Waterway we now enjoy. Half way up the last flight of locks is a building which may not be noticed as a boat is locked down, so well does its weathered grey stone blend into the landscape around it. Its wooden doorway offers us a journey back in time: for this is the old workshop of the Royal Engineers, the workshop of Colonel By, maintained in many respects in its original condition. Exactly 125 years after the turning of the first sod for the building of the Canal, on September 26, 1951, this fine building was officially turned over by the federal government to the City of Ottawa, which, in turn, leased it to the Women's Canadian Historical Society of Ottawa (its more general title, the Historical Society of Ottawa, was adopted in 1955). This relatively small group of enthusiasts was almost alone in having kept fresh the memory of Colonel By in the city which is so much in his debt. Devoted individuals, in particular the late Hamnett P. Hill, K.C., had worked hard to win recognition for the builder of the Canal, but it required the corporate activity of a group such as the Historical Society to accumulate through the years those relics which could still be found of Colonel By and his associates in Bytown. For many years, these interesting historical objects were crowded into the small old Ottawa Registry Building, but with the taking over of the workshop, the Society at last had an opportunity of displaying its collection. It is now available for all to see during summer months, when members of the Society are present to explain to interested visitors the highlights of the exhibits.

It is the By collection, of course, which will take the attention and imagination of the Rideau traveller. Here is simple furniture which was once used in the house on the opposite hill and some of the smaller domestic fittings such as candlesticks and snuffers. Included also is a little seraphine, a common musical instrument at the time of the canal building, which must have been a pleasant addition to the small household in the forest. There is also a Bible, brought back to Ottawa from England by a former mayor of Ottawa who visited By's grave and final home at Frant. To know that John By used this book is to understand to some degree his fortitude amidst all the trials and difficulties of the construction. Perhaps the most personal of all the exhibits is upstairs, in the small room known as the By room, which overlooks the locks. Here is the Colonel's own chair and here he regularly sat to write those reports on the building which gave meaning, colour, and strength to the stirring history of the Rideau Waterway.

Bytown and Ottawa

OTTAWA is a name now recognized around the world. Its citizens and its guests alike know it to be a young city, striving to keep pace with the steadily increasing demands upon it as the seat of Canada's government, and also as a centre of small but important industrial enterprises. Every part of it is a development of the last century and a third, a short time indeed when compared with the life spans of other capital cities. Its future is assured; its eventual size no man can tell. But however it may develop, its waterways will remain a central feature of its plan. The Chaudière Falls of the Ottawa River and the background of the Laurentian Hills give Ottawa a noble setting; the beauty of its waterways give it special distinction. The Gatineau River bringing wood and power from the hills to the north, the Ottawa River flowing from the northwest and then on to Montreal, and its own twin waterways, the Rideau River and the Rideau Canal, combine to make Ottawa unique amongst the capitals of the world. Even though the Rideau waterways divide the city, with all the complications that bridges bring to traffic and service problems, their quietly flowing waters and tree-shaded pools provide ample compensation. This, then, is the city of today, furnished with all modern conveniences for urban living, the home of more than a third of a million Canadians.

In the heart of this busy city, from the shade of the trees which surround the convenient platform at the doorway of Colonel By's old workshop, we can look out upon almost the same scene as the Superintending Engineer would have seen on summer days over one hundred years ago, provided we ignore the high walls of the Château Laurier and the passage of a train along the shaded track half way up the rocky cliff on the other side of the little valley. The locks look today almost exactly the same as they did when built and the surrounding trees are not dissimilar to those left by the Sappers when they cleared the ground around the site. Facing the workshop then would have been another stone building, similar in appearance, and behind it would have been visible the quarry from which Thomas McKay was obtaining his stone for all the masonry construction in this area. This included not only the buildings but also the big stone arch of the Sappers Bridge, which was in almost the same position as the nearest arch of the great modern structure which now supports the Plaza. That would have been the view looking up to the right, apart from trees and the access road. Ahead, and atop the rock cliff on the other side of the locks, the observer would probably have been able to see the two houses erected for Colonel By and his assistant officers. Down to the left, and to the right of the exit from the locks, there would be a glimpse of the two wharves which had been built first for the ferry service over to Hull, and later for the berthing of the Montreal steamers which came direct to Bytown either to discharge their cargo there, or to pause on their way into the Canal system.

The ground now occupied by the Château Laurier and the adjacent Daly Building, and by the Parliament Buildings, constituted at this time the two main cleared areas at the top of the hill. The first was the chief workshop area, the service yard for the entire Canal project, complete with small buildings, mostly of logs, for the use of blacksmiths and other craftsmen. The clearing on the brow of the great hill to the west of the Canal had three stone barracks, with the military hospital building—another fine stone structure—near by. From the earliest days, the ground around these military buildings was carefully tended. A cedar picket fence was soon erected around the reserved area and we are told that it was used as a sort of park by the earliest residents. Fortunately it is still so used now that the Parliament Buildings of Canada have replaced the simple low-lying stone buildings of the original encampment of the Royal Engineers and the Royal Sappers and Miners. This was but one of innumerable ways in which the building of the Canal paved the way, first for the building of the village of Bytown but eventually, and just as certainly, for the great modern city of today. As we have travelled along the Waterway, we have had occasion to consider the influence of the Canal upon the development of some of the attractive towns and villages on the route. At the end of this journey we find a splendid climax in the change which has transformed a simple construction camp into the national capital of the Dominion of the North.

When Colonel By arrived to start work on the Rideau Canal, in the early fall of 1826, the high rugged south bank was completely tree covered (old records show that beech trees and hemlocks predominated) and still untouched apart from the few narrow lines cut for the first surveys and the isolated clearings of the first settlers. Six houses only, with several log cabins, made up the full register of buildings in 1826 for the entire townships of Gloucester and Nepean. Ira Honeywell had been the original settler, clearing for himself an area on the Ottawa River at Britannia Bay. He was followed by Bradish Billings with his home on the Rideau River. Captain Wilson was establishing himself in Ossian Hall. Down at the Richmond Landing, Caleb Bellows had built a small dock and store; the point was even known to some as Bellows Point. Not far away was the log cabin of Ralph Smith whose chief distinction is that he built the first still on the south shore and with it made the first whisky to be distilled in this part of Upper Canada. Isaac Firth operated a small inn at the landing; he had come over from Yorkshire to marry Miss Dalmahoy, a remarkable young Scots woman who had arrived in 1818 at the foot of the Chaudière Falls, alone, after a long journey from Edinburgh by way of London, Quebec, and Montreal. She was a milliner, and her fame in making black otter caps for the workers on the Canal was rivalled only by the conviviality of the entertainment at the Inn, known far and wide as "Mother Firth's." Finally, there was Nicholas Sparks, a young Irishman who had saved enough to enable him to purchase a large area of land between the landing and the valley which was soon to be used for the start of the Canal.

Much of the forest land was owned by absentee landlords: we know that in November 1826 three of them, together with Bradish Billings and Nicholas Sparks, offered to Colonel By such parts of their estates as might be required for the building of the Canal, without requesting any payment for the land. They were probably wise enough to see how the Canal would lead to the development of this untouched area though the actual development of even the next six years must have far exceeded their calculations. Sparks must have been the most surprised man of

all. He had already found that his land was not too good for
farming. With the start of the Canal, however, he subdivided
some of it and was soon disposing of lots at what must have
seemed ridiculous but exhilarating prices. Today, the original
Sparks property is assessed at over one hundred million dollars!
Colonel By accepted the offer of the land, when the route of the
Canal had been fixed, requesting two hundred feet on either side
of the line of the Waterway for necessary bank development.
This was the real beginning of the town planning which the
Superintending Engineer pursued so vigorously, and which has
shaped the growth of central Ottawa over the years.

The land had actually been examined with a view to development a few years before the start of the Canal, on the instructions
of the Earl of Dalhousie, who had in mind the building of a
strongly fortified town to defend this critical point on the water
route to the West up the Ottawa. Major Elliot reported to the
Governor-General in 1824 that a village could be laid out in what
is now Lower Town and he did prepare a plan, but he found the
land so swampy and overgrown with thick bush that he was
unable to penetrate it in order to conduct the necessary surveys.
Had these early plans been carried out, Parliament Hill might
have been the site of a military fortress. Before any action could
be taken, however, the decision to build the Rideau Canal had
been made and so all planning was made subservient to the immediate needs of the construction of the Waterway. Lord Dalhousie's continuing interest in the sound development of the
land around the Canal is shown in the instructions which he gave
to Colonel By in the form of a letter written while he was at Hull
on September 26, 1826. Since this letter is the real charter for
the planning of Ottawa and surely one of the earliest statements
regarding town planning in Canada, it may properly be quoted in
the context of our consideration of the influence of the Canal on
Bytown and Ottawa:

These [lots] not only contain the site for the head locks, but they offer a
valuable locality for a considerable village or town for the lodging of
artificers and other necessary assistants in so great a work. I propose that
these should be clearly surveyed and laid out in lots of two to four acres,
to be granted according to the means of settlers and to pay a ground rent
of 2/6d per annum to the Crown annually. The location to contain the
positive condition of building a house within twelve months from the date
of the ticket and to place the house on the line of streets according to plan

to be made of it. Allow me to caution you against the immediate rush of applicants for these lots that will be made. Make particular inquiries as to individuals and others before you consent to their petitions. It will be highly desirable to encourage half pay officers and respectable people should they offer to build on these lots. As the purchase was made by me for the public services and has already been approved, I place the whole in your hands for the purpose I have now explained.

They proved to be capable hands. Colonel By immediately reserved the main areas of land on both sides of the entrance locks for military purposes and so Parliament Hill and Major's Hill Park were secured for public use for all time. He laid out the main streets which he saw to be necessary, arranging with Nicholas Sparks that he would give a strip of land 66 feet wide adjacent to a strip 33 feet wide on the government's property; he thus ensured the broad streets which we know today as Wellington and Rideau Streets, roadways much wider than one finds in most pioneer communities. The land required for these initial streets, as well as for Queen Street and Sussex Street, was cleared to By's direction by the men of the Royal Sappers and Miners. As early as 1831, arrangements were made for these roads to be maintained by statute labour. The earliest plans of Bytown, drawn up while the Canal was still under construction, show Rideau Street as running from the locks as far as the Rideau River, and Wellington Street connecting the locks with the crossing of the Chaudière. Bridges were therefore obviously an early necessity.

We have already seen something of the building of the great Union Bridge across the Chaudière, the precursor of the motley collection of bridges to be seen there today. There was another gully to be crossed on the south shore in order to give connection with Wellington Street. The job of constructing this further bridge was entrusted to Lieutenant Pooley and the bridge he built, in the first instance of large cedar logs, soon came to carry his name; the name is perpetuated in Pooley Street. A bridge was also necessary to connect Wellington with Rideau Street. The building of a permanent structure at this location was therefore one of the first masonry contracts to be executed at the site of the locks; indeed the familiar Sappers Bridge was completed before the locks themselves. It continued to serve as the vital link between Upper Town and Lower Town from 1827 until 1912, when it was finally demolished to make way for a modern and larger structure. There were many Ottawa residents who were sorry to see it go. Some can still remember the remarkable difficulty which was experienced in removing it, so solid was the stone work and so well set the mortar. Blasting, with all the limitations of the crowded site, proved to be ineffective. The bridge was finally demolished by dropping very heavy weights on it, and its final collapse drew many thrilled spectators. The wide bridge of Confederation Square replaced it: so wide as finally extended that many who cross it must be unaware that they are on a bridge until they notice the Canal on both sides still leading to the locks.

Applications for the new building lots in the town came in just as Lord Dalhousie had expected. Colonel By obtained permission to make much smaller lots in view of the demand. The rental was increased; and the leases in perpetuity were soon changed. Within the first two years, almost one hundred and fifty houses had been built, grouped in the two areas even then known as Upper Town and Lower Town. The name Bytown, incidentally, seems to have been given to the little settlement in the first instance almost as a joke. It was apparently used in a jocular reference at a small dinner party of some of the officers engaged upon the construction, held in 1827. Clearly, however, the name was quickly adopted for general use for it is found in official correspondence and in all the references of visitors from early in 1828. Fortunately, we have an account of the little settlement at this time from one of these visitors, Bouchette, who was at Bytown in the summer of 1828. "The streets are laid out with much regularity, and of a liberal width that will hereafter contribute to the convenience, salubrity and elegance of the place. The number of houses now built is about 150, most of which are constructed of wood; frequently in a style of neatness and taste that reflects great credit upon the Inhabitants. On the elevated banks of the Bay, the Hospital, an extensive stone building, and three Barracks stand conspicuous; nearly on a level with them, and on the eastern side of the Bay, is the residence of Colonel By, Commanding Royal Engineer at that Station." In addition to homes and structures of stone, there were also a few shanties in what came to be known as Corktown, a settlement which grew up along the sides of the Deep Cut, made up of some of the Irish workmen who were responsible for much of the essential hand labour which actually built the Canal. By the time the Canal was

opened, in 1832, the population of Bytown was almost 1,500.
Thereafter, despite doubts as to the possibility of any permanent
town developing at this end of the Canal, the increasing timber
trade down the Ottawa, the Gatineau, and the Rideau Rivers
supported a slow but steady growth in numbers. By the year 1880
the population had reached about 25,000 but the opening of the
rail route to the West and allied events seem to have acted as a
catalyst since the rate of growth suddenly increased. Today, as
we have said, Ottawa has over a quarter of a million people.

There are many tales to be told with regard to the way in
which land was passed from one owner to the other—operations
which have been giving the legal fraternity of Ottawa much
tedious but profitable work ever since. Under the terms of the
Rideau Canal Act, for example, Colonel By obtained from
Nicholas Sparks an additional area of land between the Canal and
Bank Street, and from Laurier Avenue to Wellington Street. It
was intended for a military use, By being always concerned
about the defence of the works he was constructing. Eventually
it became clear that the land would not be needed for military
purposes and it was subdivided. Protracted legal negotiations
then began, on the grounds that the Act permitted the expropri-
ation of land for the construction of the Canal only, and not for
strictly military purposes. The area was returned to the Sparks
Estate in 1848, and it is this land which has become the business
centre of Ottawa.

Not nearly so familiar to the people of the capital as the transfer of the Sparks property is the fact that, just before he returned
to England in 1832, Colonel By himself purchased a large area,
lying to the south of the Sparks property. For £1,200 he obtained
the land which now lies between Bronson Avenue on the west
and the Rideau River on the east, and from Laurier Avenue to
Gladstone Avenue, a total of six hundred acres. The purchase has
a melancholy aspect since it is almost certain that John By bought
this land only because he expected to return one day to the
country with which his career had been so closely involved. This
was not to be, and the estate was managed by one of his faithful
assistants who did stay in Bytown, John Burrows. When all the
members of John By's family died so tragically soon, the estate
passed to his brother, Henry By, and from him, in turn, to a
distant cousin, Charles William By, who at the time he was
adjudged to be the rightful heir to the estate was a waterman on

the River Thames in England. He arranged for it to be handled by trustees, in whose care it remained for almost forty years, but in 1878 all that remained was sold and so the final connection with Colonel By disappeared. Even this tale of normal property transfer has its special feature. Charles By had a sister, one of whose sons, in his wanderings around the world, chanced to come to Ottawa where he learned that there had been a change in the laws of Upper Canada which seemed to give him some grounds for a claim to share the By estate with his uncle. He was poor and unable to obtain the assistance of a lawyer so in desperation he used squatter's rights, settling down on a vacant part of the By property and demanding rent from all the tenants. The resulting legal tangle can be imagined; it finished up before no less a man than young Edward Blake, then at the start of his career in Toronto, and was referred to a former Chief Justice of Canada. Charles William By was found to be the legal heir.

Let me hasten to say that this strange legal complexity seems to have been the only unfortunate legacy to Ottawa from Colonel By. Much that he did laid the foundation for many of the features which make Ottawa the attractive city of today. We have already seen that the basic city plan follows the lines originally laid down by him to the instructions of the Earl of Dalhousie, but the planning of the Superintending Engineer did not stop at a street lay-out. As early as August 1829, he had spent £160 of his rental income for the building of a market place and a market building on what is now Lyon Street. Those who wonder why the small section of this street between Wellington and Sparks Street is so wide can be told that the Canal and Colonel By are to be thanked for a minor feature of Ottawa that is today proving to be fortunate in connection with the erection of major governmental buildings. The tradition of a country market has persisted strongly in Ottawa ever since; the Bytown Market of today is one of the very few uses of the name of Colonel By in the city.

Municipal services of over a century ago were meagre in the extreme but it is on record that a regular water supply was arranged by the men of the Royal Sappers and Miners after drilling on Barracks Hill, as it was then known, had failed to reveal any underground water supply at convenient depth. Water was hauled by cart every day, in four or five trips up from the river, by six men. When the men were not available, the Barrack Sergeant had to purchase his supply. This was probably obtained from the "By-wash" which ran out of the beaver meadow at the head of the locks, since a pump was installed there at an early date to obtain water from this convenient but rather dubious source of supply. In those days there would be little question as to the quality of the water; the population was so small that the disposal of rubbish and of sewage was no real problem with the Ottawa River close at hand. In this one respect, no progress can yet be reported despite the intervening century since Ottawa still discharges all its sewage into the handy Ottawa River. Nevertheless let it be said quickly in reassurance that public health is of vital concern to modern civic authorities. Actually the beginning of public health activity can also be traced back to the Canal, if not exactly to its building then certainly to the aftermath of building, for on June 20, 1832, a few days after the Canal had been officially opened, a Board of Health for Bytown was appointed by the Governor to deal with the scourge of cholera which was then sweeping Upper and Lower Canada. With very few breaks, there have been similar boards for Bytown and Ottawa ever since.

Fire prevention, as might be expected, has also a long and honourable history. In his progress report for October 26, 1827, Colonel By mentions the expenditure of £127-15-0 for necessary expenses for extinguishing a "fire in the woods in the immediate vicinity of the Public Buildings and Storehouses." Fire was to be a constant worry, although fortunately Bytown escaped the devastation which wiped out so many small pioneer communities. Bad fires did occur. One completely destroyed the first place of worship built in Bytown, a Methodist chapel in the vicinity of the modern Chapel Street. In Upper Town a small fire engine was purchased by a group of citizens and kept in a shed on a piece of ground donated by Nicholas Sparks (at the corner of Lyon and Queen Streets)—the modest forerunner of the Ottawa Fire Service of today which has such an enviable record.

Another municipal service, originally operated locally but now a federal responsibility, was the handling of the mail. It was owing to the construction of the Canal that Matthew Connell was appointed as the first postmaster of Bytown on April 6, 1829; up to that time mail for Colonel By and his officers had been delivered in Hull and then ferried across the river. The first post office was located on what is now the north side of Rideau Street, near Sussex Street, adjacent to one of the barracks buildings.

In other aspects of life, related to culture, we find the same pattern of a modest start by those responsible for the building of the Canal of features which distinguish the life of the Ottawa of today. Education was always difficult in pioneer communities; Bytown, however, had an early lead in this field. Even before the start of the Canal, Charlotte Honeywell was teaching all the children who could reach the pioneer home which she had created with her husband Ira. In 1827 there were two little private schools in Bytown. One was operated by a Miss Napps, of whom little is known, but the other was the first school of James Maloney, one of the great figures in early Canadian education. There are definite records of these two little schools, even though they are not mentioned in the report of the redoubtable Archdeacon Strachan who had been appointed Superintendent of Education for Upper Canada in 1824 and who visited Bytown in the late fall of 1828, making the long and hazardous journey from Kingston in performance of his duties of inspection. Knowing what we do of Colonel By, it is interesting to speculate on what must have transpired when he met his archidiaconal visitor from Muddy York.

James Maloney was an Irishman "of good education and address." How he came to settle in the construction camp that was to become Bytown, soon after the start of work, the records do not show but I suspect that he was invited by Colonel By in view of the need for schooling for his own two little girls. A fleeting reference in an old book about life in the Ottawa Valley lends some support to this conjecture, and the references to Maloney in By's letters are further warrant for imagining that the Colonel was indeed the patron of the little school. It started out in a building on Rideau Street, near the By-wash, and was called the "English Mercantile and Mathematical Academy." These first quarters must have been temporary only for as soon as arrangements for the disposition of lots were completed, Maloney was offered a conveniently located lot (the area now occupied by the Roman Catholic Basilica) for the usual sum of half a crown. He refused it and chose to remain somewhat farther away from the vicinity of the Canal works. The location which Maloney did select was at what is now 112 Clarence Street, and there his school remained until his death in 1879. Throughout all these years, Maloney went on teaching, refusing all the possibilities which a move to one of the larger centres would have given to him.

He was taken in to the public system of education when the first Board of Education was appointed by the municipality of Bytown, so that his instruction went on without a break. That Maloney was still teaching at a time when some Ottawa residents of today were young children is a vivid reminder of the short life of the great city—there is almost a personal connection with the years of the building of the Canal.

Even in the early days, education was not regarded as a necessity merely for some children. The spirit of the little community is shown in the fact that Maloney also held night classes, starting at five in the afternoon and continuing until nine o'clock in the evening—a tradition maintained today in the large classes to be found at the main Ottawa schools every winter evening. Higher education was also a matter of public concern as clearly shown by an extract from the *Bytown Gazette* for January 16, 1840. "We are not a little surprised to observe that the seat of the Scotch College has been selected in the vicinity of Kingston. Being designed for the accommodation of both provinces, this institution ought to have been placed in as central a position as possible; so why not in Bytown? In the constitution of the Kirk there is already a sufficient spice of Republicanism, so why not place the seat for educating her future Ministers as remote as possible from the contagion of Democratic principles?" I have never yet dared to ask a Queen's graduate his opinion of this sprightly suggestion.

As with education, so with the arts. We know that John By himself was musical, from the little seraphine in the Bytown Museum. There are incidental references to music in many of the old letters and records but no definite indication of any corporate activity until some years after the completion of the Canal. With the theatre, the record is more specific. The first theatrical performance in Bytown was given on February 6 and 7, 1837, when soldiers from the 15th Regiment, stationed in the barracks by the Canal (many of them had probably worked on its building), presented *The Village Lawyer*. One of the rooms in the barracks was arranged as a little theatre; this was almost within a stone's throw from the hall which has been used in recent years for the performances of the Canadian Repertory Theatre. The standard of acting must certainly have improved in the interval: the young soldiers acted all the parts, male and female. But the military association with the theatre was no isolated incident. The companies of Royal Engineers who pioneered some years later in opening up the new province of British Columbia showed similar interests beyond their notable survey and construction work. Amongst other things they were responsible for the first plays performed on Canada's Pacific Coast; again all the parts were played by young men, recently out from England by way of the long sail round the Horn. Canada's own *Dumbbells* of the First World War were clearly following in an established tradition.

The care of men's bodies had, of course, to be given equal attention from the start. One of the first buildings to be erected by Colonel By on Barracks Hill was a military hospital with twenty beds. Civilian patients were admitted to it whenever possible, and civilian doctors were permitted to attend them. Hospitals have had an honoured role in the life of Ottawa ever since this early beginning. The first special isolation hospital was hurriedly erected, on the site of the present Public Archives Building, in the summer of 1832 to provide for those afflicted with cholera; it was dismantled within a few years. The first regular civilian hospital was started in 1845 by four devoted nuns sent to Bytown from Montreal, at the request of Bishop Phelan of Kingston. Thus began the history of the Ottawa General Hospital, and a few years later began the correspondingly long story of the Civic Hospital with the admission in 1852 of the first patient to a small hospital building at the corner of Wurtemburg and Rideau Streets.

Burial was a real problem in the early days of the settlement. Until 1828, the bodies of those who died in Bytown had to be ferried across the Ottawa to the graveyard in Hull. So many deaths occurred in 1828, however, caused by the first inroads of the dreaded swamp fever, that some other arrangement had to be made. A lot of land was therefore set apart from the military reserve for use as a burial ground. It had an area of half an acre and was bounded by what are today Elgin, Metcalfe, Queen and Sparks Streets. This area was divided into three parts, for Anglicans, Presbyterians, and Roman Catholics respectively, and served these groups for many years until the steady development of the central part of the city necessitated its removal.

There was at least one early burial in Bytown, however, in what must have been unhallowed ground. Another Burrowes on Colonel By's staff was Thomas Burrowes who became Assistant Overseer of Works. He had come up from Worcester, Mass., and was recommended to By by his own commandant at Quebec,

Colonel Durnford. Thomas Burrowes arrived at Hull on September 23, 1826, and quickly got to work. He arranged for his wife to follow him up the Ottawa River and although she was expecting a child she made the difficult journey. She arrived on November 22, and was installed by her husband in a log cabin. There, three days later, she had her fourth baby, a son, the first child to be born in Bytown. Unhappily, he survived only until June 27 of the next year; the site of his necessarily simple grave was selected by the ever helpful MacTaggart.

The religious life of early Bytown seems to have benefited to an unusual degree from the calibre of the men associated with the building of the Canal. They were God-fearing men who took their religious duties seriously. John Burrows was one who gave the lead in seeing that a place of worship was available, soon after construction work started. He was an early settler in the vicinity of the Richmond Landing, who had come there in 1819 from England because of his strong religious and political views. He was a Methodist and a Whig, an unpopular combination in the early years of the last century. In his log cabin near the Falls of the Chaudière, he expected to lead an isolated life, and to assist his anonymity he changed his name from John Burrows Honey by dropping his surname. He was a well-trained young man and a good worker and when Colonel By arrived, John Burrows was one of the first of the local residents to offer his services. He was gladly accepted and became one of John By's most trusted assistants. It was in his hands that the Colonel put the management of his estate when he left Bytown, a clear indication of his esteem. Burrows' simple diary is now one of the treasures of the Bytown Museum and it is to be hoped that the notes of this good man and keen observer may one day be published. He remained in the employ of the Royal Engineers until his death in 1848; his descendants have made notable contributions to the later development of Ottawa.

With the sudden influx of men for the Canal work, John Burrows could no longer pursue his life as a hermit. He knew the strength which can come from corporate worship and so organized a small Methodist congregation, building in 1827 at his own expense a little chapel on Rideau Street near what is now Chapel Street. For some time this was the only place of worship in Bytown. Regular services were held from 1827. John Burrows found a lay preacher, in the person of Sergeant Coombs of the

Royal Engineers, to assist him in the simple services. It was this chapel which was the casualty in the early fire and it had to be rebuilt, on a new site on Sparks Street. When a stone building was erected, the site was changed again, this time to the corner of Metcalfe and Queen Streets; Dominion United Church is the direct descendant of this first church of Bytown. The Presbyterians were not far behind the Methodists, however, as was to be expected with so many Scottish masons in Bytown for work on the Canal. They, too, organized themselves into a congregation and soon acquired a site from Nicholas Sparks, a site still in use by the congregation of St. Andrews. For the first St. Andrews Church they were favoured by being able to plan more than the usual wooden chapel; a solid structure of stone was built for worship by the masons engaged on the locks in time that could be spared from the Canal work or when the weather was inclement. Thomas McKay undertook supervision of the work and he donated all the stone, no small gift since the building measured 55 by 45 feet. It served its congregation until January 1872, when the fine stone church still in use today was built.

The Anglicans already had a small church in Hull when the first work on the Canal was begun and during the early months those in Bytown who wished to worship would go over on Sundays to Hull. In May 1828, however, their chapel was very kindly made available by the Methodists for the use of the Anglicans, who numbered by that time between two and three hundred people. They then started regular services every Sunday at nine in the morning, before the regular Methodist service. The two companies of the Royal Sappers and Miners regularly marched from their barracks to the chapel, and in winter time piled their snowshoes outside the little church. The services were conducted by the resident minister in Hull. Such co-operation between the various Christian denominations was not unique in these pioneer communities, and has revived today in a different form in the steady development of the ecumenical movement. The *Perth Independent Advertiser*, in June 1829, gives news items from the several congregations at Bytown and applauds their spirit: "Each of these places of worship [in Bytown] has been built by public subscription, and it is a just tribute to the liberality of religious feelings in Bytown (the surest test of a Christian's principles) to state that those of the different persuasions have mutually contributed to aid each other in this object."

There was much discussion about the building of a permanent

Anglican Church, discussion which was only heightened when Nicholas Sparks donated a site on the promontory overlooking Richmond Landing. This site was regarded as too remote from the town and in their annoyance some Anglicans refused to pay their share of the building costs. Sparks was so anxious to get the church erected that he even paid the shares of the delinquents. It required a visit of the eminent Archdeacon Mountain, on a special mission from Quebec City, to get the matter settled. The church was completed, despite all difficulties, and was soon found to be too small for the congregations which wished to attend, even though two services were held consecutively. In 1839, the incumbent petitioned the government to provide money for an enlargement or, as an alternative, to pay for the transport every Sunday to Hull of the troops of the garrison, who formed a large part of his congregation—it had to be done by ferry since the Union Bridge had collapsed and had not been replaced. An enlargement was built and dedicated in 1843, and this original building was eventually replaced in 1872 by the present Cathedral, the east window of which is a memorial to Nicholas Sparks.

Archdeacon Mountain made the long journey to Bytown by way of Montreal, Cornwall, and Hawkesbury. From Cornwall to the Ottawa River he rode on horseback and so came through Glengarry. There he called on the first Roman Catholic bishop in Upper Canada, Bishop Macdonell, who received him most kindly "giving directions, in Gaelic, to his people." Bishop Macdonell must also have been a visitor to Bytown; he contributed a letter of appreciation to the Foreword of John MacTaggart's book in which he writes of his conversations with Colonel By. A native of Glen Urquhart, Scotland, he was educated in Spain, but later organized and served as chaplain in the Glengarry Fencibles, a Catholic Highland regiment which had duty in Ireland. In 1804 he had come out to Glengarry, Upper Canada, with several hundred Highland settlers. Appointment as Bishop of Kingston or Regiopolis in 1826 brought to his care a widely scattered flock but he devoted to it faithful and warm-hearted service. He died back in his own Scotland in 1840 and was buried in St. Mary's Church in Edinburgh, but in 1862, so affectionately was he remembered, his remains were brought back to Canada; on its way to the final interment in the Roman Catholic Cathedral in Kingston, the cortege stopped for homage at familiar points such as Lancaster and Cornwall all along the St. Lawrence.

It was under Bishop Macdonell's guidance that Mass was celebrated for the first time in Bytown in 1827, in a house at the north end of Bank Street, by Rev. Father Heron who was stationed at Richmond. On September 7, 1828, a delegation headed by the Bishop interviewed Colonel By with a request for a suitable lot for the eventual building of a church, a request which was readily granted. As they had no place for worship, the Roman Catholic congregation used a weigh house in Wellington Street and made some progress towards the start of a church in this vicinity. It was finally decided to change the location to Lower Town, where most of the Roman Catholics of Bytown were then living. Colonel By assisted this further move by the grant for the land upon which the Basilica now stands, together with the necessary area for the ancillary buildings. The first wooden church was opened for regular services in 1832. The present building was started in 1841 and so is one of the oldest structures in Ottawa, its twin spires having long been an easily recognized feature of the Ottawa skyline.

The first Baptist congregation was organized only a few years after the four churches already mentioned; services began in 1844 and a Baptist Meeting House was opened in 1845. In keeping with the traditions of the Baptist communion, a public baptism was held shortly after the regular services had been started, and the chosen location was the Rideau Canal, near the turning basin which had been excavated in the beaver meadow. The solemn service was unfortunately marred by the behaviour of youths who gathered on the other bank of the Canal and rudely interrupted the proceedings; their action put an end to this most unusual use of the waters of the Rideau.

This account of the establishment of distinguishing features of the life of the community on the Ottawa has centred around the years when the Canal was built and those just after its opening. We should now move on to a later period. But before we leave "Bytown" for "Ottawa," let me complete the early record by a story about the final flight of locks. One of the most intriguing, if rarely profitable, pastimes of those interested in history is to speculate on the "Ifs" of history, and there is a big "If" in connection with this section of the Canal which will encourage such musing.

The story starts at a dinner which was given in the tiny military settlement of Richmond in the year 1820 by the half-pay

officers then starting their residence there, with the Earl of Dalhousie as their guest. They urged upon him the necessity of a
warehouse at the Richmond Landing on the Ottawa, where their
goods often lay about for some days after discharge from the
boats from Montreal. The land was owned by Robert Randall.
The Governor immediately made known his intention to purchase
the land for this constructive use. Present at the dinner was a
Captain John Le Breton. He later claimed that he knew nothing
of the Governor's stated intention but the fact remained that he
purchased all the land in question from Randall, when he heard
that it was to come up for sheriff's sale in December of the same
year. He paid £499 for it and then proceeded to offer it to the
government at a price of £3,000. The Governor was understand-
ably annoyed. Le Breton was unofficially accused of breach of
trust and appears to have been black-listed in official circles. We
shall never know the true facts of the case since the records which
remain are to some extent conflicting. The balance of the evidence
is certainly in the direction indicated by the attitude of the
Governor-General and this view is substantiated to a degree by
the fact that the early settlers at the Richmond Landing, the
Firths with their inn and Caleb Bellows with his little store,
refused to move off or to pay any rent at all to Le Breton.

The legal aspects of the purchase were debated at length and
with them we are not concerned; the land itself has long been
subdivided and is today an undistinguished part of industrial
Ottawa. What does concern us is the consequence of this trans-
action when the time came to plan the Rideau Canal. Lord
Dalhousie did not make the same mistake twice. He arranged to
purchase the land leading up from Entrance Bay, upon which it was
decided to build the flight of locks, from Hugh Fraser of Three
Rivers, before any public announcement was made so that no
land speculation could recur. He awaited the arrival of Colonel
By and they jointly examined the ground in September 1826,
before the final decision was made to place the entrance of the
Canal where it is today. In those discussions, it is almost certain
that one possibility was ruled out from the start: to take off from
the Ottawa River at the spot used by all early travellers on the
south bank, at the Richmond Landing. There would have been
difficulties in construction, but it was only two miles from Richmond Landing to Dows Great Swamp so that a considerable
length of canal could have been saved. If Captain Le Breton had

not been present at that dinner, if he had not asked such a pre-
posterous price for a small area of cleared forest land at the foot
of the Chaudière Falls, the Canal might have followed this other
route, along approximately the line of Bronson Avenue today.

The historical "If" continues. If the Canal had followed this
alternative route it is almost certain that a short connection between this route and the Ottawa River *above* the Chaudière
Falls would also have been constructed. This was so obvious a
connection that it was frequently mentioned in the early reports.
MacTaggart assumed in his reports to Colonel By that it would
be made. It was certainly officially considered, for Sir John
Colborne reported in a dispatch dated February 7, 1832, that the
branch to Lac Deschenes had actually been planned but that the
Imperial government had decided that it was not needed. And
there the matter rested; the short spur was never built. The
trouble which developed over the cost of the Rideau Canal itself,
the slow but gradual decrease in the military significance of the
Canal, and the subsequent growth of interest in other means of
transportation all combined to make this small additional piece of
canal construction more and more problematical. Had it been
built—a prolongation again of the historical "if"—the fate of the
much studied Georgian Bay Ship Canal might quite well have
been other than it was. The abortive attempt to build a canal at
Quyon, around the great Chat rapids at the north end of Lac
Deschenes, would then have had some meaning. The alternative
route would of course have meant that the entire planning of the
city of Ottawa as we know it today would have been changed,
with the foot of Bronson Avenue possibly the heart of the nation's
capital instead of the square affectionately, but facetiously, known
to Ottawans as Confusion Square, and to the world more properly
as Confederation Square, hallowed as the site of Canada's
National War Memorial, the hub of Ottawa's busy traffic and
found where it is just because it is at "the head of the locks."

The "If" remains now merely as an interesting conjecture. The
Canal was planned and constructed as it is now to be seen, and
the excitement of its building and opening was succeeded by the
steady mercantile progress of Bytown as a centre for the entire
Ottawa Valley, through which passed the traffic of the Canal and
the timber of the Ottawa forests on its way to the markets of the
Old World. Gradually the signs of construction headquarters disappeared as the temporary buildings were removed and the more

permanent ones were assigned to other purposes. The barracks buildings remained for many years, however, and were used by the troops who were stationed in Bytown to maintain the Rideau Canal until in 1853 it ceased to be regarded as a military water-way. The Superintending Engineer of the Canal continued to occupy the house erected by Colonel By for his own use; Major Bolton lived in it after By's recall to England, followed by Major Thomson who was its occupant when a fire destroyed the entire building in 1861. Although the troops were stationed here for military purposes, there were many civic calls upon them for assistance in maintaining the peace. On one occasion at least they were turned out to assist the local magistrates. Politics were taken seriously in those days but disturbances in Bytown seem slight when compared to those in other Canadian cities such as the riots in Montreal in 1849 over the Rebellion Losses Bill, dis-orders which contributed, in some degree, to the eventual decision to move the capital of the country to Ottawa as the young Do-minion came into being.

Bytown's maturity came fully into public view when, on February 8, 1853, a petition was presented to the Executive Coun-cil praying that the name of the town be changed to Ottawa and that the status of a city be given to the settlement. This first request was not granted; a second request made in September 1854 was agreed to, and the necessary Act was passed on Decem-ber 18 of that year in Quebec City. On January 1, 1855, the name originally bestowed almost jocularly in 1827 was given up for all time and replaced by Ottawa. The modern city was born. Even before the change in name, the Bytown Council had brought to the attention of the Executive Council the advantages of Bytown as the site of the national capital, following the disastrous fire which had destroyed the Parliament Buildings in Quebec City with their many valuable records. So began the long argument as to where the capital of Canada should be, an argument only settled finally by a direct appeal to Queen Victoria.

In the complex, but fascinating, tangle of the political ma-noeuvrings connected with this argument, it would be tempting to lose oneself, but our main concern must continue to be the Canal. It does have a place, however, in the story of the choosing of the capital. All Canadians are familiar with the pleasant anecdote of how Lady Head, wife of the Governor, was so im-pressed by the beauty of Ottawa that she made a sketch while taking lunch on Major's Hill, under canvas, and sent this to the Queen; the sketch has been held to be responsible to some degree for the Queen's decision. What was probably more helpful to Her Majesty was the confidential dispatch on the topic from Sir Edmund Head himself. It contains, for instance, a strong military argument based on the fact that the location of Ottawa was remote from the American border. Sir Edmund and his advisers were much concerned about the difficulties of defending Canada in the event of an attack from the south, with the few troops at their disposal. It is not surprising, therefore, to find his argument finishing with the statement that "Stores and troops could be sent to Ottawa either from Quebec or Kingston, without exposure on the St. Lawrence to the American frontier." The original purpose of the Rideau Canal thus came into its own again, as a factor in a vital discussion. Another argument of Sir Edmund Head also refers to the Rideau Canal though His Excellency admitted that it was a "secondary consideration": ". . . the Rideau Canal, now handed over to the Provincial Government, would probably increase its traffic, and become more productive by the transfer of the seat of Government to Ottawa. At present, this great work is a dead loss so far as money is concerned. . . ." We can be reasonably sure that Ottawa was not selected as the national capital merely to provide a little more traffic for the Rideau Canal but it is not unreasonable to suppose that the military argument did weigh heavily with those who had the responsibility of advising Queen Victoria on the decision which she had to render for her North American outpost.

In the vigorous years, then, of the opening up of the Ottawa Valley and of the great reaches of Canada beyond, "Bytown" became "Ottawa" and the capital city and thus part of the national story. Further careful planning after the start given by the Earl of Dalhousie and the first Superintending Engineer has transformed the "sub-Arctic village converted by royal mandate into a political cock-pit" of Goldwin Smith, into Sir Wilfrid Laurier's dream of a "Washington of the North." The name "Bytown" has gone from official records, except to describe the market place now used by neighbouring countryfolk for the street sale of their produce, and as the name of one of Ottawa's small hotels and of four local commercial enterprises.

The visitor will naturally ask, "But what of Colonel By, the founder of the city?" He may well ask the question for a founder has seldom been so neglected by those who have reaped the benefit of his work. All that could be pointed out until the year 1954 was a cube of granite well hidden in the garden by the side of the Canal, immediately on the south side of the Plaza bridges, with By's name engraved upon it. It was unveiled in 1932, with due ceremony, as the foundation for a statue of Colonel By which it was hoped would be erected at a later date. A model of the statue was actually made but nothing was done for twenty years more. Then, in 1953, the Ottawa Branch of the Engineering Institute of Canada became concerned over this neglect of a fellow engineer. With the sympathetic interest of the Engineering Institute itself, of the Historic Sites and Monuments Board of the federal government, of the Federal District Commission, and of the City of Ottawa, plans were slowly developed for the erection of a suitable monument, a simple one such as would have appealed to Colonel By himself. On October 5, 1955, in the presence of a distinguished civil and military gathering, and saluted, fittingly, by an honour guard of the Royal Canadian Engineers, this memorial was unveiled. It stood in a garden plot near the head of the locks and exactly on the site of the beaver meadow which helped Colonel By so much in his early construction. Dignity and interest had been added by the incorporation of a fountain of red granite from Aberdeenshire, made up from parts of the two original fountains which were erected in Trafalgar Square shortly after the Rideau Canal was completed and which served in the heart of London for over a century. Because of recent major building projects in this part of Ottawa, the memorial had to be moved from this most appropriate location and placed in temporary storage; it is intended to re-establish it in Major's Hill Park.

In 1954, under the guidance of the Chief Magistrate of Ottawa, Dr. Charlotte Whitton, herself an historian of note, the name of Colonel By was at last restored to public use in the city of Ottawa. During the visit to Ottawa of Her Majesty the Queen Mother, the old road down from Hog's Back, past Hartwells Locks, to Dows Lake was named the Colonel By Drive by the royal visitor. The new bridges just above the Falls of the Rideau were similarly named, by the Queen Mother, the Bytown Bridges (the name is inscribed on a suitable tablet). Colonel By thus began to catch up with his own officers and his contractors whose names have been officially used for many years in the city of Ottawa. Major's Hill Park, for example, is named after Major

Bolton, the second resident of the house Colonel By built for his own use. Major Bolton is remembered also in Bolton Street, as are Lieutenant Colonel Boteler and Lieutenant Pooley in streets which carry their names. Contractors are commemorated in Drummond, Redpath, and McKay Streets. The special interest of Thomas McKay in New Edinburgh is shown by the naming of a number of streets in that locality after members of his family: Creighton Street bears his wife's maiden name and Charles, John, and Thomas Streets those of three of his sons. Civilian employees of the Canal were not forgotten: there are McTaggart Street (spelled incorrectly, unfortunately) and streets bearing the names of Clegg (one of the senior paymasters), Cooper, and Slater. The neglect of Colonel By has an ironic contrast in the fact that Mann Avenue was named after Major General Gothar Mann, the Master General of the Ordnance, in London, to whom By reported. These, however, are but superficial remembrances of the names of some of the men who were responsible for the start of Bytown, and so for the foundation of Ottawa. It is surely the Canal and the city itself which are the true memorial of all those who participated in the building, as they are of Colonel By himself.

Happily it is now possible to visualize what Colonel By looked like as he directed the Canal works since there now stands in Major's Hill Park a life-like statue of this great man, looking towards Parliament Hill. The statue, the work of sculptor Emile Brunet, was unveiled on a lovely Saturday morning, 14 August 1971, by His Excellency Roland Michener, Governor-General of Canada, in the presence of an honour guard of Royal Engineers who had come over from England especially for the occasion. Unveiling of this fine statue in such an appropriate location was the culmination of years of devoted work by members of the Historical Society of Ottawa under the inspired leadership of their President, Dr. Bertram Mackay, and Brigadier General J. M. Melville, Vice-President. The statue will always be a point of pilgrimage for lovers of the Waterway. It provides a fitting starting point from which to see the Canal works in Ottawa, its informative plinth giving a most useful introduction. And over by the Museum, on the other side of the Canal, another modest memorial may be seen, one of the old coping stones from the lock walls, also dedicated while the men of the Royal Engineers were in Ottawa in August 1971, and confirming the links that exist between this most famous Corps of the British Army and the city of Ottawa.

The happy results of the labours of these men have been a constant theme of this study of the construction of the Rideau Waterway and of the landscapes and communities that line its route. The study now approaches its conclusion, and a final tribute to the success of their work. Perhaps the most stimulating setting for a last consideration of the efforts of over a century ago is the place which offers the most impressive of all views of the memorial city of Ottawa, Major's Hill Park. It was once suggested that the residence of the Governor-General of Canada should stand on this site to the east of the entrance locks, with its magnificent panorama of the Ottawa River and high cliff of Parliament Hill across the way, the majestic buildings upon which now fill the skyline. It is surely better, however, that this area has been kept as an open space in the midst of the steadily expanding city, for the enjoyment of citizens and guests alike. The pleasant little park has other reminders of the past in addition to the sweep of stone, tree, river, and rock. Near the centre, in the unbroken grass, is a strange monument, made up of two blocks of stone, on one of which some carving can still be made out with difficulty. An inscription tells that the stones came from the famous Sappers Bridge, having been salvaged when the bridge was demolished. The carvings on the bridge, the last remains of which are to be seen here and which must have looked somewhat incongruous when the bridge stood almost alone in the forest, were carried out, records show, by Private Thomas Smith of the Royal Sappers and Miners. The inscription tells also that the stones mark the site of Colonel By's own house. Now that the statue of Colonel By has been added, the small park will be still further associated with the Canal, the fountain and new landscaping that is planned making it an even more attractive area.

To those who come to know the Waterway, this can be indeed a place of memories, where a retrospective view of all that the skill and foresight of Colonel By and his fellow workers have meant to the development of the Ottawa of today, will seem inevitable and just. The hum of city traffic, the noble pile of the Château, the soaring Peace Tower keep the busy life of the modern city ever present to ear and eye; at the same time they urge upon the attention the amazing changes which took place not only in the little settlement that was Bytown but also in the young colony after the days when Colonel By and his family made their home on this commanding site.

It was on a day in September 1826 that a little company

gathered on the Ottawa around the Countess of Dalhousie as she
turned the first sod to mark the beginning of work on the Rideau
Canal. On that day, emblazoned with the trees of the autumn
forest, the Earl of Dalhousie made a short speech in which he
displayed his enthusiastic belief in the future of this seemingly
military project: "The public interest and the public prosperity
will advance beyond the short sighted views which any of us
here can yet imagine." Short sighted views? Surely few men in
the pioneer days of Canada were more far sighted than the
Governor-General and the Superintending Engineer, whose sen-
sible arrangements for the land around the entrance to the Canal,
for the junction of waterways, and for the first broad streets and
permanent buildings are the essential elements of the National
Capital Plan of today. This Plan, already being implemented,
will make the Ottawa of the future not merely a reflection of
another capital but a national city world-renowned in its own
right and for its own peculiar dignity. It stands forth now
as the final superb gift of Canada's unusual legacy from a military
work: regal in appearance and meaning, it sets off to glorious
advantage the lovely chain of rivers and lakes fashioned in a
master piece of early engineering—the Rideau Waterway.

Appendix A

REFERENCES

REMARKABLY little has been published about the Rideau Canal. The list which follows is believed to be reasonably complete in its references to the Canal; for the district served by the Canal, and for the cities of Kingston and Ottawa, it is merely an introductory guide to an extensive literature.

All quotations have been taken from the publication mentioned in the adjacent text, from one of the sources noted below, or from the invaluable "C" volumes in the Public Archives of Canada.

THE RIDEAU CANAL

From *Papers on Subjects connected with the Duties of the Corps of Royal Engineers* (London: J. Crane), dates as noted:

Frome, Lieut. "Account of the Causes which led to the Construction of the Rideau Canal connecting the Waters of Lake Ontario and the Ottawa; the Nature of the Communication prior to 1827; and a description of the Works by means of which it is converted into a Steam-boat Navigation," vol. I, pp. 73–102, 4 pl., 1837.

Denison, Lieut. W. "Rideau Dams," vol. II, pp. 114–121, 3 pl., 1838.

—— "Detailed Description of the Works on the Rideau Canal, and of the alterations and improvements made therein since the opening of navigation," vol. III, pp. 133–138, 3 pl., 1839.

—— "Description of a Series of Bridges erected across the river Ottawa, connecting the provinces of Upper and Lower Canada, and especially of a wooden arch of 212 feet span which crossed the main branch of the river," vol. III, pp. 158–163, 2 pl., 1839.

Burgoyne, Sir J. F. "Memoranda on Blasting Rock," vol. IV, pp. 27–91, 1840.

Bolton, Major D. "Account of the Dam constructed across the Waste Channel at Long Island, on the Rideau Canal, in 1836," vol. IV, pp. 131–135, 2 pl., 1840.

Ainslie, M. *Waterways to Explore—The Rideau Lakes*, 32 pp., ill., 1947, Ontario Department of Travel and Publicity, Toronto.

Billings, C. E. (Mrs. Bradish). "The Rideau Canal," *Trans. Women's Can. Hist. Soc. of Ottawa*, vol. II, pp. 46–55, 1909, Ottawa.

Bovey, Colonel Wilfrid. "Builders of Canada; the Rideau Triangle," *The Legionary*, vol. XXVII, pp. 22–23, September 1952.

Drummond, A. T. "Some Notes on the Rideau Canal, the Sources of its Water Supply, and its Early History," *Canadian Record of Science*, vol. V, pp. 459–471, October 1893.

Friel, H. J. "The Rideau Canal and the Founding of Ottawa," *Trans. Women's Can. Hist. Soc. of Ottawa*, vol. I, pp. 31–35, 1901, Ottawa.

Harrington, Lyn. "Historic Rideau Canal," *Canadian Geographical Journal*, vol. XXXV, pp. 278–291, December 1947, Ottawa.

Hill, H. P. "The Construction of the Rideau Canal, 1826–1832," *Ont. Hist. Soc., Papers and Records*, vol. XXII, pp. 117–124, 1925, Toronto.

Lake, Dr. E. J. *Chart of the Rideau Lakes Route between Kingston and Ottawa*, 3rd edition, 68 pp., ill., 1920, Kingston.

MacTaggart, John. *Three Years in Canada etc.*, 2 vols., xi + 347, vii + 340 pp., 1829, H. Colburn, London.

COLONEL JOHN BY

Blue, C. S. "John By: Founder of a Capital," *Canadian Magazine*, vol. XXXVIII, 1912, Toronto.

Hill, H. P. "Lieutenant Colonel John By, a Biography," *Royal Engineers Journal*, vol. XLVI, pp. 522–525, ill., December 1932, Chatham (Eng.).

KINGSTON

Glover, T. R., and D. D. Calvin. *A Corner of Empire*, 178 + x pp., ill., 1937, Cambridge University Press.

BYTOWN AND OTTAWA

Blythe, G. R. "Bytown 1834 to Ottawa 1924," *Trans. Women's Can. Hist. Soc. of Ottawa*, vol. IX, pp. 5–10, 1925, Ottawa.

Brault, Lucien. *Ottawa Old and New*, 349 pp., ill., 1946, Ottawa.

Card, Anson. *The Hub and the Spoke*, xiv + 371 + 174 pp. of photographs, 1904, Endeson Press, Ottawa and New York.

Carr-Harris, B. W. *The White Chief of the Ottawa*, iv + 252 pp., ill., 1903, Briggs, Toronto.

Davies, Blodwen. *Ottawa: Portrait of a Capital*, 186 pp., ill., 1954, McGraw Hill, Toronto.

Hill, H. P. *Robert Randall and the Le Breton Flats*, 62 pp., 1919, James Hope and Sons, Ottawa.

Hunter, W. S., Jr. *Hunter's Ottawa Scenery*, 19 pp., 13 pl., 1855, pub. by the author, Ottawa, Canada West.

Kenny, F. G. "Some Account of Bytown," *Trans. Women's Can. Hist. Soc. of Ottawa*, vol. I, pp. 22–30, 1901, Ottawa.

Ross, A. H. D. *Ottawa, Past and Present*, 224 pp., ill., 1927, Thorburn and Abbott, Ottawa.

Scott, R. W. *Recollections of Bytown*, 30 pp., prob. 1908, Mortimer Press, Ottawa.

Simpson, J. R. "Some Reminiscences of Bytown," *Trans. Women's Can. Hist. Soc. of Ottawa*, vol. VII, pp. 5–11, 1917, Ottawa.

Stewart, McLeod. *First Half Century of Ottawa*, 84 pp., ill., 1910, Esdale Press, Ottawa.

Whitton, Dr. C. *I belong on the Ottawa*, 12 pp., 1952, Runge Press, Ottawa.

REGION SERVED BY THE RIDEAU CANAL

Chapman, L. J. and D. F. Putnam. *The Physiography of Southern Ontario*, 284 pp. + maps, 1951, University of Toronto Press, Toronto.

Earle, E. P. *Leeds the Lovely*, 174 pp., 1951, Ryerson, Toronto.

Fleming, Clint. *When the Fish are Rising*, xv + 205 pp., with maps, 1947, Duell, Sloan and Pearce, New York.

Gourlay, A. M. *History of the Ottawa Valley*, 288 pp., 1896, Ottawa.

Leavitt, T. W. H. *History of Leeds and Grenville, Ontario, from 1749 to 1878*, 1879, Recorder Press, Brockville.

New Historical Atlas of Carleton County, Ontario, 70 pp., ill., 1879, H. Belden, Toronto.

GENERAL AND HISTORICAL REFERENCES

Aitken, H. G. J. *The Welland Canal Company*, ix + 178 pp., 1954, Harvard University Press, Cambridge.

Canada and Dominion Sugar Co. Ltd. *Redpath Centennial—One Hundred Years of Progress*, 40 pp., ill., 1954, Montreal.

Creighton, D. G. *The Commercial Empire of the St. Lawrence*, vii + 441 pp., 1937, Ryerson, Toronto.

Denison, Wm. "A Series of Experiments on Different Kinds of American Timber," *Trans. Inst. Civil Engs.*, vol. II, pp. 15–32, 1838, London.

Denison, Sir Wm. *Varieties of Viceregal Life*, 2 vols., 514 and 446 pp., 1870, Longmans Green, London.

Glazebrook, G. P. deT. *A History of Transportation in Canada*, xxv + 475 pp., 1938, Ryerson, Toronto.

Hill, Captain Basil. *Travels in North America in 1827 and 1828*, 1829, Caddel and Co., Edinburgh.

Kingsford, William. *The Canadian Canals; their History and Cost, with an inquiry into the policy necessary to the well-being of the province*, 191 pp., 1865, Rollo and Adam, Toronto.

Stacey, C. P. "An American Plan for a Canadian Campaign," *Am. Hist. Review*, vol. XLVI, pp. 348–358, 1941.

—— "The Backbone of Canada," *Can. Hist. Association Report*, 1953, pp. 1–13, Ottawa.

—— "The Ships of the British Squadron on Lake Ontario," *Can. Hist. Review*, vol. XXXIV, pp. 311–323, 1953, Toronto.

Appendix B

THE SUPERINTENDING ENGINEERS

Under the Royal Engineers
1826–1832	Lieutenant Colonel John By
1832–1843	Lieutenant Colonel Bolton
1843–1847	Lieutenant Colonel Thomson
1847–1853	Captain C. E. Ford
1853–1856	Captain Chayter

Under the Board of Works of Upper and Lower Canada
1856–1858	A. Killaly
1858–1867	J. D. Slater

Under the Department of Public Works
1867–1872	J. D. Slater
1872–1879	F. A. Wise

Under the Department of Railways and Canals
1879–1894	F. A. Wise
1894–1934	A. T. Phillips
1934–1935	J. Murphy

Under the Department of Transport
1935–1938	J. Murphy
1938–1954	A. R. Whittier
1954–	L. W. Clark

Appendix C

A CONVENIENT and comprehensive guide for sailing on the Rideau Canal is available in the form of an illustrated brochure entitled *Navigation Canals: Rideau, Trent, Quebec* published by the Department of Transport. It is available, with supplements as needed to bring it quite up to date, from:

> *The Superintending Engineer,*
> *Rideau Canal,*
> *P.O. Box 3188, Station "C,"*
> *Ottawa.*

All inquiries about the use of the Waterway should be addressed to the Superintending Engineer.

Two other most useful publications should always be in the possession of all users and prospective users of the Waterway:

Canal Regulations
  (1966 edition, with supplement included)

Boating Safety Guide
  (1971, giving details of lights etc.)

Both publications are prepared by the Department of Transport as further service to boatmen; copies may be obtained from Information Canada, the former for 35 cents a copy, the latter free.

No permits for using the Canal are now necessary but all regulations regarding the licensing and equipment of vessels must be strictly followed.

CHARTS

The route of the Canal was shown on two of Canada's official Hydrographic (or "nautical") charts; these are:

CHART 1575; Kingston to Narrows Lock; and
CHART 1576; The Narrows Lock to Ottawa.

Copies of these charts were obtainable for 50 cents each but they are now being superseded by the following entirely new charts and so will soon be out of print. Copies will still be around, however, and can serve as a useful guide but the following newer charts should always be used for actual navigation:

CHART 1513; Rideau Waterway, Small Craft Chart; Smiths Falls to Kingston, including Tay Branch to Perth; 1971 edition, 5 sheets in attractive folder; $4.00.

CHART 1512; Rideau Waterway, Small Craft Chart: Ottawa to Smiths Falls; to be issued in 1972 in similar form.

Charts may be obtained from:

> *Canadian Hydrographic Service,*
> *Marine Sciences Branch,*
> *Department of the Environment,*
> *Ottawa.*

They are also available from the Rideau Canal Office and the Lockmasters at Kingston Mills, Chaffeys Locks, Smiths Falls and Ottawa.

All motorists know well the excellent series of road maps issued by the various gasoline companies; these will assist with visits to the Rideau country but for any detailed journeys the appropriate Topographic Maps (as listed in the next section) should always be used. A few of the gasoline companies issue corresponding maps for Inland Waterway Cruising; these are also useful in a general way but for navigational purposes the latest official charts, as noted above, are essential.

TOPOGRAPHICAL MAPS

The route of the Rideau Waterway is well shown in the National Topographical Series of Maps of Canada. Prepared by the Surveys and Mapping Branch of the Department of Energy, Mines and Resources, and the Army Survey Establishment, the Series includes maps on scales of 16, 8, 4, and 2 miles to the inch but it is the maps to a scale of 1:50,000 (approximately 1¼ inches to 1 mile) that will be of most interest and use to those who wish to visit the Canal.

An index sheet of the 1:50,000 and 1:63,360 map sheets of the National Topographic Series covering this area to a scale of 50 miles to the inch is available from the Department of Mines and Technical Surveys. From this it will be seen that the entire route of the Canal is shown on the "31" map of the 16 miles to the inch group. The index map explains the coding used in sub-dividing the "31" area, which results in the following index numbers to the (1:50,000) maps, each of which includes a part of the Canal route:

Code number	Name	Year of issue
31/5	Ottawa	1968
31/4	Kemptville	1969
31/13	Merrickville	1969
31/16	Perth	1969
31/9	Westport	1969
31C/8 East Half	Gananoque	1962
31C/8 West Half	Gananoque	1962
31C/1 West Half	Wolfe Island	1962

The cost of each of the full sheets is $1.00, and of the last three half sheets 50 cents.

Remittances in payment for both charts and maps should be made out in favour of the Receiver-General of Canada. Orders for maps should be sent to:

Map Distribution Office,
Department of Energy, Mines and Resources,
Ottawa.

A publication of the provincial government of Ontario will be of further assistance to users of the Waterway: *Ontario Boating.* It may be obtained by writing to:

Ontario Department of Tourism and Information,
185 Bloor Street East,
Toronto 5, Ontario.

GEOLOGICAL INFORMATION

There is no single publication from which an over-all picture of the geology of the route of the Rideau Canal can be obtained since it traverses several distinct geological provinces. Geological information must therefore be sought in a number of reports which deal with parts of the area through which the Waterway runs. Typical of those issued by the Department of Mines of the Province of Ontario, now unfortunately out of print but available at many libraries, are:

The Geology of Kingston and Vicinity. By M. B. Baker: Annual Report, Vol. XXV, part III, 71 pp., 1916.

Geology and Minerals of the County of Leeds. By M. B. Baker: Annual Report, Vol. XXXI, part VI, 26 pp., 1922.

The geology of the Ottawa end of the Canal is covered in a publication of the Geological Survey of Canada (c/o Department of Energy, Mines and Resources, Ottawa), which also contains an extensive and most useful bibliography:

Geology of the Ottawa–St. Lawrence Lowland, Ontario and Quebec. By Alice E. Wilson: Memoir 241, 65 pp., 1946.

There is now available a splendid illustrated guide to the geology of the city of Ottawa and its immediate environs, one that can be warmly recommended to all visitors to the nation's capital:

Guide to the Geology and Scenery of the National Capital Area. By David M. Baird: Miscellaneous Report No. 15, issued by The Geological Survey of Canada, 1968; copies available from Information Canada at $2.50 each.

The physiography of the region served by the Canal is naturally described in the work by Chapman and Putnam mentioned appreciatively in the text and so listed in the "References" in Appendix A; it may usefully be noted again:

The Physiography of Southern Ontario. By L. J. Chapman and D. F. Putnam: University of Toronto Press, 2nd ed., 400 pp., illus., map, 1966.

Another useful publication is the *Soil Survey of Carleton County*, which is Report No. 7 of the Ontario Soil Survey, published in 1944 jointly by the Experimental Farms Service of the federal Department of Agriculture and the Ontario Agricultural College.

Appendix D

FISHING ON THE RIDEAU WATERWAY

FULL INFORMATION about fishing in the Rideau Waterway (and elsewhere in Ontario) may be obtained by writing to the Department of Lands and Forests, Legislative Building, Queen's Park, Ontario. For detailed information reference should be made to the Game and Fish Act, 1961–62, and the Ontario Fishery Regulations, but the Department has prepared a complete consolidation of the Regulations that is available on request. A useful and convenient summary, *Ontario Fishing*, is available, issued each year as a pocket-sized folding brochure. This contains a complete map of the province, marked with the Divisions that are mentioned below, and containing an illustrated summary of the current regulations together with miscellaneous interesting and useful information. (As an example it is noted that there is no restriction on the taking of bullfrogs in Ontario except in the Counties of Lanark and Leeds where the open season is from July 1 to October 15, with a limiting daily catch of 25.) The most recent copy of this pocket guide, available throughout the region at hardware and sporting goods stores and from the District Office of the Department in the Provincial Government Building in Kemptville, should always be consulted for up-to-date information. The following typical dates are taken from *Ontario Fishing 1972*.

The Rideau Waterway lies in Divisions 9 and 10 of the Department's subdivision of the province; the following limits apply to both Divisions unless so stated, in which case the limit for Division 10 is for the Counties of Lanark and Leeds, that for Division 9 for the remainder of the Canal area.

OPEN SEASONS
(All dates are inclusive)

Pike	Division 9	May 13 to March 31
	Division 10	May 13 to Feb. 28
Yellow Pickerel	Division 9	May 13 to March 31
	Division 10	May 13 to Feb. 28
Bass, Large and Small Mouth	Division 9	June 24 to Nov. 30
	Division 10	June 24 to Oct. 15

Maskinonge	June 17 to Nov. 30
Brook and Brown Trout	Jan. 1 to Sept. 30
Rainbow Trout	Jan. 1 to Sept. 30
Lake Trout	Feb. 26 to Sept. 30

LIMITS OF CATCH

Pike	Six in one day
Yellow Pickerel	Six in one day
Bass, Large and Small Mouth	Six in one day
Maskinonge	Two in one day
Brook Trout	Fifteen fish or ten pounds plus one fish, whichever is the lesser
Brown Trout	Five in one day
Rainbow Trout	Five in one day
Lake Trout	Five in one day, except in Division 10 where the limit is three in one day

Possession limit shall not exceed one day's legal limit. Fish are considered to be in possession of an angler whether they are on hand, in cold storage, in transit, or elsewhere. Sizes of Bass must not be less than 12 inches in Division 10; sizes of Yellow Pickerel in Division 10 must not be less than 14 inches; Maskinonge must be not less than 28 inches in both Divisions.

LICENCES

All non-resident anglers must have a licence. These are procurable at Ontario Government Reception Centres, hardware and sporting goods stores, licensed fishing and hunting camps, the District Office of the Department of Lands and Forests in Kemptville, as well as from a wide list of licence issuers throughout the province. Licences may also be obtained by mail from the Department by writing to its headquarters in Queen's Park, Toronto. Licences are not transferable. Non-residents under the age of seventeen may angle without a licence if accompanied by a member of their family who has a licence, but the fish which he takes shall be regarded as a part of the catch of the licence-holder.

LICENCE FEES

Non-resident angling licence (valid for entire season)	$8.50
Non-resident three-day angling licence	$4.00
Non-resident bow-and-arrow and smelt-fishing licence	$5.00

The foregoing information has been abstracted from *Ontario Fishing 1972* by kind permission of the Department of Lands and Forests. It is intended as a general guide only. Reference should be made to official publications of the Department, such as the guide just noted, for more complete information and useful suggestions.

Appendix E

TABLE OF MILEAGES, LIFTS, AND CLEARANCES

Dimensions of all Locks: 134 feet by 33 feet.
Draught: Normal 5 feet 6 ins.: Minimum 5 feet 0 ins.

Ottawa River: Mean Level 131 feet above Mean Sea Level.
  (at Ottawa)
Lake Ontario: Mean Level 246 feet above Mean Sea Level.
  (at Kingston)

Total Lift in Locks ascending from Ottawa to Upper Rideau Lake:
              33 Locks—277 feet.
Total Lift in Locks descending from Upper Rideau Lake to Kingston:
              14 Locks—162 feet.

This table has been abstracted from information given in *Navigation Canals: Rideau, Trent, Quebec*, published by the Department of Transport in which information additional to that in the table may be found.

Miles from		Structure	Average lift of locks	Clearance at bridge
Ottawa	Kingston			
			feet	*feet*
0.00	123.53	Ottawa River, Ottawa		
0.00	123.53	OTTAWA LOCKS, 1 to 8, in flight	79.00	
0.22	123.31	Plaza concrete arch and steel bridge		26.50
0.40	123.13	Mackenzie King concrete fixed span bridge		26.00
0.54	122.99	Laurier Avenue steel arch bridge		27.25

Miles from		Structure	Average lift of locks	Clearance at bridge
Ottawa	Kingston			
			feet	feet
1.50	122.03	Fixed concrete bridge carrying the Queensway		22.00
1.56	121.97	Bridge 1—vertical lift— Pretoria Avenue		22.00
2.81	120.72	Bank Street concrete arch bridge		27.00
3.42	120.11	Fixed concrete bridge carrying Bronson Avenue		22.00
4.17	119.36	HARTWELLS LOCKS, 9 and 10, in flight	21.50	
5.10	118.43	Fixed concrete bridge carrying Heron Road		22.00
5.23	118.30	HOG'S BACK LOCKS, 11 and 12, in flight	14.50	
5.25	118.28	Bridge 4—swing—Hog's Back; canal enters Rideau River		
7.43	116.10	C.N.R. high level bridge		31.00
9.25	114.28	LOCK 13—Black Rapids	9.16	
14.25	109.28	LONG ISLAND LOCKS, 14 to 16, in flight	25.33	
14.33	109.20	Bridge 5—swing—Long Island, over Lock 16		
16.03	107.50	Fixed concrete bridge at Manotick		22.00
23.33	100.20	Fixed concrete bridge at Kars		22.00
30.48	93.05	Channel to Kemptville	South Rideau Branch to Kemptville	
33.38	95.95	Kemptville Wharf		
31.93	91.60	Becketts high level fixed bridge		27.00
38.93	84.60	LOCK 17—Burritts Rapids	9.00	
39.43	84.10	Bridge 9—swing— Burritts Rapids		
41.83	81.70	FLIGHT LOCK 18—Nicholsons	6.50	
42.09	81.44	FLIGHT LOCK 19—Nicholsons	8.00	
42.10	81.43	Bridge 10—swing— Nicholsons, over Lock 19		
42.50	81.03	LOCK 20—Clowes	7.58	
44.30	79.23	C.P.R. high level bridge— Merrickville		40.00
44.65	78.88	FLIGHT LOCK 21—Merrickville	8.66	
		FLIGHT LOCK 22—Merrickville	10.00	
		FLIGHT LOCK 23—Merrickville	6.00	

Miles from		Structure	Average lift of locks	Clearance at bridge
Ottawa	Kingston			
			feet	*feet*
44.81	78.72	Bridge 11—swing—Merrick-ville, over Lock 23		
52.81	70.72	LOCK 24—Kilmarnock	2.00	
52.82	70.71	Bridge 13—swing—Kilmarnock, over Lock 24		
56.22	67.31	LOCK 25—Edmunds	9.16	
57.72	65.81	C.P.R. high level bridge—Smiths Falls		30.00
57.72	65.81	OLD SLYS LOCKS, 26 and 27, in flight	16.00	
57.77	65.76	Bridge 15—swing—Old Slys		
58.52	65.01	SMITHS FALLS COMBINED LOCKS, 28, 29, and 30, in flight	26.00	
58.58	64.95	Bridge 17—swing—Beckwith Street		
58.86	64.67	Bridge 19—swing—Abbot Street		
58.88	64.65	SMITHS FALLS DETACHED LOCK 31	8.50	
58.98	64.55	C.N.R. bascule lift bridge		
60.98	62.55	LOCK—32 Poonamalie	5.75	
61.58	61.95	Entrance to Lower Rideau Lake		
65.10	58.43	Diversion to Tay Branch	Tay Canal to Perth	
65.80	59.13	Canal entrance—Beveridge Bay—Rideau Lake		
66.00	59.33	LOCK 33—Beveridges	12.00	
66.09	59.42	Bridge 21—fixed—Beveridges		22.00
66.32	59.65	LOCK 34—Beveridges	13.00	
71.52	64.85	Bridge 22—fixed—Craig Street, Perth		22.00
71.77	65.10	Bridge 23—fixed—Beckwith Street, Perth		22.00
71.86	65.19	Bridge 24—fixed—Drummond Street, Perth		22.00
71.92	65.25	Perth Basin wharf		
71.96	65.29	Bridge 25—fixed—Gore Street, Perth	(Total length, Tay branch, 6.12 miles)	22.00
67.02	56.51	Bridge 26—swing—Rideau Ferry		
72.42	51.11	Diversion to Portland	Channel to Portland Wharf	
78.90	57.59	Portland wharf	on south shore, Big Rideau Lake	

Miles from		Structure	Average lift of locks	Clearance at bridge
Ottawa	Kingston			
			feet	*feet*
80.02	43.51	LOCK 35—The Narrows	3.00	
80.02	43.51	Bridge 27—swing—The Narrows		
80.08	43.45	Entrance to Upper Rideau Lake (summit level 408.0 above M.S.L.)		
80.08	43.45	Diversion to Westport	Channel to Westport wharf	
85.33	48.70	Westport wharf	on west shore, Upper Rideau Lake	
84.43	39.10	Bridge 29—high level, highway		27.50
84.74	38.79	LOCK 36—Newboro	7.75	
89.74	33.79	C.N.R. high level bridge		34.00
90.00	33.53	LOCK 37—Chaffeys	10.75	
90.00	33.53	Bridge 30—swing—Chaffeys		
92.15	31.38	LOCK 38—Davis	9.00	
96.45	27.08	LOCK 39—Jones Falls	13.75	
96.48	27.05	Jones Falls basin		
96.59	26.94	LOCKS 40 to 42, in flight— Jones Falls	44.75	
96.63	26.90	Bridge 33—swing—Jones Falls, over Lock 41		
99.38	24.15	Diversion to Morton		
101.00	25.77	Morton dam but no wharf		
100.88	22.65	Diversion to Seeleys Bay	Channel to Seeleys Bay	
101.53	23.30	Seeleys Bay wharf	village and wharf	
103.08	20.45	Bridge 36—swing—Brass Point		
107.28	16.25	LOCKS 43 and 44, in flight— Upper Brewers	18.00	
107.58	15.95	Bridge 37—fixed concrete for county road		22.00
109.06	14.47	Bridge 39—swing—Lower Brewers, over entrance to Lock 45		
109.06	14.47	LOCK 45—Lower Brewers or Washburn	13.00	
118.81	4.72	LOCK 46—Kingston Mills	9.83	

Miles from		Structure	Average lift of locks	Clearance at bridge
Ottawa	Kingston			
			feet	*feet*
118.81	4.72	Bridge 41—swing—Kingston Mills		
118.83	4.70	Kingston Mills basin		
118.91	4.62	LOCKS 47 to 49, in flight—Kingston Mills	35.16	
118.93	4.60	C.N.R. high level bridge, over Locks 47–48		30.00
119.56	3.97	Fixed concrete bridge carrying Highway 401		24.00
123.53	0.00	Kingston–Lasalle Causeway bascule bridge		

PLEASE HELP TO KEEP ONTARIO VACATIONLAND GREEN

An unending battle is being waged by the Ontario Department of Lands and Forests to prevent forest fires, and you can help. Each fire season, which includes the period between April 1st and October 31st, numerous forest fires occur owing principally to little acts of carelessness on the part of summer vacationists. The discarded cigarette butt along a trail or portage, the lack of proper care in the selection of a place to light a camp-fire and then not bothering to extinguish it—dead out—are some of the causes of fire. Please watch your step while in the woods and you will be able to return year after year and find the same beauty awaiting you.

PLEASE HELP TO PREVENT FOREST FIRES

Index